ERIC VOEGELIN: PHILOSOPHER OF HISTORY

Eugene Webb is Chairman of the Comparative
Religion Program and professor of comparative
literature at the University of Washington. He
is the author of *Samuel Beckett: A Study of His
Novels* (1970), *The Plays of Samuel Beckett*
(1972), and *The Dark Dove: The Sacred and Secular in Modern Literature* (1975), all published
by the University of Washington Press.

Eric Voegelin

Philosopher of History

by
EUGENE WEBB

UNIVERSITY OF WASHINGTON PRESS
Seattle and London

Excerpts from the poems "Dry Salvages" and "Little Gidding," by T. S. Eliot, are reprinted from his volume *Collected Poems, 1909–1962* by permission of Harcourt Brace Jovanovich, Inc.; copyright 1936, by Harcourt Brace Jovanovich, Inc.; copyright 1963, 1964, by T. S. Eliot.

Copyright © 1981 by the University of Washington Press
Printed in the United States of America

Library of Congress Cataloging in Publication Data

Webb, Eugene, 1938–
  Eric Voegelin, philosopher of history.
  Bibliography: p.
  Includes index.
  1. History—Philosophy.   2. Voegelin, Eric,
1901–   I. Title
D16.8.W37   901   80–51078
ISBN 0-295-95759-X

For Eric and Lissie Voegelin

Preface

Although Eric Voegelin is one of the major philosophical thinkers of the twentieth century, his work is only beginning to be studied widely and intensively. It is my hope that the rapidly growing appreciation of his importance among historians, political philosophers, and scholars of comparative religion will bring him a larger and broader audience among the public at large. As I indicate in the Introduction, there are various reasons why many readers have found the approach to his thought difficult. My own purpose in writing this book has been to help the potential reader overcome such difficulties by providing an overview and some clarification of Voegelin's basic concepts. I hope that the book will prove helpful to specialists and non-specialists alike, that it will make the thought of this important figure more readily available to those who have not studied it before, and that even those who have studied it may be helped to a deeper understanding of its theoretical foundations.

The present work is in three parts. The first is theoretical; it seeks to elucidate Voegelin's philosophical principles and concepts and to explain how he developed them, both with reference to contemporary philosophical discourse and through the study of the history of thought. The second part briefly summarizes the main lines of Voegelin's study of history as he has interpreted it in the light of those theoretical principles. The third part focuses on the two themes most central to Voegelin's concern: the philosophy of religion and the philosophy of history. Because Voegelin uses many technical terms that may not always be readily clear from the context or easy to remember from one chapter to the next, I have appended a glossary in addition to a topical index.

I have many individuals to thank for helpful comments on the manuscript, a list too long to be included here. I would like to name at least a few, however, whose help I believe made the book better than it would otherwise have been: Michael Anderson, Dante Germino, William Havard, Robert B. Heilman, Rodney W. Kilcup, Thomas J. McPartland, and Donald W. Treadgold.

Most of all, I wish to thank Eric Voegelin himself for encouraging me in my work on this project, for reading and commenting on the manuscript at every stage of its development, and for his unfailing kindness, hospitality, and generosity in making both himself and his unpublished manuscripts available to me. I doubt that there has ever been a subject both so interesting to work on and so pleasant to work with.

This is not to say, of course, that either Professor Voegelin or any of the others I have named is in any way responsible for any inaccuracies or deficiencies of interpretation that may remain. If there are such, I hope there will be many future scholars of this subject eager to correct them.

Seattle, June 1980

Contents

ERIC VOEGELIN: PHILOSOPHER OF HISTORY

Introduction

THE thought of a major philosopher is always a challenge. Whether the philosopher is traditional or contemporary, his thought reaches beyond the horizon of his reader, and to study him is to explore experiences and perspectives that are unfamiliar, in which one often is uncomfortable, and which require a stretching that must be spiritual as well as intellectual. It is, of course, for this very reason that we call such a philosopher major. It is easy so to label a thinker from the past whom time has judged worthy. We accept, to some degree, the judgment of history. Approaching a contemporary, we become more suspicious and more guarded, less willing to put both our judgment and our habitual patterns of thinking at risk.

If this were the only obstacle to the reading of Eric Voegelin, however, the task of discussing him would be less formidable than it is. More than other contemporary philosophers, Voegelin seeks from his reader a radical shift in perspective from the one that has prevailed in modern thought for centuries. Moreover, there are a number of additional problems. Although Voegelin is widely known, he is far less widely read; his works have the reputation of being forbidding. This is not surprising, since he demands not only a radical shift in perspective but also a familiarity with the entire history of Western thought—mythological, philosophical, and religious. And the fact that he has chosen to unfold the main lines of his own thought in a magnum opus—*Order and History*—that now runs to four volumes and will include one more when it is finished tends to make him one of those authors consigned to a list of monuments to be gazed at respectfully from afar.

Many who have heard of Voegelin have also picked up mistaken impressions of his way of thinking. That he is a "right-wing" thinker in both politics and religion is probably the most wide-spread of these misconceptions. This attitude is due ultimately to the unfamiliarity of his perspective; one tends to assimilate him to familiar patterns. If one notices that he is not a doctrinaire liberal, for example, then it is difficult not to assume that he must be a doctrinaire conservative. Moses Hadas, reviewing *Order and History* in the *Journal of the History of Ideas*, even suggested that he is a crypto-Fascist.[1] Those who have studied Voegelin's thought more carefully have recognized that, as Dante Germino says, "as a politi-cal philosopher, Voegelin defies classification according to the lan-guage of political struggle: he is not left, right, or center, but is engaged in the critical study of politics."[2]

William Havard, whose acquaintance with Voegelin dates from his own freshman year as a student at Louisiana State University in 1943, the year that Voegelin began his sixteen years of teaching there, has said, "Perhaps the real measure of the neglect of Voege-lin's efforts by American political scientists is the fact that he has not been ignored nearly as often as he has been dismissed with categorical labels, most of which indicate that the labeler has either not bothered to read him or, if he has read him, has not taken the trouble to understand him."[3] Havard tells several amusing stories of such virtual refusals to understand: "On one occasion a fellow graduate student (now a rather prominent social scientist who has shown great skill, as Voegelin said with reference to Harold Laski, 'in his expert surf-riding on the wave of the future') remarked, after hearing Voegelin examine the pragmatic necessity for social demo-cratic reforms under certain historical conditions, 'I didn't know the man was a Socialist; I always thought he was a reactionary.'" And

1. 19 (1958): 444.

2. "Two Conceptions of Political Philosophy," in George W. Carey and George J. Graham, Jr., eds., *The Post-Behavioral Era* (New York: David McKay, 1972), p. 248.

3. William C. Havard, "Voegelin's Changing Conception of History and Consciousness," in Stephen A. McKnight, ed., *Eric Voegelin's Search for Order in History* (Baton Rouge and London: Louisiana State University Press, 1978), p. 2.

on another occasion: "A senior colleague for whom I have great respect once astonished me by bluntly asserting that he could not make the written tribute to Voegelin for which he had been called on because 'Voegelin never said anything against the Nazis after he came to this country.' It continues to puzzle me that so well-informed a man could have missed Voegelin's articles on 'The Growth of the Race Idea' . . . , 'Extended Strategy' . . . , and 'Some Problems of the German Hegemony.'" [4]

What makes Voegelin's thought difficult to grasp for any person accustomed to the more common type of philosophical exposition is that he is not in any sense an ideological thinker. He does not present a system of ideas that could be labeled according to any of the traditional designations—such as "materialist," "idealist," "empiricist," "realist," and so on—and, what must be still more disconcerting to many, he does not even present a standard philosophical argument of the sort that leads the reader from premises to a conclusion through the force of formal logic. This, of course, might make it sound as if he is a dogmatic thinker; but that would be to return to the supposition that a philosopher's aim must be to present and win assent for a doctrine. Voegelin, however, has a quite different conception of philosophy, and it will be the first, and perhaps the most important, task of the present study to make clear what that conception is. It will take time to do so, and that effort will have to wait for the main body of this study, but it will be helpful at this point—having said something about what type of philosopher Voegelin is not—to indicate at least briefly what philosophy does mean to him.

Perhaps the best way to do this is to describe the manner in which

4. Ibid., pp. 12–13. One might also mention in such a connection the writings published earlier in German that had contributed to Voegelin's dismissal from his position as Extraordinary Professor at the University of Vienna after the Anschluss in 1938 and to his subsequent flight. These included the monographs, *Rasse und Staat*, and *Die Rassenidee in der Geistesgeschichte von Ray bis Carus*, both published in 1933, *Der autoritäre Staat* (1936), and *Die politischen Religionen* (1938). Voegelin's escape from the Gestapo was a close one; they were actively searching for him and were watching his house on the day he fled.

his conception of the nature of his philosophical task took shape and finally crystallized in its present form during the 1940s. Voegelin began his career as an intellectual historian specializing in legal and political philosophy. In the early 1940s he undertook what was to have been the major scholarly enterprise of his career, a history of political ideas from ancient to modern times. He worked on this project steadily for several years and produced the equivalent of several volumes of manuscript, some parts of which have subsequently been published.[5] In 1945, however, while working on Schelling's theory of mythology and revelation, he arrived at what seemed to him a crucial realization that eventually made his entire endeavor to that point seem fundamentally misconceived.[6] This

5. The largest section yet published appears in *From Enlightenment to Revolution,* ed. John H. Hallowell (Durham, N.C.: Duke University Press, 1975). Also from this work came the articles "Siger de Brabant" (1944), "Machiavelli's Prince: Background and Formation" (1951), and "More's Utopia" (1951). There is also considerable remaining material not yet published. A large additional portion of the manuscript, including material stretching from the Middle Ages to the seventeenth century, is being edited for publication by William Havard.

6. Voegelin has not described this episode in detail in print, but some commentators have given brief accounts of it. See, for example, Havard, "Voegelin's Changing Conception," pp. 14–16, 24, and Hallowell's preface to *From Enlightenment to Revolution.* Havard and Hallowell locate it simply in the 1940s. Voegelin himself has discussed the important advances in his thinking—focusing on his radical break with Husserl's phenomenology—that took place in 1943 in the new first chapter, "Remembrance of Things Past," of the English edition of *Anamnesis,* trans. Gerhart Niemeyer (Notre Dame and London: Notre Dame University Press, 1978), pp. 3–13, but the final crystallization of his approach to the study of history did not take place at that time. When I asked Voegelin in July 1977 for a more precise date for the crucial realization that led to the shift from the history of ideas to the history of experiences and their symbolizations, he said that this came in 1945, remembering that it was approximately two months before the explosion of the atomic bomb at Hiroshima. He continued, however, to work on the history of political thought that was already under way; the basic shift in conception began in 1945, but he says that its full implications did not become clear until the late 1940s, so that he did not discontinue the earlier project until then. For a later criticism of what Voegelin refers to as the "doxographic history of ideas," see *Anamnesis,* pp. 181–82. The German edition of this work, *Anamnesis: Zur Theorie der Geschichte und Politik* (Munich: Piper, 1966), is not identical to the English version, which contains the new first chapter just

realization was that ideas are not what is most fundamental in thought, and have no life of their own, but rather are the symbolic expressions of various kinds of experience and existential stance. Or at least this is what they are at root; they may also become uprooted from their engendering experiences and thereby lose their substance, and in this form they may become both elements and objects of argumentation. The history of ideas as conventionally practiced, in other words, came to seem to Voegelin no more than a game of shadows founded on the illusion that essential meaning could be captured in the form of the husks left behind when philosophy itself had vanished.

From this negative realization, Voegelin proceeded over the years between then and the early 1950s to develop his positive conception of the philosophical enterprise as the rediscovery of the philosophical quest itself through the recovery of its experiential ground. By the time he delivered his Walgreen lectures at the University of Chicago in 1951 (subsequently published as *The New Science of Politics*),[7] it was clear to him that philosophy in its essential reality was not a set of ideas but a phase—the most reflectively conscious—of an existential process in which one experiences and freely yields oneself to what Voegelin has come to call the "tension of existence," the deep longing of the soul for truth and for fullness of life, the pull at the core of the philosopher's being toward a goal that will remain always mysterious but which draws him with imperative force.

---

referred to as well as an important recent article, "Reason: The Classic Experience," originally published in the *Southern Review*, n.s., 10, no. 2 (Winter 1974): 237–64, and which also leaves out seven sections of the original edition. When it is necessary to refer to the German original, I will identify it as *Anamnesis* (German).

7. *The New Science of Politics* (Chicago: University of Chicago Press, 1952). The original title of the lectures was "Truth and Representation," a title Voegelin prefers because it identifies their central theme, which is the constitutive role played in every society by its symbolic self-representation and by the manner in which this may relate to various levels of truth, that is, to the representation of various levels within the hierarchy of being.

This is a process that embraces the whole of the philosopher's existence, its levels of comparative unconsciousness as well as its luminous heights. Philosophy, from this point of view, may be said to be in continuity with a range of wondering, questioning, and aspiring that has varying degrees of conscious clarity and expresses itself in many symbolic forms, of which ideas are only one and not always the most adequate. The ideational expression of philosophy is the most superficial level of the philosophic life. At its best, this level has the advantage of a high degree of explicitness and self-awareness, but its very clarity may also involve some loss of the richness and complexity of the fundamental experience, which is at root the experience of the mystery of existence, something that can never be rendered fully explicit. Existence, as Voegelin approaches it, is not something we can turn into an object of contemplation—as though it were a field we could step outside of to grasp it intellectually in a single view. Rather we are immersed in it fully, with all of our being, and it will always remain a mystery: both an action and a passion, luminous and yet unfathomable.

As a consequence, there are, and will always be, aspects of our existence that require for their expression and exploration the analogical language of myth. Philosophy, mythology, and religion, from this point of view, are linked in essential continuity. This is why in his major work, *Order and History*, Voegelin went back for his starting point, in the first volume, *Israel and Revelation* (1956), to the mythic and religious thought of the Mesopotamians, Egyptians, and Israelites, and why he began his study of Greek thought in volume 2, *The World of the Polis* (1957), with Homer and Hesiod. Similarly, one of the distinctive features of the third volume, *Plato and Aristotle* (1957), is its emphasis on the role of myth in the thought of Plato; it seems safe to say that no other major study of Plato has devoted so much attention not only to the myths, both traditional and original, that Plato uses in the course of exploring philosophical issues but also to the manner in which Plato treats myth itself as an essential instrument of philosophical reflection. The fourth volume, *The Ecumenic Age* (1974), has continued Voegelin's treatment of this theme, with special reference to Christianity, and it is expected that the fifth and final volume, *In Search of Order*, will continue it further.

For Voegelin the intellectual enterprise of the philosopher—who by the very nature of his task must be simultaneously a historian of philosophical thought and a philosopher of history—has become the recovery of the experiential ground of philosophy, the descent by way of historical memory through the various levels of symbolization, mythic and conceptual, to the deepest motivating center of the philosophical quest, which at its root is the spiritual quest of man for true existence.

To speak of philosophy of history, of course, is to broach the question to which the present study as a whole is an attempt at an answer: what are the features of an adequate philosophy of history and what does Eric Voegelin uniquely contribute to this subject? It is also to touch on another of the points at which misunderstanding may arise for one initially approaching the study of Voegelin's thought. The normal expectation when one hears of a "philosopher of history" is that he will claim to have discovered laws that govern history as an immanent course of events and to be able, on the basis of this knowledge, both to explain the past and to predict the future. Eilert Løvborg, in Ibsen's *Hedda Gabler*, is a parody of such a figure, based on a model exemplified elsewhere in a less Dionysiac style by such figures as G. W. F. Hegel, Karl Marx, and Henry Thomas Buckle. The fountainhead of this conception in the modern period was Giambattista Vico, who claimed that the philosophy of history, his "new science," could have far greater certainty than the currently prestigious sciences of nature.[8] The title of Voegelin's *New Science of Politics* alludes to the Viconian enterprise and attacks explicitly its more recent, positivist exemplars.

Voegelin's own conception of the philosophy of history is entirely different. In fact it is quite the opposite. He does not seek to identify determining forces that would enable a philosopher to ex-

8. Vico, *The New Science*, trans. T. G. Bergin and M. H. Fisch (Ithaca: Cornell University Press, 1948), bk. 1, sec. 3, no. 331.

plain or predict an immanent course of events. Rather he conceives of history as a function of the life of man, which means that there is always in history an irreducible element of freedom, both the possibility and the obligation of choice on the part of the historical agent, the individual human being. His choices may be either more conscious and rational or less so, depending on the degree of clarity with which the individual responds to the values of truth and responsible action, but nonetheless a measure of freedom always remains. For Voegelin the philosophy of history is the analysis of human life in its historical dimension, that is, of human life as a process in which choices are made and in which, through the values that are served or not served, one may or may not live up to the calling of one's potential humanity. History is an enterprise, in other words, in which one may succeed or fail, and what the philosophy of history must offer is criteria by which that success or failure may be measured.

These criteria can be found, Voegelin believes, by the study of man and his history. The opening sentence of *Order and History* states this as the fundamental principle of that work: "The order of history emerges from the history of order."[9] The philosophical historian discovers, in other words, that there is an order to human nature that has manifested itself historically. This order and the essentials of the human condition have been known implicitly by thinkers of every period of recorded history—even if many have failed to recognize or acknowledge them. Now and then these central truths of man's existence have been rendered explicit by means of various symbolisms. It is the task of the philosopher of history to recover these insights from forgetfulness, restore them to clarity, and where necessary to carry further the process of their explication.

Voegelin does not seek, therefore, to predict events or to speculate on the final shape of history in its temporal completion. Rather his effort is to illuminate man's historical life by elucidating the choices human beings have made and can make. The philosopher of

9. *Israel and Revelation* (Baton Rouge: Louisiana State University Press, 1956), p. ix. This volume will subsequently be abbreviated as *OH*, 1.

history is himself a man, faced with the same challenges as any other. He cannot stand above the course of history so as to see its end, but must dwell in the midst of it and there enact as best he can the drama of his fidelity.

It should now be clear, at least in a preliminary way, why Voegelin's philosophical thought could not take the customary form of a logical argument. He aims deeper, and he offers something different: an avenue of entry into the fundamental experience that underlies philosophy as such. Each person has a field of experience, but may notice more or less of its discernible features. Complicating this is the fact of human freedom and the spiritual dimension of our involvement in existence: we may choose not to notice what we do not wish to recognize. If this happens, we fall from what Voegelin calls "existence in truth" or "open existence" into what he calls "closed existence." The perspective of closed existence on reality will fail the experiential test of its validity—at least for one who, willing to recognize a greater range of experiential data, notices what has been left out. One who is not willing to notice, however, cannot be compelled. The extent to which interpretations of reality may be founded on attempts at systematic self-deception, is now, especially since Freud, widely recognized.[10] As James L. Wiser said in a commentary on *The World of the Polis*: "Philosophy cannot compel assent. It can only hope to initiate a conversion experience by supplying intimations of a fecund reality which is unavailable to the closed form of existence."[11] Nor is it necessarily a matter of

10. For several perspectives on the philosophical implications of the type of psychology of which Freud is probably the best known representative, see Paul Ricoeur, *Freud and Philosophy: An Essay on Interpretation,* trans. Denis Savage (New Haven: Yale University Press, 1970), Ernest Becker, *The Denial of Death* (New York: Free Press, 1973), and Lionel Trilling, *Sincerity and Authenticity* (Cambridge, Mass.: Harvard University Press, 1972). Literary studies of the principle are numerous; one might consider Mann's *Death in Venice,* Gide's *Pastoral Symphony,* or Camus's *The Fall,* to name only a few.

11. "Philosophy and Human Order," *Political Science Reviewer,* 2 (1972): 158. See also p. 140, where Wiser says philosophy suggests a perspective within which one may encounter transcendence. For a more recent treatment by Wiser of the same theme, see his "Philosophy as Inquiry and Persuasion," in McKnight, ed., *Eric Voegelin's Search for Order in History,* pp. 127–38.

willingness or perversity; it may also be a matter of lack of language or of the obscurity of symbols. What we cannot name or represent is difficult even to notice.

What Voegelin has set out to do in *Order and History* and his other mature works is to recover the roots of philosophical thinking that for most of us lie buried under layers of uprooted symbols that have accumulated for centuries. He does so by tracing the symbols that we call ideas to their origins in the philosophical experience of the thinkers who first developed them. This does not mean that he thinks the first expressions of philosophical thought are necessarily complete, so that they constitute what might be called classical norms for all later thought. It only means that it is to the origins that he looks for the experiences that engender ideas and give them their meanings.

Philosophy is constantly being lost, and if it is to continue, it must constantly be rediscovered. The rediscovery is a process of appropriation and reappropriation that involves both a movement back into the past of human thinking and downward into its depths. Both movements are concrete and empirical; both can be tested according to criteria that are genuinely objective, even if they make severe demands of intellectual and spiritual maturity on the part of those who would apply them.[12] The two movements, moreover, may be evaluated independently; that one may acquire a valid fundamental perspective on the human experience of existence

12. Dante Germino, in his chapter on Voegelin in *Beyond Ideology: The Revival of Political Theory* (New York: Harper and Row, 1967), p. 183, offers a good description of the challenges involved in evaluating the quality of philosophical reflection when it is conceived of in this way as compared with the positivistic approach: "Within the positivistic universe of discourse, all propositions must be verified by experience. But the only experience accepted as objective—and therefore in the realm of science—is that observable by the physical senses. Other dimensions of experience, apprehended through the *nous* or eye of the mind instead of the eye of the physical body, are treated as subjective because they are not as universally shared and readily communicable as experiences on the level of physical sensation." The result, he says, is a positivistically conceived science appealing not to persons of mature mind and character but to a lowest common denominator.

does not necessarily mean that the interpretation of a text or event from the past will have a matching validity, though a comprehensive view of man will be of great advantage in the interpretation of a thinker of rich experience and complex insights. What I hope to do in the present study is first to render explicit the theoretical framework of Voegelin's thought and then to show his interpretive application of it to the historical data on which it is based. If I succeed in presenting these two sides of his work with clarity, the reader should be in a position to make an appropriate assessment of Voegelin's achievement both as a philosopher and as an intellectual historian. I hope the reader will then share my judgment that Voegelin deserves to be ranked among the major philosophers.

PART 1

THEORIA

The Principles
of Voegelin's Thought

CHAPTER 1

Philosophy and History

"VERY deep is the well of the past," wrote Thomas Mann in the opening line of *Joseph and His Brothers*.[1] Mann's symbol of history as a deep, perhaps bottomless well that we attempt to sound in order to discover the deep sources from which our life rises to us expresses precisely the intimate and paradoxical relation that Voegelin, too, sees between the study of the human past and that of the depths of man as such. From the accustomed modern point of view, history tends to be seen as a record of past events in space and time, but for Voegelin *anamnesis*, or memory, is, as it was for Plato, a complex symbol. It points toward the historical past, but it also points inward and downward—into the depths of the historical present. Historical inquiry, therefore, is an exploration not only of past events and their interrelations but also of the structure of human existence as a process of participation in being. This means that history as a study is in its essential character a philosophical discipline. Similarly, to Voegelin philosophy itself is a process of reflection in which the structure of human existence and its historical character become conscious. As he put it in his essay, "Eternal Being in Time," written in 1964, history and philosophy mutually constitute one another (*Anam.*, p. 133). History is a philosophical inquiry, and philosophy is intrinsically historical in structure. Both engage in a double movement that is simultaneously a movement backward in time to reappropriate the past and a movement into the depths of the perpetual present, what Voegelin has called the "flow

1. Trans. H. T. Lowe-Porter (New York: Alfred A. Knopf, 1968), p. 3. Voegelin considers Mann's *Joseph* to offer one of the great philosophies of history in our time.

17

of presence," to appropriate, as far as this is possible to reflective consciousness, the essential structure of human existence.[2]

The starting point for philosophical reflection is always the philosopher's present historical situation, his own questioning consciousness as it has been shaped by the concerns, the questions, and the language of those who have sought understanding before him. As Karl Jaspers said at the beginning of his *Philosophy*, philosophical questions "arise from a *situation* in which, coming from a past, I find myself."[3] The philosopher discovers himself as a historical being, both in the sense that his own life is woven into the web of events around him, including the events of philosophical questioning and aspiration, and in the sense that he is himself a being in process. Again as Jaspers put it, "I can see the situation only as a motion that keeps transforming me along with itself." Perpetually changing, surrounded by darkness, longing for light, beset by fears of the loss of understanding and of existence itself, the historical individual is drawn into a web of questioning in which immemorial generations have been caught in the same way. As Paul Ricoeur has put it, "The philosopher does not speak from nowhere, but from the depths of his Greek memory, from which rises the question: *ti to on?* what is being?"[4]

The question of being, when asked by one motivated by the experience of his own historicity, is a special kind of question. It is

2. For the concept of the "flow of presence" or "flowing presence," see "Immortality: Experience and Symbol," *Harvard Theological Review,* 60 (1967): 235–79, and *Anam.*, p. 133.

3. Karl Jaspers, *Philosophy,* trans. E. B. Ashton, 3 vols. (Chicago: University of Chicago Press, 1969–71), 1:43. This three-volume work was originally published in 1932. As will be described below, Voegelin attended Jaspers's lectures at Heidelberg in 1929.

4. Paul Ricoeur, *The Symbolism of Evil,* trans. Emerson Buchanan (Boston: Beacon Press, 1969), p. 20. Voegelin's basic conception of philosophy is similar to Ricoeur's, although he cannot be said to have been influenced by him, since his own thought was already well formed by the time he read Ricoeur. Both men developed their ways of thinking against the immediate background of Jaspers and Husserl (for Ricoeur there was also the important influence of Gabriel Marcel). For an approving reference to Ricoeur by Voegelin, see *Anam.*, pp. 209–10.

not a question about an object that can be examined from a detached viewpoint; rather it is an attempt to reach toward the clarification of a mystery that will not cease to be mysterious. Nor is it only an attempt at understanding. Clarity of reflective consciousness, to the extent that it can be developed, is itself an event in reality, an act of participation in being, as Voegelin frequently puts it. The question of being is not simply a question about the nature of something, but a question about how to be. "I would like," said Jaspers, speaking of this type of inquiry, "an answer that will give me *support*."[5] The question of being is itself an existential project, and the questioner looks for guidance on how to carry it out.

Ricoeur said that the question of being arises from the depths of the philosopher's Greek memory, for it was the Greeks who first taught us to ask it, and much of Voegelin's philosophical research has been an effort to recover a precise sense of that question, its symbolism, and the experience that gave rise to it. The question is always asked, however, in a particular way, which one learns less from the Greeks than from one's contemporaries and more recent forebears. Before a philosopher can acquire a Greek memory, as Voegelin eventually did, he must dwell in the memory of his own historical starting point, his own place and time. For Voegelin in his formative years this was early twentieth-century Vienna—from the last years of the Hapsburg monarchy through the period of the Austrian Republic, until he was forced to flee from the Nazis shortly after the Anschluss in 1938.

Voegelin was born in Cologne, Germany, in 1901 and between the ages of four and nine lived in Oberkassel and Königswinter, small towns on the Rhine just south of Bonn. In 1910 his family moved to Vienna, where he later attended the university, receiving his doctorate in political science, and eventually becoming a professor in the Faculty of Law.[6] Despite the long association with Vienna, however, Voegelin's experience was not at all narrowly

5. Jaspers, *Philosophy*, 1:43.
6. The title of his degree was *Doctor rerum politicorum*. It was awarded in 1922 by the Law Faculty of the University of Vienna.

localized. It was customary at that time for a scholar to prepare himself by traveling to numerous major universities and attending the lectures of distinguished authorities in his field. Voegelin's own field, political thought, was broad, and his opportunities for travel were even wider than those of most students at the time, because he had received a Laura Spelman Rockefeller Memorial Fellowship for study in the United States from 1924 to 1926. This took him to Harvard, where he attended the lectures of Alfred North Whitehead and others, and to the University of Wisconsin, where he was especially impressed by the thought of the political economist, John R. Commons. This visit resulted in Voegelin's first book, *Über die Form des amerikanischen Geistes (On the American Mind)*, published in 1928.[7]

The return from America and the writing and publication of that book did not terminate Voegelin's scholarly *Wanderjahre*. In 1929 he spent a term at Heidelberg University, where he attended the lectures of Karl Jaspers, who at that time had written his *General Psychopathology* and *Psychologie der Weltanschauungen (Psychology of World Views)* and was developing the ideas that four years later would be published in his *Philosophy*. It was Jaspers, says Voegelin, who started him on what was to become an extensive reading of Kierkegaard. He also read Heidegger, Husserl, and Bergson during this period, as well as such literary figures as Mallarmé, Valéry,

7. This book discusses C. S. Peirce, William James, and George Santayana, as well as the American Puritans and Anglo-American legal theory. There is a chapter devoted to John R. Commons. Voegelin praises in particular Commons's analysis of abstract political entities into sequences of transactions on the part of individuals, which, as he puts it, brings men and institutions onto a single plane and does away with the idea that society and its institutions have a preeminent reality under which that of the individual person is subsumed. He also praises Commons for his recognition that there is a continual, unavoidable tension between the ideal goals of an individual on the one hand and his concrete practice of life in society on the other; resolutions of conflicts within society must take place through the reasonableness of men who have "common sense." Voegelin interprets Commons as basically within the "common sense" tradition of philosophy deriving from Thomas Reid. For further observations by Voegelin on Reid and "common sense" philosophy, see *Anam.*, pp. 212–13.

Proust, Joyce, Mann, Kraus, and George.[8] Somewhat later, from 1933 to 1938, he read extensively in the literature of the neo-Thomist movement, which was then becoming intellectually prominent. He says that his special reason for the study of neo-Thomist thought was that it was very influential in the Christian Socialist Party, the majority party in Austria during those years, and that as a political scientist he had to understand the pattern of thought underlying the thinking of that party.[9]

To understand the development of Voegelin's thought it is important to remember his situation as a political scientist during the 1920s and 1930s. When he was seventeen years old, he saw the end of a political order that to the Austrians of the early part of the century had seemed virtually indestructible.[10] During the next decade or so, he saw the beginnings of a new political order emerge, and he saw this from a point close to the center of events, since from 1923 he was closely associated, as a teaching assistant and research assistant, with Hans Kelsen, the neo-Kantian legal theorist, who was the author of the Austrian Constitution and served as expert adviser to the Austrian Republic and later as a member of the Austrian Constitutional Court.[11] Voegelin also saw the crumbling of the Austrian and German republics in the 1930s as the Nazis rose to power, and he analyzed the process in which this took place in

8. Interesting in connection with Voegelin's literary reading, which has continued throughout his career, is the following observation from *Anam.*, p. 191: "If . . . one wishes to inform oneself about the great problems of thinking about order in Germany, one would do better to read the literary works of Robert Musil, Hermann Broch, Thomas Mann, Heimito von Doderer, or the dramas of Frisch and Dürrenmatt, rather than the professional literature of politics."

9. Conversation of April 27, 1978.

10. For a description of the Viennese intellectual milieu in the early part of this century, see Allan Janik and Stephen Toulmin, *Wittgenstein's Vienna* (New York: Simon and Schuster, 1973).

11. One of Voegelin's early published articles was a review article on Kelsen's *Allgemeine Staatslehre* (1925), "Kelsen's Pure Theory of Law," *Political Science Quarterly*, 42 (1927): 268–76. He says (conversation of April 27, 1978) that Kelsen played an important role in his getting the Laura Spelman Rockefeller fellowship, which enabled him to study in the United States, and that his association with Kelsen continued after his return to Vienna.

various articles and books that he published during this period, particularly *Rasse und Staat (Race and State, 1933), Die Rassenidee in der Geistesgeschichte von Ray bis Carus (The Idea of Race in Intellectual History from Ray to Carus, 1933), Der autoritäre Staat (The Authoritarian State,* 1936), and *Die politischen Religionen (Political Religions,* 1938).

During the time, then, that Voegelin's philosophical interests were forming, his own historical situation was that of a political scientist vitally concerned with the problems of justice and the order of society. He saw these threatened from several directions. On the level of national politics they were threatened by irrational, virtually demonic forces that the National Socialists were able to exacerbate, harness, and direct. On the level of the individual person they were threatened, well before the advent of Nazism as a movement, by the internal disorder of a mode of existence dominated by passion and appetite and lacking the orientation toward a transcendental *summum bonum* that the spiritual traditions of Christianity and Judaism had attempted to encourage. On the level of intellectual culture they were threatened by various obstacles to a serious search for solutions to the problems of right order in society and in the individual soul. These obstacles included a scientistic theory of knowledge that placed severe limits on inquiry and fostered an externalizing conception of existence.[12] They included also a positivistic, immanentist theory of man, and a widespread belief in a supposed dichotomy between facts and values.[13]

Voegelin's inclination from early on was to interpret the prob-

12. Voegelin was later to criticize this type of thought in detail in "The Origins of Scientism," *Social Research,* 15 (1948): 462–94.

13. Voegelin has studied the origins and development of the modern immanentist theory of man in *From Enlightenment to Revolution* (1975). The introduction to *The New Science of Politics* (1952) is devoted to a critique of positivism in the social sciences and the idea of the fact-value dichotomy, especially as represented by Max Weber. For some early articles by Voegelin in which he can be seen wrestling with the idea of the fact-value dichotomy, see, for example, "Max Weber" (1930) and "Das Sollen im System Kants" (1931). For a general introduction to the idea of the fact-value dichotomy in Viennese intellectual history, see Janik and Toulmin, *Wittgenstein's Vienna,* pp. 164–66, 234–37, 244.

lems of political and social order as founded on the order or lack of it in the souls of the individual members of society. This is how his studies as a political scientist led him inevitably into political philosophy and eventually to philosophy of history. The various roadblocks to philosophical inquiry mentioned above, however, made difficult the search for an understanding of such issues; and the academic philosophy of the time, even to the extent that it was not an active impediment, offered little help in overcoming these difficulties. Jaspers, who like Voegelin came to philosophy from the vantage point of another discipline (in his case psychology), because the more searching questions growing out of his own research forced him toward it, has described the philosophical scene of the 1920s and his relation to it in terms that Voegelin would probably consider to echo his own feelings at that time:

> It seemed to me that the philosophy of the academicians was not really philosophy; instead, with its claims to be a science, it seemed to be entirely a discussion of things which are not essential for the basic questions of our existence. In my own consciousness I myself was not originally a philosopher. But when the intellectual world is empty of philosophy, it becomes the task at least to bear witness to philosophy, to direct the attention to the great philosophers, to try to stop confusion, and to encourage in our youth the interest in real philosophy.[14]

Voegelin was later to say regarding Plato's conception of philosophy, "His philosopher does not exist in a social vacuum, but in opposition to the sophist."[15] Philosophy is not simply an academic subject matter, but an active struggle for truth, moral, spiritual, and intellectual: "Justice is not defined in the abstract but in opposition to the concrete forms which injustice assumes. The right order of the polis is not presented as an 'ideal state,' but the

14. "Philosophical Autobiography," in *The Philosophy of Karl Jaspers*, ed. Paul Arthur Schilpp (New York: Tudor, 1957), p. 34.

15. *Order and History, vol. 3: Plato and Aristotle* (Baton Rouge: Louisiana State University Press, 1957), p. 63. This volume will subsequently be abbreviated as *OH*, 3.

elements of right order are developed in concrete opposition to the elements of disorder in the surrounding society. And the shape, the Eidos, of Arete [true excellence] in the soul grows in opposition to the many *eide* of disorder in the soul."

First comes the struggle, motivated not by an idea or theory but by an initial, inchoate sense of a true good to be won or lost, something mysteriously precious that the soul will lose at its peril. One need not be a philosopher to sense the urgency of the struggle and to join in it. Paul Ricoeur has said of the Israelite prophets, "The prophet does not 'reflect' *on* sin; he 'prophesies' *against*."[16] Still, when the struggle is carried out with fidelity to the goal of truth, eventually it generates reflection by its very nature; it may begin in darkness, but it is a struggle for light. As Voegelin, again, has put it in his discussion of Plato: "Nevertheless, the struggle itself becomes a source of knowledge. In suffering and resisting the soul discerns the directions from which the pulls come. The darkness engenders the light in which it can distinguish between life and death, between the helper and the enemy. And the growing light of wisdom illuminates the way for the soul to travel" (*OH*, 3:62).

In the urgency of its struggle for true life, the soul looks, as Jaspers said, for support, and where this cannot be found in the philosophy of the academicians, it will be sought outside the academy. Jaspers himself found it in Kierkegaard and Nietzsche especially. Voegelin says that in his own youth, the only philosophers who were widely read in the German-speaking countries were Schopenhauer and Nietzsche, neither of them academically fashionable. He first began reading both at the age of about fifteen, and to them he joined, at about eighteen, the Upanishads. Voegelin has always been selective in what he has taken from any thinker for use in his own philosophical quest, and he has spoken critically of Nietzsche in some of his later writings.[17] In his youth,

16. *Symbolism of Evil*, p. 54.

17. See for example, *Science, Politics, and Gnosticism* (Chicago: Henry Regnery, 1968), pp. 28–34, 54–65. For an earlier, less harsh, appraisal of Nietzsche's place in German intellectual history, see "Nietzsche, the Crisis and the War," *Journal of Politics*, 6 (1944): 177–212.

however, he heard in him a voice calling and encouraging the reader to aspire to heights of reflective self-awareness, to a rigorous honesty of thought that would amount to a form of spiritual renewal. Jaspers has said of Kierkegaard and Nietzsche that one of the principal features they have in common is that "reflection is for both preeminently self-reflection. For them, the way to truth is through understanding oneself." [18] Unlimited self-reflectiveness could, however, as Jaspers goes on to say, lead to a sterile introspectiveness and self-preoccupation, "a slavish rotation about one's own empirical existence." From Schopenhauer and the Upanishads Voegelin learned to recognize, in the depths of man himself, a radical thrust toward self-transcendence, a deep longing for a good beyond the limited existence of man. The profound impression that this early awakening of a sense of transcendence made on him, well before he became acquainted with Jaspers and Kierkegaard, may be seen already in his book on the American mind where he argues against the idea that being could ever become, as Hegel had hoped, a closed rational system, because it has a transcendental dimension that is an openness making any closure into system impossible; being, he says, is never a secure and certain possession but a movement reaching beyond itself toward a goal that is correlative to the indwelling tension (*immanente Spannung*) of our existence. [19] Despite the changes that have taken place in his thinking in the intervening years— which were in fact only clarifications of the initial thrust of his thought—this early description of man's quest for truth as a movement of transcendence was echoed again almost precisely nearly

18. Karl Jaspers, *Reason and Existenz*, trans. William Earle (New York: Noonday Press, 1955), p. 33.

19. *Über die Form des amerikanischen Geistes* (Tübingen: J.C.B. Mohr, 1928), p. 20: "Das Sein is nicht Eins und nicht Zwei; d.h. es hat als Ganzes keinen Stützpunkt außerhalb seiner; und es ist kein geschlossenes rationales System im Innern, denn das Transzendieren in die Existenz ist eine Offenheit, die jede Schließung zum System essentiell unmöglich macht. Es ist also niemals ein beruhigtes Haben, ein absolut gewisses Besitzen, sondern immer eine über sich hinausgerichtete Bewegung, deren Ziel aber weder endlich, noch im Unendlichen gegeben ist, sondern nur als Symbol für eine immanente Spannung verstanden werden darf."

forty years later in the foreword to the German edition of *Anamnesis*, when he said, "The illusion of a 'theory' [that would give a precise description of being and of consciousness as though from a vantage point outside affording a comprehensive view] had to be abandoned in favor of the reality of the meditative process, a process that had to traverse phases of increasing experience and insight."[20]

Voegelin has spoken in various places of the necessary grounding of philosophy in meditative experience and of the need for "precautions of meditative practice" lest the original meaning of spiritually engendered symbols be lost from view.[21] In his Ingersoll Lecture on Immortality at Harvard in 1965, for example, he began with the observation that "when the experience engendering the symbols ceases to be a presence located in the man who has it, the reality from which the symbols derive their meaning has disappeared," and he went on to say, "There is no guaranty whatsoever that the reader . . . will be moved to a meditative reconstitution of the engendering reality; one may even say the chances are slim, as meditation requires more energy and discipline than most people are able to invest" ("Immortality," pp. 235–36). One might say also that we live in a time in which the very idea of experiential understanding of spiritual symbols tends to be rejected on principle as "unscientific" and "lacking in methodological rigor." Those who wish philosophy as an academic discipline to compete for respectability with the natural sciences are led to deny any claim to knowledge that cannot be validated by an observer whose objectivity is thought to be guaranteed precisely by his lack of the type of meditative experience that Voegelin considers essential. For Voegelin, on the other hand,

20. "Die Illusion der 'Theorie' hatte der Realität des meditativen Prozesses zu weichen; und dieser hatte seine Phasen zunehmender Erfahrung und Einsicht zu durchlaufen," *Anamnesis* (German), p. 7.

21. *Order and History, vol. 4: The Ecumenic Age* (Baton Rouge: Louisiana State University Press, 1974), p. 56. This volume will subsequently be abbreviated *OH*, 4. For some other places in which Voegelin has written about the practice of meditation and its importance, see *OH*, 4:52; *Anam.*, pp. 14–35, 175–76; *Anamnesis* (German), pp. 33–36; *Science, Politics, and Gnosticism* (1968), pp. 111–14; and "Immortality: Experience and Symbol" (1967).

it is this very type of knowledge, which he describes not as knowledge of information but as a "truth experienced," that must not be lost: "The truth conveyed by the symbols, however, is the source of right order in human existence; we cannot dispense with it" (p. 236).

In his own life the meditative movement of the soul as it pursues the sense of transcendence past all finite objects of knowledge or enjoyment has been the fountainhead of his thinking from his youth, when he first learned it by following the *neti neti* ("nay, nay") of the Upanishads:

> GARGYA: He who is the being in the sun and at the same time the being in the eye; he who, having entered the body through the eye, resides in the heart [of man] and is the doer and the experiencer—him I meditate upon as Brahman.
>
> AJATASATRU: Nay, nay! Do not speak thus of Brahman. That being I worship as transcendental, luminous, supreme. He who meditates upon Brahman as such goes beyond all created beings and becomes the glorious ruler of all.
>
> GARGYA: The being who is in the moon and at the same time in the mind—him I meditate upon as Brahman.
>
> AJATASATRU: Nay, nay! Do not speak thus of Brahman. That being I worship as infinite, clad in purity, blissful, resplendent. He who meditates upon Brahman as such lacks nothing and is forever happy.[22]

And so on. The kind of meditative practice that is here described, and that is at the heart of Voegelin's own philosophical experience, is a process of looking beyond all particular forms of reality, all finite objects of contemplation and enjoyment, toward absolute perfection of being. The particular forms of reality, to the extent that they represent degrees of perfection or fullness of being (of intelligibility, beauty, loveliness, and so on), suggest analogically still

22. "Brihadaranyaka," *The Upanishads: Breath of the Eternal,* trans. Swami Prabhavananda and Frederick Manchester (New York: Mentor Books, New American Library, n.d.), p. 82. Voegelin discusses this Upanishad in *OH,* 4:319–22. See also *Anam.,* p. 8.

higher degrees and in this way point in a direction that leads ultimately beyond all limited degrees toward a supreme perfection that
may be spoken of as their "ground," in which they "participate," in
the sense that it is said in the literature of meditation to be through
likeness to that supreme splendor that these forms of reality
exemplify, as sunbeams embody the light of the sun, the limited
perfection that is theirs.[23] The meditative practice itself, conceived
in this way, is not so much a seeing as a looking—a looking beyond
all that can be seen toward that which always remains, strictly
speaking, the ultimate Unknown, even though, by virtue of the
analogies that point beyond themselves and by virtue of the "indwelling tension" (immanente Spannung) mentioned earlier, one is
not totally ignorant of it either. One does not "see" the supreme
perfection, but one discovers intimations of it by "reading" or "sens-
ing," as it were, the directional tendency in the tension to which the
goal of the looking is correlative. One experiences the love, and by
knowing it, one also comes to know, "as in a glass darkly," what it
is one loves.

When asked to describe what he means by meditation, Voegelin
sometimes refers to the anonymous fourteenth-century classic of

23. For one of the more fully articulated theoretical expressions of the kind of
thinking referred to here, see Thomas Aquinas, *Commentary on "The Divine Names"
of Pseudo-Dionysius*. Aquinas says, for example: "Created beauty is nothing other
than a likeness of the divine beauty participated in things. . . . God, Who is
'supersubstantially beautiful, is called Beauty,' as Dionysius says, because He
confers beauty upon all created beings according to the peculiar nature [the
limited form of being] of each one. . . . God bestows beauty inasmuch as He is
'the cause of harmony (consonantia) and splendor of form (claritas) in all
things'. . . . Now Dionysius shows how God is the cause of splendor of form,
saying that He transmits to all creatures, with a certain lightning-like brightness,
a ray of his own brilliant light, which is the source of all illumination. And these
lightning-like communcations of the divine ray of light are to be understood
according to analogical participation; and as Dionysius says, they are 'beautify-
ing,' that is, productive of beauty in things." *An Introduction to the Metaphysics of
St. Thomas Aquinas*, trans. James F. Anderson (Chicago: Henry Regnery, 1969),
pp. 88–89. The nature of the "participationist" language that Aquinas uses here
will be a principal theme of the next chapter.

spirituality, *The Cloud of Unknowing*.[24] An excerpt from that may serve to further illustrate the character of the process in question:

> But now you will ask me, "How am I to think of God himself, and what is he?" and I cannot answer you except to say "I do not know!" For with this question you have brought me into the same darkness, the same cloud of unknowing where I want you to be! For though we through the grace of God can know fully about all other matters, and think about them—yes, even the very works of God himself—yet of God himself can no man think. Therefore I will leave on one side everything I can think, and choose for my love that thing which I cannot think! Why? Because he may well be loved, but not thought. By love he can be caught and held, but by thinking never.[25]

There is no claim here to privileged knowledge, to an intuition by which one grasps the supreme perfection as though it were an object one could master. Such an intuition would amount to what Voegelin calls *gnosis*, the Greek term for the type of knowledge that directly "sees" its object and possesses it with the certainty of intuition. Rather, there is not only an acknowledgment of ultimate ignorance but a recognition that ignorance, the "cloud of unknowing," is essential to the meditative quest, because what is looked toward is a fullness that is not only beyond the limits of all present conceptual forms but beyond all possible conceptual limits. It is by a "naked intention" (*The Cloud of Unknowing*, p. 61) directed toward the Unknown that the work of meditation is carried out.

This same passage from *The Cloud of Unknowing* points also, however, to a major problem that can arise for any thinking concerned with the transcendental: the problem that what is essentially beyond all limited forms may come to seem so absolutely unknow-

24. For a published reference to *The Cloud of Unknowing*, see *Anamnesis* (German), p. 35. He has referred frequently to both *The Cloud* and the Upanishads in conversation with me.

25. Trans. Clifton Wolters (Baltimore: Penguin Books, 1961), pp. 59–60. A helpful commentary on *The Cloud* is William Johnston, *The Mysticism of "The Cloud of Unknowing"* (St. Meinrad, Ind.: Abbey Press, 1975).

able that no thinking or language can apply to it. This would make the meditative experience that Voegelin speaks of as the "source of right order in human existence" unthinkable and incommunicable, which would defeat the philosopher from the start. From the point of view of the mystical contemplative, total silence might not be an unsatisfactory conclusion to the spiritual quest, but for the philosopher, and especially for the political philosopher, it would be a dead end: what can never be communicated cannot be *socially* effective. Unless the spiritual substance of the order within the soul can be communicated through symbols, it can never become the ordering principle of a society. Problems of the nature and mode of functioning of language, therefore, must be central to the concern of a thinker such as Voegelin, and the next chapter will explore them in some detail.

First, however, it may be helpful to consider the ways in which the orientation of Voegelin's thought through the meditative experience awakened by his early reading helped him to find his way past the major intellectual obstacles of his time. These included an externalizing conception of being, an immanentizing conception of man, the belief in a dichotomy between facts and values, and a tendency to deny genuine cognitive status to modes of knowing not of the form exemplified in the natural sciences. Collectively these have a common feature that might not be immediately evident but which can be discerned upon reflection and which for Voegelin seemed the very heart of the problem: a tendency to conceive of reality in such a way that it seems reduced from a mystery in which we are overwhelmingly involved to a problem we can master. Ultimately this amounts to the reduction of existence to ideas.

In the 1920s and 1930s Voegelin found himself in a world in which the most representative thinkers seemed to be trapped inside their own heads, lost in a forest of concepts, unable to root their thinking in the solidity of actual experience. Even thinkers such as Husserl and Heidegger, whom he saw as making a serious and important effort to return to the experiential roots of thought, seemed to him to have fallen victim to the tendency to place stifling limits on the experience to which they appealed. Heidegger he read primarily in 1929, but he was later to describe him as the willing victim of "the shutting off of immanent from world-transcendent being" (*Science, Politics, and Gnosticism*, p. 47). Husserl he read over a much longer period. In the new first chapter of the English *Anamnesis* he describes how his wrestling with the implications of Husserl's thought finally came to a head in 1943 after he had an opportunity to read Husserl's *Crisis of European Sciences*.[26] There were two points that particularly struck him. One was the attempt through the Husserlian phenomenology to establish philosophy once and for all (in its *Endstiftung*) as an apodictically certain science.[27] The other was Husserl's schema of history, which divided it into three phases: (1) an irrelevant prehistory, (2) the beginnings of philosophy among the Greeks, with a long hiatus between them and Descartes, and (3) a final phase of perfection inaugurated by the "apodictic beginning" set by Husserl's own work. "I still remember the shock when I read this 'philosophy of history,'" writes Voegelin: "I could not help recognizing the all-too-familiar type of phase constructions in which had indulged the Enlightenment philosophes and, after them, Comte, Hegel, and Marx. It was one more of the symbolisms created by apocalyptic-gnostic thinkers,

26. This was first published in the periodical *Philosophia I* (Belgrade, 1936). It was based in part on a lecture "Philosophy and the Crisis of European Humanity," presented before the Vienna Cultural Society, May 7 and 10, 1935, which Voegelin attended. Both the book and the lecture are contained in Edmund Husserl, *The Crisis of European Sciences and Transcendental Phenomenology*, trans. David Carr (Evanston: Northwestern University Press, 1970). A letter of September 17, 1943, from Voegelin to the sociologist Alfred Schütz giving his response to this work at the time is reprinted in *Anamnesis* (German), pp. 21–36.

27. *Anam.*, pp. 9–10. See also *Anamnesis* (German), p. 24. For a description of Husserl's intention to make philosophy a rigorous science, see Maurice Natanson, *Edmund Husserl: Philosopher of Infinite Tasks* (Evanston: Northwestern University Press, 1973), pp. 5, 161. Natanson says Husserl considered philosophy the search for radical certitude and wished to locate in experience the kind of necessity found in mathematics.

with the purpose of abolishing a 'past history' of mankind and letting its 'true history' begin with the respective author's own work" (*Anam.*, p. 10).

Although, as he wrote in his letter to Alfred Schütz at the time, he had no wish to call into question the intellectual brilliance of Husserl, since the limitations of Husserl's thought were those prevailing in his historical setting, Voegelin was able to recognize, standing out clearly against the background of epistemological and methodological discussion, the essential features of a consciousness rotating about itself in sterile self-preoccupation (*Anamnesis*, German ed., p. 36). Even before he could formulate theoretically the reasons for his dissatisfaction with this way of conceiving of man and being, he had a clear "feeling that the analysis of consciousness is a dead end," a feeling of virtual suffocation (*Anam.*, p. 15). "Something had to be done. I had to get out of that 'apodictic horizon' as fast as possible" (p. 10).

This meant, however, that he would have to "formulate the alternative to Husserl's conception of an egologically constituted consciousness" (p. 10). This in turn meant the he would have to develop a more adequate theory of consciousness that would take into account the radical openness of the horizon of consciousness—involving transcendence both into the world and toward what is beyond the world (p. 36). It would also have to take account of the historicity of consciousness: "Husserl's apocalyptic construct had the purpose of abolishing history and thereby to justify the exclusion of the historical dimension from the constitution of man's consciousness; the alternative, therefore, had to reintroduce the historical dimension Husserl wanted to exclude" (p. 10). This was not a matter of introducing a "history of ideas" approach; that would simply compound the problem of imprisonment in subjectivity. It was a matter of recognizing that the historicity of consciousness was a function of its radical finitude, its rootedness in the flesh, and its involvement in a world and a total context of reality that transcends it:

The historical dimension at issue was not a piece of "past history" but the permanent presence of the process of reality in which man participates with his conscious existence. Reality, it is true, can move into the position of an object-of-thought intended by a subject-of-cognition, but before this can happen there must be a reality in which human beings with a consciousness occur. Moreover, by virtue of their consciousness these human beings are quite conscious of being parts of a comprehensive reality and express their awareness by the symbols of birth and death, of a cosmic whole structured by realms of being, of a world of external objects and of the presence of divine reality in the cosmos, of mortality and immortality, of creation into the cosmic order and of salvation from its disorder, of descent into the depths of the *psyche* and meditative ascent toward its beyond. [Pp. 10–11]

This effort of retheorization implied, in fact, as the traditional, even somewhat archaic flavor of the list of symbols just recited indicates, the kind of extensive reappropriation of human historical experience and symbolization that eventually was to become the task of *Order and History*.

At the moment, however, in 1943, it meant both a clarification of the nature of Voegelin's theories in relation to Husserl's and an initial effort to identify more precisely the experiential foundations of adequate philosophizing. The first task was carried out in the letter to Alfred Schütz and in a subsequent essay, "On the Theory of Consciousness"; the second began with a set of "Anamnetic Experiments" in which Voegelin attempted to trace through recollection the prereflective roots of transcendental experience in his own childhood.[28] Voegelin concludes the "Theory of Consciousness" essay

28. All three of these were written in 1943, although they were not published until 1966 in *Anamnesis* (German). The original title of "On the Theory of Consciousness" was, probably significantly, "Zum Theorie des Bewußtseins" (*Toward* the Theory of Consciousness), since it is Voegelin's contention, as opposed to a thinker such as Husserl, that a comprehensive theory of consciousness that would exhaust its dimension of mystery is not possible. On this point, see Dante Germino, "Eric Voegelin's *Anamnesis*," *Southern Review*, n.s., 7 (1971): 70–72.

with the judgment that "the basic subjectivity of the egological sphere" in Husserl's thought is the symptom of a "spiritual nihilism" in that "the creation of the transcendental I as the central symbol of philosophy implies the destruction of the cosmic whole within which philosophizing becomes at all possible" (*Anam.*, p. 35). Voegelin's own contrasting conception situates philosophy firmly within the historical world and within the concrete existence of the philosopher:

> Inasmuch as the consciousness of philosophizing is no "pure" consciousness but rather the consciousness of a human being, all philosophizing is an event in the philosopher's life history—further an event in the history of the community with its symbolic language; further in the history of mankind, and further in the history of the cosmos. . . . the systematic reflection on consciousness is a late event in the biography of the philosopher. The philosopher always lives in the context of his own history, the history of a human existence in the community and in the world. [P. 33]

The problem with Husserl ultimately, as Voegelin wrote to Schütz, was that despite his claims he was not really a radical thinker at all in the sense of developing clarity regarding the roots of his thinking: "his radicalism, which he constantly emphasized, is not a radicalism of philosophical existence, but only radicalism in the following out of a special problem" within the framework of questioning set up historically by such thinkers as Descartes and Kant.[29] Husserl could not be a radical thinker in Voegelin's sense precisely because the tradition of thought within which he was working had cut itself off from the thinker's own real experiential roots: "The development of the transcendental critique down to Husserl is characterized by the dissolution not only of traditional symbolic systems but also by the exclusion of the underlying areas of experi-

29. "Sein Radikalismus, den er immer betont, ist nicht ein radikalismus der philosophischen Existenz, sondern der Radikalismus in der Verfolgung eines Speziaiproblems, eben des transzendentalphilosophischen." *Anamnesis* (German), p. 25.

ences and problems from the orbit of philosophical reflection (*Anam.*, p. 35).

That this loss of the experiential ground should have happened, says Voegelin, was not accidental; it is itself historically rooted in the modern Western civilizational crisis in which much of the traditional symbolism had ceased to function effectively to mediate the experiences of transcendence that originally engendered them (p. 34). For Voegelin, on the other hand, such symbols retained some degree of transparency. The task he now set himself was to retrace his way to the prereflective experiential roots in his own life that gave present vitality to such traditional symbols as cosmos, mortality and immortality, God and the gods, the Beyond, and so on. Between October 25 and November 7, 1943, he engaged in the experiments of recall now recorded in "Anamnetic Experiments." His purpose was to locate within his early years, before age ten, "the experiences that impel toward reflection and do so because they have excited consciousness to the 'awe' of existence" (p. 36; the various recollections appear on pp. 38–51). There are twenty recollections, each numbered. They show the origins, as early as fourteen months of age, of a sense of time as passing and as an inner constitutive presence. The memory of a Mardi Gras Parade of Fools as seen from a balcony involved a sense of phenomena as evanescent processes in time (the parade was constantly drawing new "fools" at the same time as it was crumbling at the rear). This memory involved also an oppressive feeling of anxiety, the first intimations of the threat of death, which became more fully articulated around age seven or eight in the fear that Halley's comet would destroy the earth. The memory of the legend of a monk who is said to have walked for a day lost in meditation only to return to his cloister to find a hundred years had passed suggests an early sense of the paradoxical intertwining within consciousness of temporal flow and timeless contemplation. Several memories involved the sense, experienced with varying degrees of poignancy and acceptance, of an unattainable Beyond: the legend of a Never-Never Land beyond the mountains, or of a

Paradise far away in China, or of a Cloud Castle on the Wolkenstein and of the "vague, sad, lost figure" of the knight who dwells there. Some memories involved a sense of the mysteriousness of space and perspective. One recalled an initial awareness of the uncertainty of induction (rain is not caused by the dark clouds of smoke emitted by freighters on the Rhine). Another had to do with a clash between appearance and reality (mistaking a splendidly helmeted attendant for the Kaiser when the imperial procession passed through Oberkassel). Several had to do with the magic of fairy tale and legend and generally with the evocativeness of symbols. Some Dutch ships he saw on the Rhine bore exotic names such as Kriemhild, Siegfried, and Xante, while others brought prosaic men with prosaic wares: the result was two different Hollands, one for saga and one for cheese. Similarly illustrative of the power of symbolism and its relation to the indwelling tension in the soul was the memory of what it was like as a schoolboy to study the history of Prussia backwards, proceeding from the ordinary recent monarchs to those who took on increasing stature as they became more remote in time. "That seemed to be the right perspective," says Voegelin: "to look from the humanly comprehensible present into the depth of time and see the horizon closing with ever-larger figures that provided security. Whatever capacity I have today to understand mythical images of history, like that of the Greeks, must have developed on occasion of this reversed Prussian history. I have always taken it for granted that the present was to be measured, with Thucydides, in human terms, that with increasing distance men grew to the size of a Solon and Lycurgus, that behind them there cavorted the heroes, and that the horizon was securely and dependably closed by the gods" (pp. 47–48, no. 15).

What the experiments of recall accomplished for Voegelin at the time was the development of greater clarity regarding the basic motives of his thinking: "I was confronted with the question of why I was attracted by 'larger horizons' and repelled, if not nauseated, by restrictive deformations. The answer to this question could not be found by pitting truth against falsehood on the level of 'ideas'. . . . The reasons had to be sought, not in a theory of consciousness, but concretely in the constitution of the responding and verifying consciousness. And that concrete consciousness was my own" (p. 12). The childhood experiences recalled were important, he says, "because they were living forces in the present constitution of my consciousness" (p. 13). In his most extensive theoretical essay, "What Is Political Reality?" (written in 1966) Voegelin said that non-noetic (i.e., pretheoretical) symbolisms expressed in myth and legend precede the noetic ones by thousands of years and that "the non-noetic interpretations not only precede the noetic ones in time, but, after the emergence of noetic interpretation, they also remain the form of society's self-interpretation" (p. 144).[30] Just as society may be described as man written large, so individual consciousness shows a parallel relation between theoretical and pretheoretical levels of constitutive self-understanding. Voegelin's anamnetic experiments of 1943 traced the deepest accessible symbolizations of the ordering experiences that had been operative in his adult consciousness for the preceding two decades, that had turned his mind to meditative thinking from his adolescence, that had led him to speak of an indwelling tension within human experience as early as his book on the American mind, that had led him to study such philosophers as Schopenhauer, Nietzsche, Husserl, Heidegger, and Jaspers, and that drove him to rebel decisively against the ideological restrictions that had trapped so much of modern thought within a wilderness of abstractions and closed off from consciousness the full range of philosophical experience, the heights and depths of the life of the soul.

It would be a mistake to think that the breakthrough of 1943 was a radical new turn in Voegelin's thought. His conscious revolt

30. Voegelin's conception of *noesis* will be discussed in detail in chapter 3. For the moment it may be described as articulated reflective understanding involving critical self-awareness on the part of the inquirer based on some degree of understanding of the nature of inquiry as such.

against the ideologizing restriction of horizons had already been under way for two decades or more before that time, and in fact that "breakthrough" was really only a clarification of insights that had been developing continuously. Nor should the well-documented reflections of 1943 be interpreted as the final step in this process. The so far undocumented realization in 1945, mentioned in the Introduction, that mythic symbolism would always be indispensable to philosophy, that the conceptual articulation of theory will always lie between a pretheoretical myth and a philosopher's myth that reaches out into an inexhaustible frontier of consciousness, was at least equally important, in his opinion. There have been further new realizations since then, as will be discussed in the eighth chapter. None of these, however, have involved any departure from Voegelin's basic conception that the roots of philosophical thinking, in the true sense of the word (that is, of an existential quest for being through the right ordering of the soul), lie in the fundamental experience of what he has come to call the "tension of existence."

In Voegelin's own life this tension expressed itself first in the childhood experiences of wonder, awe, fear, perplexity, and longing. Later it expressed itself as the force of philosophical questioning and the revolt against restrictive horizons. Retrospectively he discovered that the tension had always been present, but that it could take a variety of forms according to the intellectual, moral, and spiritual situation of the person in whom it lives. It is not an emotion, but something more basic; it can express itself in the form of emotion, but it can also express itself in the form of worship, inquiry, moral concern, poetry, the arts, and so on. As the term "tension" indicates, what it is most basically is a tendency or tending, a fundamental reaching toward a fullness that can be apprehended under many aspects, but that is not exhausted in any of them. It is a longing for life, for maximal participation in being. It is an unrestricted, radical "Question" that hungers and thirsts after all possible truth—not just the answers to particular, determinate questions, but understanding of all forms of reality and, beyond them, of an ultimacy that in their various, limited ways they analogically exemplify.[31] Similarly, this tension may be described as an unrestricted love rising from the deepest level of the soul and longing for enjoyment of all possible good, both limited goods and the unlimited good beyond them of which they serve as intimations.

That this tension or longing is unrestricted does not, however, immediately become apparent. For the child, or for the adult lacking reflectiveness and maturity of experience, the experienced tension may take the conscious form only of particular appetites: for pleasure, for power, for prestige, for perpetual mundane existence free from the threat of death, and so on. Many before Voegelin have noticed both the tension and the difficulties of knowing it. Saint Augustine, for example, speaks in the first chapter of his *Confessions* of the fundamental experience of the *cor inquietum*, the restless heart, that reaches past all earthly goods toward the divine ground: "tu excitas, ut laudare te delectet, quia fecisti nos ad te et inquietum est cor nostrum, donec requiescat in te" ("you arouse us, that we may love praising you, for you have made us for yourself and our heart is restless until it rests in you").[32] At the time Augustine wrote this, however, despite the immediacy of the experience, more intimate to us than we are to ourselves, it was a hard-won realization, and the rest of the *Confessions* is largely a description of the long, often faltering process by which he came to the self-knowledge here expressed. T. S. Eliot in "Little Gidding," the last of the *Four Quartets*, used the symbol of the shirt of Nessus to suggest the inexorability and even anguish of the same longing that for Augustine eventually became an inexhaustible joy:

> Who then devised the torment? Love.
> Love is the unfamiliar Name
> Behind the hands that wove

31. Voegelin develops the symbol of the unrestricted "Question" in *OH*, 4:316–35.

32. Augustine, *Confessions*, with an English trans. by William Watts, 2 vols. (Cambridge, Mass.: Harvard University Press, 1912), 1. 1. (my translation).

> The intolerable shirt of flame
> Which human power cannot remove.[33]

C. S. Lewis spoke in his autobiography of the force of "an unsatisfied desire which is itself more desirable than any other satisfaction" and which he called Joy, but which he also said might "almost equally well be called a particular kind of unhappiness or grief," yet which one who had once tasted it would never wish to exchange for all the pleasures in the world.[34] These are all Christian examples, but others could be given from different religious traditions, from ancient Egyptian Pyramid texts, the poetry of medieval Sufis, Tamil devotional hymns, and so on, and of course Voegelin's own early reading of the Upanishads has already been mentioned.[35] Each of the three Christian authors cited, moreover, was referring to an experience he considered to be universal, even if not always clearly noticed.

Voegelin does not consider himself to be at all original in the sense of developing ideas never before thought. On the contrary, he considers the universality of the experience of existential tension to be its most philosophically important feature. The adequacy of present philosophical reflection must depend, he believes, on its fidelity to what has often been noticed and symbolized over millennia. "The test of truth . . . ," as he puts it, "will be the lack of originality in the propositions."[36]

There will probably be many, on the other hand, to whom the proposition that human existence is characterized by a fundamental,

33. *The Complete Poems and Plays, 1909–1950* (New York: Harcourt, Brace and World, 1952), p. 144. The image of the shirt of Nessus (that killed Hercules) is from the *Trachiniae* by Sophocles.

34. C. S. Lewis, *Surprised by Joy: The Shape of My Early Life* (New York: Harcourt, Brace and World, 1955), pp. 17–18.

35. Voegelin's article, "Immortality: Experience and Symbol," is in large part a commentary on the expression of this sort of experience in the Egyptian "Dispute of a Man, Who Contemplates Suicide, with His Soul," from the First Intermediate Period, ca. 2000 B.C.

36. "Equivalences of Experience and Symbolization in History," in *Eternità e Storia: I valori permanenti nel divenire storico* (Florence: Valecchi, 1970), p. 222.

direction-giving tension will seem debatable at best. Certainly its truth is not directly evident from the form of the proposition, nor is it analytically derivable from any other self-evident truth. For one who does not recognize the experience to which it refers, it will seem to be simply an idea, deriving from a history of such ideas, and serving as a presupposition from which Voegelin's thought will seem to be a set of deductions. It will be best to recognize straightforwardly the problem this presents. The experience of existential tension is indeed the starting point of Voegelin's thought, which may be described generally as the working out of the implications of that experience. And it cannot be logically proved, precisely because it is not an idea or a proposition but an experience. From a logical point of view it is indeed a presupposition. But from the point of view of the individual who recognizes the experience as his own, there can be no question regarding the reality of the experience and the truth of the proposition that describes it: for him it is empirically confirmable, even if not according to positivistic canons of what constitutes the empirical.[37] For such a reader Voegelin's thought will not be a deductive system, even if it may be systematic in the sense of coherent and inclusive; that is, it will not be a *System* in the German sense associated with Hegelian thought, but a *Zusammenhang*.

The question of the universality of the experience is another matter entirely, and here the theoretical legitimacy of a skeptical point of view must be acknowledged. Clearly there are those who, whether the tension is present within them or not, have no consciousness of it. How can this be explained? Certainly the supposition that no existential tension is present is one possible explanation. Another is that it is present but has not been noticed. In the

37. Cf. Augustine *Tract. in Joh.* 26. 4: "Give me a man in love: he knows what I mean. Give me one who yearns; give me one who is hungry; give me one far away in this desert, who is thirsty and sighs for the spring of the Eternal Country. Give me that sort of man: he knows what I mean. But if I speak to a cold man, he just does not know what I am talking about." Quoted in Peter Brown, *Augustine of Hippo* (Berkeley and Los Angeles: University of California Press, 1967), p. 375.

history of thought there have been those who have spoken in this way on the basis of their own experience of having come to notice what they later recognize should always have been obvious to them, but which, whether out of negligence or out of deliberate self-deception, they never attended to. Augustine's *Confessions* (book 10, chap. 27) again offers an excellent example of such a self-observation: "Sero te amavi, pulchritudo tam antiqua et tam nova, sero te amavi! et ecce intus eras et ego foris, et ibi te quaerebam." ("Too late I loved you, O beauty so old and so new, too late I loved you! and behold, you were within and I was without, seeking you out there.") The type of experience here recorded involves a recognition both of the constancy of presence of what was previously unacknowledged and also of culpability for the failure to acknowledge it. To the one who has had this sort of experience of belated recognition of the deep reality of his life—and those who undergo any radical conversion of perspective frequently echo Augustine's cry of "too late"—this is at least a potential explanation for the fact that there are others who have no consciousness of the tension.

This can give him no certainty, however, that the experience so central to his own life is universal, conscious or not, and some speak of it as indeed not universal but special, as when Augustine says of those who belong even in this life to the heavenly Jerusalem, "they are set apart by a holy yearning."[38] But then on the other hand, any person, including Augustine, who seeks to elicit in his hearers an interest in questions of truth and of the true good, appeals over and over to a common experiential basis for this that he hopes is already present. One of the profound aspects of Plato's *Gorgias* lies in the way in which—in the conflict between Socrates and Callicles—he leaves permanently open this question of the universality of the *eros* to which Socrates appeals. An underlying issue of that dialogue is the question which one is truly representative of human nature, the spokesman for the love of wisdom or the spokesman for the lust for

38. "Etsi adhuc corpore permixti sunt, desiderio tamen sancto discernuntur" (*Enarrationes in Psalmos* 64. 2. 48).

power, the appeal to friendship or the threat of force; the reader is left at the end to make a choice that amounts to an act of faith.[39] And this must remain the situation of any philosopher, ancient or modern: one always has to hope that the interlocutor, too, is motivated by a radical love of truth, that he has a feeling for the imperative force of the question of the good, and so on.

The problem of levels of consciousness and unconsciousness regarding features of the field of experience can be seen upon reflection to be an inevitable one, because it grows out of the paradoxical structure of consciousness as such. Consciousness, at least insofar as it may be known in human experience, always involves the structure of intentionality—the fact that consciousness is *of* something (it is a subject's consciousness of an object).[40] But at the same time consciousness also is characterized by nonintentional self-presence. Or to put it another way, consciousness may be seen to involve both a level of immediacy, in which the knower and the known are one, and a level of mediation in which what is known, even in the case of self-knowledge, is known in the mirror of interpretive models—whether these are analytic concepts or the symbols of myth. Jaspers has described the movement of self-reflective consciousness as one of loss and recovery of immediacy: "Essentially, each act of self-reflection is . . . the transitory medium of an immediacy that has been lost and is to be restored" (*Philosophy*, 2:38). Yet one can say that if it is lost, it is lost only in a sense, for self-presence is as intrinsic to consciousness as such as is the relation to intentional

39. Socrates even places the objective reality of the *eros* in his own soul at issue when he says at 486e that if he can bring Callicles to agree with him, he may then know that his own soul is truly golden. Callicles, however, holds out to the end. See Keith Algozin, "Faith and Silence in Plato's *Gorgias*," *The Thomist*, 41 (1977): 237–46.

40. Husserl, following Brentano (in turn following the Scholastics), made this theme prominent in twentieth-century philosophical discussion, but according to Janik and Toulmin, *Wittgenstein's Vienna*, p. 153, Schopenhauer was already a source in the early part of the century of the idea that "representation" is a primordial fact of consciousness and that consciousness is always structured in terms of subject and object.

objects. And if it is restored through the medium of reflection, it may become greatly enriched in the process, as the self-knowledge of Augustine's *cor inquietum* involved, it seemed to him, a greatly different quality of self-awareness than did his earlier blind thrashing about. The love in the heart may be there in some form all along, but to know what you love so that you can love it consciously is a considerable achievement, and a liberation.

Kierkegaard put the matter well, in terms that Voegelin could be expected to approve. In the *Concluding Unscientific Postscript* Kierkegaard says that one can never begin with the immediate, "since the immediate never is as such, but is transcended as soon as it is."[41] This is to say that in human consciousness there is no immediacy that is not simultaneously mediated by reflection and linguistic articulation. To gain access to the level of immediate experience, it is necessary to begin from the mediate level and then trace one's way back to the immediate by way of a process of reflective self-appropriation: "The beginning which begins with the immediate *is thus itself reached by means of a process of reflection*."[42] Although Voegelin considers himself a "mystic-philosopher," his is not a mysticism of *gnosis* that would claim to bypass the need for critical reflection or one that would withdraw from language into interior silence.[43]

It was a quest for such mediated immediacy that Voegelin carried out in his own search for a practical answer to the philosophical and spiritual problems with which his world confronted him. What he discovered was the fundamental ordering experience that he has

41. Trans. David F. Swenson and Walter Lowrie (Princeton: Princeton University Press, 1941), p. 102.

42. Ibid. This is also a major theme of the thought of Paul Ricoeur; his *Symbolism of Evil* offers an excellent example of such tracing.

43. Gregor Sebba, "Prelude and Variations on the Theme of Eric Voegelin," *Southern Review*, n.s., 13 (1977): 665: "To me Eric Voegelin has always been an exemplary representative of rationality in the Greek sense, but when I argued that against a statement calling him a mystic philosopher he wrote back: 'This will shock you, but I *am* a mystic philosopher.'"

termed the tension of existence and that can be described succinctly as a radical love of the true and the good. From the point of view of his own experience, this was not a subjectively created idea but an imperative that grips the soul, a passion to which one may submit or which one may resist but which one does not dream up. It manifested itself not as a proposition to be proved but as an appeal to be responded to and a force to be trusted. As an experience it had an immediacy that made it palpable, even if this was an immediacy that could never be arrived at once and for all but would have to be endlessly pursued through a lifelong process of critical self-appropriation. The reality that disclosed itself was not an object to be looked at but a life to be entered. The answer it promised to one who entered would not be simply intellectual but existential: the philosopher would have to live in the truth and participate in the reality of which he was in search. He was presented not with a simple fact but with an invitation, a call to decision. If he decided to withhold his trust, the life he was invited to would never become real, at least for him. If he did decide to trust it, he could live in its truth, but he would know it only in the dark glass of trust, hope, and love.

That combination of experience and decision became the starting point for Voegelin's work as a philosopher. The experience to which it opened access, which it allowed to come forward, one might say, into the light of reflective consciousness, became the existential answer to each of the major philosophical problems described earlier. It broke open the subjectivist prison in which the philosopher can study only ideas, while at the same time it overcame the narrowly restrictive and objectivizing claims of scientism by offering access to experienceable truth transcending the realm of physical phenomena. It countered an externalizing conception of being by opening up the experience of existence from within. It broke out of the framework of the fact-value dichotomy by discovering an experiential reality that was itself worthy of love and that was the source of orientation toward the good as such.[44] Finally, and most important for an understanding of the relation between philosophy and history, it burst the boundaries of the immanentizing conception of man by opening up human consciousness to the transcendental dimension constituted by the experience of a tension that reaches beyond the realm of finite particulars toward the unlimited goal that could alone bring it to rest.

When the fundamental tension of existence becomes conscious, so that one realizes its unrestricted character and its directional tendency, then one can begin to appropriate one's existence as structured by the tension. This means that one's historical existence ceases to be a movement bounded by particular mundane goals and becomes a movement directed beyond the world—a movement that Voegelin, drawing characteristically on the historically developed ancient symbolism for the tension, refers to as an Exodus.[45]

It is in the light of the symbolization of this tension as a movement of Exodus that the intimate linkage between philosophy and history becomes fully clear. It is not merely that philosophical reflection takes place in time and leaves a trail of symbols that need to be reappropriated through historical memory. This is indeed true, but the link is much closer and deeper than that: the fundamental constitutive form of both philosophy and history is the

44. Dante Germino, speaking of "the basic positivist dichotomy (running back to Comte but reiterated, only in a more refined form, by the neopositivist avant-garde of the Vienna Circle) between objective fact apprehended by sense-experience and epiphenomenal, subjective value," has said: "The term 'value-judgment' did not come into the philosophical vocabulary until the late nineteenth century (with the neo-Kantians). Classical ethics always spoke of 'the good' which is a very important 'fact' or datum confronting the consciousness" (*Beyond Ideology*, p. 183). In fact, as the next chapter will explain, the fact-value dichotomy can be traced back much further than Comte—through David Hume and ultimately to the nominalists of the late Middle Ages.

45. See, for example, *OH*, 4:311–12, and 1:133, where Voegelin, in connection with this symbol, criticizes Oswald Spengler and Arnold Toynbee for dissolving history into a sequence of civilizational courses in which there is no movement toward a goal but only typical, recurrent situations and responses.

spiritual Exodus that is the conscious realization and willing acceptance of the tension of existence with its transcendental dimension.

This is a bold statement and one that will not meet with universal acceptance, moving as it does counter to the widespread modern tendency to conceive of history as constituted by what Voegelin would term "world-immanent" events, that is, events that are located in space and time and observable through the senses.[46] What is often overlooked is that the superior "reality" of such a world and such events is founded on epistemological and metaphysical assumptions that are frequently left unexamined or even entirely unnoticed because to the unreflective they seem so obvious. This is a problem that will be examined in more detail in the next three chapters. The principal question for the moment is what constitutes real change, since most would agree that history is made up of changes of one sort or another. There are various ways that change can be conceived, but if it is granted that there can be degrees and qualities of change and that of these some may be considered more significant than others, then it will not seem unreasonable to speak of history as constituted by significant change. Events may transpire, but in such a way that little or no real change is experienced.

Charles Baudelaire, for example, explicating the *ennui* of his age, speaks of time that does not move at all but simply piles up and buries one:

> Et le Temps m'engloutit minute par minute,
> Comme la neige immense un corps pris de roideur. . . .[47]
>
> [Minute by minute, Time engulfs me,
> As an enormous snowfall does a stiffening body. . . .]

46. Michael Murray, *Modern Philosophy of History* (The Hague: Martinus Nijhoff, 1970), p. 4, says, on the other hand, that the Greeks never used the term *historia* in the sense of a collection of events, but used it to refer to investigation generally, thereby giving it the character of a quest for truth. Cf. Voegelin, *Order and History*, vol. 2: *The World of the Polis* (Baton Rouge: Louisiana State University Press, 1957), p. 49, on Herodotus's use of the term. This work will subsequently be referred to as *OH, 2.*

47. "Le goût du néant," *Oeuvres complètes*, ed. Y.-G. Le Dantec and Claude Pichois (Paris: Gallimard, 1961), p. 69.

Samuel Beckett's Unnamable uses a similar image to express his own despairing experience of directionless time: "the question may be asked, off the record, why time doesn't pass, doesn't pass from you, why it piles up all about you, instant on instant, on all sides, deeper and deeper, thicker and thicker, your time, others' time, the time of the ancient dead and the dead yet unborn, why it buries you grain by grain neither dead nor alive."[48] And the speaker of T. S. Eliot's "Dry Salvages" asks:

> Where is there an end of it, the soundless wailing,
> The silent withering of autumn flowers
> Dropping their petals and remaining motionless;
> Where is there an end to the drifting wreckage . . . ?[49]

All of these are images for an experience of time that is widely recognized but seldom reflected on for its significance in a philosophy of history: time in which events take place, but nothing really happens, in which there is no real change, no meaningful movement. The events of this time may even seem dramatically imposing from the point of view of externalizing, empiricistic observation, but they do not constitute the sort of movement that Voegelin considers genuinely to merit the name of history.

On the other hand, there can be events, scarcely perceptible to the observer and unaccountable from an immanentizing point of view—the emergence of a new conception of order, the birth of a new sensitivity to the appeal of truth or of the good, the emergence of a new existential orientation on the basis of fuller experience and understanding—and these may constitute changes that can be recognized as radical and, in a phrase that Voegelin frequently uses, "epochal," in that they structure the field of experience into an irreversible "before" and "after," changing the flow of time from mere flux to a directional movement (see, for example, OH, 4:2).

Events of this sort are what make up history in the full meaning of the term, according to Voegelin—history in the sense of the

48. *The Unnamable* (New York: Grove Press, 1959), p. 143.
49. *Complete Poems and Plays,* p. 131.

symbol as it was developed in ancient Israel, the preeminent sense that refers to a movement through time, on a meaningful course, toward an anticipated fulfillment. This, as Voegelin phrases it, is history as a "form of existence" (*OH*, 1:127). History, as he put it in an essay of 1944, is not a "chronological encyclopedia," but the "unfolding of a pattern of meaning in time."[50] This unfolding, however, is not an inevitable process, as a philosophy of history of the Hegelian or Marxist type would interpret it. Rather it depends on the free response of individuals within the concrete societies they make up; without that response there may be incidents but no history. What Voegelin's statement means, as his subsequent works have gone on to make clear, is that history in the proper sense of the word—history as lived by one who attends and responds to the calling implicit in the experienced tension of existence—is a process of gradually emerging existential truth, of development, that is, into conscious existence attuned both cognitively and ethically to the structure of reality. In the introduction to *The Ecumenic Age* Voegelin formulated the basic conception of history in *Order and History* as "a process of increasingly differentiated insight into the order of being in which man participates by his existence " (*OH*, 4:1).[51] This is not a purely contemplative process, because man is not the mere spectator of his existence. Insight may be accepted or resisted, and in practice it is both. The acceptance and resistance are part of the field into which insight develops, and the insight is itself a victory in the struggle between them. This is why Voegelin can say that the "struggle for the truth of order is the very substance of history" (*OH*, 2:2) and that "what happens 'in' history is the very process of differentiating consciousness that constitutes history" (4:332).

50. "Political Theory and the Pattern of General History," *American Political Science Review*, 38 (1944): 748. This essay has been reprinted in *Research in Political Science*, ed. Ernest S. Griffith (Chapel Hill: University of North Carolina Press, 1948).

51. Cf. p. 304: "Through the differentiations of consciousness, history becomes visible as the process in which the differentiations occur."

Both history and philosophy are processes that take place in a field of tension between existential truth and untruth. One of the traditional symbolisms Voegelin draws on as an expression of this tension is that of Augustine's two cities: the *civitas Dei*, the city of God, which symbolizes the line of tension leading toward perfect Being, and the *civitas terrena*, the worldly city or Babylon, which is composed of the distractions that draw one away from it (see, for example, "Immortality," p. 257). These symbols combine with that of the spiritual Exodus in a passage Voegelin refers to from Augustine's *Sermons on the Psalms*: "Incipit exire qui incipit amare. Exeunt enim multi latenter, et exeuntium pedes sunt cordis affectus: exeunt autem de Babylonia" ("They begin to depart who begin to love. Many there are who depart without knowing it. For their walk of departure is a movement of the heart. And yet they are departing from Babylon").[52] Augustine's image, says Voegelin, is the classic formulation of the material principle of a philosophy of history (*Anam.*, p. 140).

It is because it has the character of a spiritual Exodus in this sense that Voegelin says the structure of history is eschatological (*OH*, 4:304).[53] History, in other words, is the incarnation as temporal process of the tension of existence in its orientation toward the divine beyond of existence.

The same is true of philosophy. The philosopher, in Voegelin's analysis, is not the technician of an academic discipline; he is simply man in the struggle for existence in truth, which is the struggle to live consciously and faithfully the tension of existence. "This is the very tension," says Voegelin, "in which the philosopher lives and moves. . . . His concern is, therefore, not with truth as a bit of information that has escaped his contemporaries, but as a pole

52. See, for example, *Anam.*, p. 140, and "Configurations of History," in Paul G. Kuntz, ed., *The Concept of Order* (Seattle and London: University of Washington Press, 1968), p. 33. The commentary of Augustine is on Psalm 64 (Latin) or 65 (Authorized Version) in *Enarrationes in Psalmos* 64. 2. 42–44.

53. Cf. p. 6: "History is not a stream of human beings and their actions in time, but the process of man's participation in a flux of divine presence that has eschatological direction."

in the tension of order and disorder, of reality and loss of reality, he experiences as his own" ("Immortality," p. 250). History is the process in which man moves, with varying degrees of consciousness, through the struggle for true being; philosophy is the same process at the point at which it becomes sufficiently reflective to be aware of its own essential structure. Man is a longing for reality, cognitive and existential; the philosopher is man conscious of his humanity; and history is man written large.

CHAPTER 2

Experience and Language

PHILOSOPHY, as Voegelin conceives it, has its starting point in the human experience of existence, which the philosopher discovers as a process of transcendence; its specific task is the elucidation of this process. When the transcendental dimension of human existence is raised by philosophy into reflective consciousness, the philosopher can freely dedicate himself to the process of transcendence into which he is called and which constitutes his true being as man.

Underlying this way of thinking are conceptions of experience and existence that may seem unfamiliar to some readers. In our lives as inquirers, we live within language, and the language to which the modern ear has become attuned has been strongly influenced by cognitive ideals growing out of a different manner of thought shaped by the prestige of the natural sciences. In this langugage, experience tends to be reduced to mere data—usually, in the Lockean manner, to sense data, as in the case of the logical positivism associated with the group usually known as the Vienna Circle.[1]

1. This group, which included among others Moritz Schlick (usually spoken of as the organizing center of the group), Rudolf Carnap, Otto Neurath, Kurt Gödel, and Friedrich Waismann, and with which Ludwig Wittgenstein and Karl Popper were more loosely associated, was active in Vienna in the 1920s and 1930s. Voegelin, who says of them that they should really be called the Schlick Circle, since "there were many circles in Vienna" at the time, had no association with them. (Conversation of April 27, 1978.) In fact they were not at all typical of Viennese intellectual life in the period; Voegelin writes (letter of August 5, 1978), "One should be aware that the Schlick-Kreis was considered in Vienna something like a lunatic fringe." The subsequent prominence of some of the members of the Schlick Circle in England and America is probably due in part to their untypicalness from a Viennese point of view; they had more in common with the Anglo-American philosophical tradition than they did with that of

Similarly, existence tends to be externalized as a property to be attributed to an external object when the hypothesis that that object exists is confirmed by empirical data of the sort just mentioned.

Voegelin's conception of experience, and of the existence that may be known from its perspective, is much broader, because it is based on a tradition of language that is older than modern scientistic thinking. His use of the term "experience" resembles that of Aristotle as outlined in the first book of the *Metaphysics*, where it is described as a cognitive mode between mere data on the one hand

---

Austria and Germany, and this made them more assimilable abroad than they might otherwise have been. The central argument of Janik and Toulmin's *Wittgenstein's Vienna* is that Anglo-American perceptions of Wittgenstein have been distorted by a tendency to interpret him against the background of Cambridge and Oxford and to forget his Viennese background, but even their extremely helpful study of the Viennese milieu tends to emphasize those features of it that lie behind Wittgenstein and thus to give special prominence to the group around Schlick. For a more accurate picture of Viennese intellectual life in the period one must turn to Viennese sources. The memoirs of the historian, Friedrich Engel-Janosi, . . . *aber ein stolzer Bettler: Erinnerungen aus einer verlorenen Generation* (Graz: Styria, 1974), though not exhaustive, describes a number of important intellectual circles active between the two world wars, some with overlapping memberships at various times. These include the group associated with the periodical *Die Österreichische Rundschau*, the circle around Stefan George, the on-going "seminar" of the economist Ludwig von Mises (which had as its theme not economics but "the understanding of understanding"), the Heinrich Friedjung-Gesellschaft (primarily historical in emphasis), and the Geistkreis, founded in 1921 by Herbert Fürth and Friedrich Hayek. Voegelin was active in the Mises and Geistkreis seminars and also was involved to some degree with the *Österreichische Rundschau* and Stefan George circles. Engel-Janosi lists Voegelin, along with Felix Kaufmann and Alfred Schütz, as one of the three most distinguished members of the Mises seminar out of approximately twenty (p. 111) and says that in the Geistkreis Voegelin led the group both in the number of his presentations and the breadth of his thematic reach, talking on "The Philosophy of Judaism," "The Meaning of Art History," "Paul Valéry," "The Problem of Time in Augustine," "Eötvös and the Authoritarian State," "The Letters of the Mongols," and "Political Religions" (p. 118). (There is a list on pp. 125–28, made up from memory by Fürth, of the contributions of the various members of the group from 1921 to 1938; Voegelin appears in each year's list except that of 1924–25.) Engel-Janosi quotes Fürth (p. 117) as saying, "Voegelin is perhaps the greatest living political scientist (and I believe the only one among us who can be described as almost a real genius)." See also Ludwig von Mises, *Notes and Recollections* (South Holland, Ill.: Libertarian Press, 1977).

and knowledge in the full and proper sense on the other.[2] Experience, from this point of view, might be described as a sort of compact, implicit mode of knowing, whereas knowledge in the full sense has been rendered explicit through critical reflection. As was said in the last chapter, the question of being is also a question of how to be. In view of this, Aristotle's observation that the man of experience is capable of sound action—and superior in this respect to one who has theory but not experience—is especially significant. Seen in this light, existential experience, the type with which Voegelin is concerned, will involve at least a pretheoretical knowledge of how to carry out the project of human existence. Theoretical philosophy, on the other hand, will be not abstract speculation but the explication of what is already present in implicit form: the universal, constant structure of human existence as a project of active fidelity to man's transcendental calling. This is not existence as known from without—as would accord with the scientistic ideal—but existence as known from within by a person fully involved in it, who has to struggle to understand it and to live up to the calling that this understanding makes explicit.

The modern reductionist tendency that opposes this way of conceiving of experience, knowledge, and existence goes back quite some time, if indeed it can be said to have any one specific point of

2. *Metaphysics* 980a–981a: "By nature animals are born with the faculty of sensation, and from sensation memory is produced in some of them, though not in others. . . . The animals other than man live by appearances and memories, and have but little of connected experience; but the human race lives also by art and reasonings. Now from memory experience is produced in men; for the several memories of the same thing produce finally the capacity for a single experience. And experience seems pretty much like science and art, but really science and art come to men *through* experience. . . . Now art arises when from many notions gained by experience one universal judgement about a class of objects is produced. . . . With a view to action experience seems in no respect inferior to art, and men of experience succeed even better than those who have theory without experience. . . . But yet we think that *knowledge* and *understanding* belong to art rather than to experience. . . . For men of experience know that the thing is so, but do not know why, while the others know the 'why' and the cause." Trans. W. D. Ross in *The Basic Works of Aristotle*, ed. Richard McKeon (New York: Random House, 1941), pp. 689–90.

beginning. The scientistic ideal became culturally prominent in the sixteenth and seventeenth centuries, but it was already in preparation in the late Middle Ages and in the nominalist theory of language that developed at that time. Descartes can serve to illustrate the transition from a fuller to a more narrow conception of experience, because he stands midway between the meditative tradition of the Middle Ages, with its sense of the fullness of spiritual as well as physical experience, and the more strictly sensationalist focus of later empiricists such as Locke and Hume. In part 1, article 9, of the *Philosophical Writings*, Descartes says: "By the term *conscious experience* . . . I understand everything that takes place within ourselves so that we are aware of it. . . . And so not only acts of understanding, will, and imagination, but even sensations are here to be taken as experience."[3] Whereas Aristotle considered experience a step beyond sensation, Descartes used the term to include sensation, and eventually the later empiricists and positivists largely confined it to sensation.[4]

3. Trans. G. E. M. Anscombe and Peter Geach (London: Nelson, 1966), quoted in Paul Ricoeur, *The Conflict of Interpretations* (Evanston: Northwestern University Press, 1974), p. 101. In the letter to Alfred Schütz, *Anamnesis* (German), p. 35, Voegelin said that Descartes's meditation had a much richer content than Husserl attributed to it and that it was fundamentally a Christian meditation in the traditional manner in search of the point of transcendence (the *apex animae*) at which the *intentio* of the soul toward God is experienced. He compares it there to the meditations of Augustine and the author of *The Cloud of Unknowing*. See also "The Gospel and Culture," in D. G. Miller and D. Y. Hadidian, eds., *Jesus and Man's Hope*, 2 vols. (Pittsburgh: Pittsburgh Theological Seminary, 1971), 2:59–101, where he describes Descartes as a transitional figure between Christian meditative experience and a new reifying objectivism: "The *Meditations*, it is true, belongs still to the culture of the search, but Descartes has deformed the movement by reifying its partners into objects for an Archimedean observer outside the search" (p. 64).

4. Husserl, in contrast, says in *Crisis* (p. 30) that sense data are not immediately given, but are really abstractions from the world as experienced. On the return in the late nineteenth and early twentieth centuries to a more comprehensive conception of experience, see Hans-Georg Gadamer's discussion of the development of the term *Erlebnis* (lived experience) among such thinkers as Dilthey, Husserl, Natorp, Simmel, Schleiermacher, and Bergson in *Truth and Method* (New York: Seabury Press, 1975), pp. 55–63. See also Voegelin's comments on how William James radicalized the empiricism of David Hume by treating relations as experienced (*Über die Form des amerikanischen Geistes*, p. 47).

If experience is limited to data coming from without, this has important implications for man's knowledge of being. What is thought to be real becomes reduced, as a corollary, to that which can be known through such data and in the manner of such data: being becomes an object to be known from the point of view of external observation and hypothecation. This has a number of consequences. For one thing, its very reality becomes highly problematic, dependent as it is on one's trust in the reliability of sensations. Descartes's difficulty with this, Berkeley's, and above all Hume's, are well known. Ultimately, with the logical positivists, this leads to a virtual denial of the possibility of philosophical knowing in the traditional sense and a reconception of philosophy as theorization of the methodology of the mathematical and natural sciences. Much more important, however, for one who like Voegelin thinks with a sense of the urgency of man's existential project, it negates the very possibility of the project by denying that being is something in which man can be involved and that he can know experientially from a point of view within it.   Voegelin is, of course, far from alone in feeling that this reductionist way of thinking is both unreasonable and constricting. In Descartes's own century one could find his slightly younger contemporary, Pascal, saying:

> I spent a long time in the study of the abstract sciences, but what little discussion there was about them tended to diminish my interest. When I began the study of man, I saw that the abstract sciences did not fit him and that by studying them I strayed more from the reality of my condition than did those who neglected them. I pardoned their ignorance. But I expected at least to find many companions in the study of man, especially since this is the study that is really suited to him. I was deceived; there are fewer studying man than geometry. It is only from ignorance of how to study man that one pursues the other studies.[5]

More recently, and from the heart of Voegelin's own philosophical milieu, Karl Jaspers has said in his "Philosophical Autobiography":

5. Blaise Pascal, *Pensées*, ed. Louis Lafuma, no. 756 (Brunschvicg, no. 144), 3d ed. (Paris: Delmas, 1960), p. 344 (my translation).

"There is a type of thinking which, from the point of view of science, is not compelling nor universally valid. . . . This type of thinking, which we call philosophic thinking, leads me to my very self; its consequences arise out of the inner activity of its own procedures; it awakens the sources within me which ultimately give meaning even to science itself' (p. 38). Similarly, one finds Heidegger in *Being and Time* speaking of the call of conscience as "concernful Being's" call from the depths of existence to the person who is not sufficiently conscious of existential concern (*Sorge*), but in whom that concern may never be totally eclipsed because it is intrinsic to existence as such. "And to what is one called," he asks, "when one is thus appealed to? To one's *own Self*." [6]

When one says this sort of thing, however, and when one says, as Jaspers does, "To analyze existence is to analyze consciousness" (*Philosophy*, 1:49), a further problem is suggested—at least when one does so using language that has over several centuries come to be colored almost irrecoverably by its use in the context of an immanentist conception of being. This is the danger that a return to the "very self" or "one's *own Self*" may be a retreat into subjectivism. Pascal may have been thinking of this danger when he concluded the *pensée* quoted above, on the study of man, with the question, "But still, perhaps even this is not the science man needs—perhaps he could be happier if he remained ignorant of himself."

When reality is conceived of as a collection of particular entities, each with its individual, self-enclosed existence, this will seem an inevitable danger. In fact this way of conceiving of being is closely related conceptually to the nominalist way of conceiving of language—in which words should always refer, preferably in a precisely denotative manner, to individual entities and their relations. Both approaches emerged in a fully articulated theoretical form in the late Middle Ages in the work of William of Ockham. In subsequent centuries they have become pervasive. A thinker is not

6. Martin Heidegger, *Being and Time*, trans. John Macquarrie and Edward Robinson (New York: Harper and Row, 1962), p. 317.

limited to such a framework of ideas, however; he can always attend to his actual, less limited experience. Voegelin has chosen to do so, and so have others. C. S. Lewis, who discovered the tension of existence in what he called "Joy," said that through this experience and the wonder it gave rise to he came to understand "that in deepest solitude there is a road right out of the self." [7] How far one will travel out of the self, of course, will depend on the person—both on the extent to which his thinking retains immanentizing tendencies and on the extent to which he is willing to pay the price of transcendence, which T. S. Eliot described as "a lifetime's death in love, /Ardour and selflessness and self-surrender." [8]

Where a nominalist style of language and the world view it implies have gained wide currency in a culture, so that language becomes flattened out or emptied of its inward, existential content and its vertical dimension of transcendence, the breakthrough to a larger view will require, as Voegelin says, "experiential reactivation and linguistic renewal" (OH, 4:56). The latter may take various forms, including both the development of new terms and the recovery of the full meaning of old ones. To break with the prevailing externalizing conception of being and to speak of being as known experientially, from within, Heidegger developed his special term—*Dasein*—and used it in a way that enabled him to dispense with such terms as "man" and "consciousness." [9] Jaspers, on the other hand, like Voegelin, continued to speak of man and consciousness, but he developed the word *Existenz* into a technical term

7. *Surprised by Joy*, p. 221. See also Ricoeur, *Symbolism of Evil*, p. 356: "Now in treating the symbol as a simple revealer of self-awareness, we cut it off from its ontological function; we pretend to believe that 'know thyself' is purely reflexive, whereas it is first of all an appeal by which each man is invited to situate himself better in being."

8. "The Dry Salvages," *Complete Poems and Plays*, p. 136. In Voegelin's opinion, both Jaspers and Heidegger were held captive, to different degrees, by immanentizing tendencies as well as by a diminished sense of existential eros. (Conversation of July 1, 1977.)

9. *Being and Time*, pp. 26–27. Cf. William Barrett, *Irrational Man: A Study in Existential Philosophy* (Garden City, N.Y.: Doubleday, 1962), p. 218.

with a meaning parallel to Heidegger's *Dasein*.[10] Voegelin's approach is similar in intent, but he is less inclined to develop a new
technical terminology (though he, too, finds that necessary to some
extent); what he attempts is to restore through historical exegesis a
sense of the fullness of meaning in traditional language, both
philosophical and mythological.

This recovery of ancient language is another way of dipping into
the well of time; for language, as Hans-Georg Gadamer has
suggested, may be described as one of the most powerful forms of
the presence of the past.[11] And just as Mann asked of that well,
"Should we not call it bottomless?" (*Joseph and His Brothers*, p. 3),
one may say of the language of transcendence that the historical
experience it can mediate for our present has inexhaustible depths.
Through the effort to sound those depths we discover ourselves, but
in a way that always involves a mingling of light and darkness. As
Jaspers put it, "No way of making existence conscious gets me to
the bottom of it" (*Philosophy*, 1:53).

Voegelin's conception is that the experience of existence is a
continuum of varying degrees of consciousness and unconsciousness
ranging from dark and inarticulate depths up through a center of
luminosity in human reflective consciousness and then beyond this
into another darkness above.[12] That segment of the experiential
continuum constituted as reflective consciousness is characterized by

10. See, for example, *Philosophy*, 1:54–60. In the "Philosophical Autobiography," p. 86, Jaspers said that he owed the concept of *Existenz* to Kierkegaard.

11. See *Truth and Method*, pp. 397–98, on "Language as Horizon of a Hermeneutic Ontology."

12. Darkness, that is, from the point of view of human consciousness. The
idea that experience can vary in its degrees of consciousness and that there can be
unconscious experience may seem paradoxical to some readers, but this has become a common theme of both psychoanalytic theory and phenomenological
philosophy. See, for example, Ricoeur, *Conflict*, p. 102, where, commenting on
Husserl's *Ideen* I, he says that the unconscious is reciprocal to consciousness as a
"field of inattention": "It belongs to the essence of consciousness to never be
entirely explicit, but always related to implicit consciousness." See also Eugen
Fink, "Appendix on the Problem of the 'Unconscious,'" in Husserl, *Crisis*, pp.
385–87.

intentional structure, the division into subject and object; those both beneath and beyond this are not so structured. On all its levels—the human, the infrahuman, and the superhuman—being, as Voegelin conceives it, is characterized by immediacy of self-presence, but on the human level this immediacy becomes refracted through the medium of human intentional consciousness. Here there is admittedly a supposition that there is more to reality in its fullness than is contained within the limits of human thought. It is a supposition not peculiar to Voegelin, however, but one which comes down to us historically in the symbolic language, both philosophical and mythological, in which human beings have for millennia given expression to their experiences of involvement in a field of reality larger than themselves. Such language, as was mentioned, has what might be called a vertical dimension by which it reaches into the heights and depths of existence. It is true that one may doubt the validity of this language for that very reason, but as Paul Ricoeur, who has probably done more than any philosopher except Voegelin to trace language to its engendering experiences, has said, unless the philosopher wishes to close himself off from the possibilities of a fuller and richer life which this language mediates, he must accept the risks that go with exploration: "A philosophy that starts from the fullness of language is a philosophy with presuppositions. To be honest, it must make its presuppositions explicit, state them as beliefs, wager on the beliefs, and try to make the wager pay off in understanding" (*Symbolism of Evil*, p. 357).

Voegelin's own wager on the place of human consciousness within an encompassing reality is made quite clear in his essay "On the Theory of Consciousness":

> That being which is the ground of all experienceable particular being is an ontological hypothesis without which the experienced reality of the ontic nexus in human existence remains incomprehensible, but it is nowhere a datum in human existence rather it is always strictly transcendence that we can approach only through meditation. It cannot be drawn from that Beyond of finiteness into finiteness itself. Our human finiteness is always within being. At one place, namely consciousness, this being has the character of illumination, but the

illumination clings to this particular level; it illuminates neither the basic being of nature nor the ground of being. [*Anam.*, pp. 32–33][13]

It does not do so directly, that is. Through the reach of analogical language, however, it can throw indirect light into distances of the experiential field that would otherwise remain totally obscure. There is an upper limit to the meditative exegesis of the experience of existence, where, as Dante said in the first canto of the *Paradiso*:

> . . . appressando sé al suo disire,
>   nostro intelletto si profonda tanto,
>   che dietro la memoria non può ire.[14]

[. . . as it draws near to its desire, our intellect enters so deep that memory cannot go back upon the track.]

And there is a lower limit as well. Between these boundaries lies the domain of the language in which the tension of existence historically has explicated itself. The tension, as Lewis described it, is imageless, but "our imagination salutes it with a hundred images" (*Surprised by Joy*, p. 221). It is experienced on one level as immediate, apperceptive self-presence, but even so it remains in a sense beyond us, beyond specifically human experience, until the images in which it expresses itself give it a mediated presence on the level of reflective consciousness. This means, paradoxically (but the paradox is the sign of fidelity to a mystery), that what is most intimate to us, the deepest reality of our lives, is something we will always have to reach toward. Even our immediate experience can never become an object of absolute knowledge.[15] Only in the mirror of language do

13. In the immediate sequel to this Voegelin says that from this point of view "neither an idealistic nor a materialistic metaphysic is tenable," for both are attempts to reduce the whole of being to one level within being.

14. Trans. Charles S. Singleton (Princeton: Princeton University Press, 1975), pp. 2–3.

15. Cf. Ricoeur, "Consciousness and the Unconscious," *Conflict*, p. 101: "Immediate consciousness does involve a type of certainty, but this certainty does not constitute true self-knowledge. . . . All reflection points back to the unreflected with the intention of escaping from itself, but the unreflected is no longer able to constitute a true knowledge of the unconscious."

we ever really know ourselves, and then only in the manner that Voegelin frequently refers to as *cognitio fidei*, knowledge in the manner of faith, through trust in the language that opens up the heights and depths of existence through analogies.[16]

The analogical language in which the tension of existence expresses itself has tended historically to fall into two basic patterns. In mythological expression it has taken the form of images of divinity. In philosophical expression it has used the image of "participation in being." Both symbolisms have now largely become either unfamiliar to the modern ear or overlaid with literalizing misreadings reinforced by the nominalist approach to language. Much of the remainder of this chapter and the next two will be an exploration of their meaning as intended by those who originally developed these symbolic forms and as interpreted by Voegelin in his historical and theoretical studies. The best way to do this is to begin with Voegelin's analysis of the experiential starting point of reflection and show how this tends to generate these mythological and philosophical languages in the process of explicating itself.

This, as Voegelin approaches it, is the experience of human existence, an experience which is intrinsically mysterious in character, because there is no possibility of a vantage point outside it from which it could be viewed as an object and reduced to conceptual clarity. Still, it is a luminous mystery. It becomes conscious in the process of questioning as the force and structure of the question itself. This is to say that human existence can become conscious of itself as a state of tension in which there is a reaching toward understanding and correlatively toward a range of closely related goals.

To seek understanding, in the proper sense of the word, is to seek understanding of the real, which means that it is a reaching toward being and toward truth. And that these are sought implies that they are apprehended, at least inchoatively, as good. In its essential

16. The concept of *cognitio fidei* will be discussed further in the following chapter. For some places in which Voegelin takes it up, see, for example: *OH*, 2:218; 3:186, 188, 275; 4:329; *The New Science of Politics*, pp. 122, 124; *Science, Politics, and Gnosticism*, p. 108; *Anam.*, p. 184.

character, the seeking itself is unrestricted. To seek true understanding is to seek an understanding that is comprehensive. It is possible that something less than a comprehensive understanding of real being may be sought, but in such a case the quest is not for true understanding. This means, as Voegelin analyzes the matter, either that the existential tension from which the quest proceeds has not realized its essential character, has not yet become fully self-luminous, or else that the seeker has chosen to close his attention to some aspect of reality, perhaps because it would threaten him with an unpleasant truth.

Closed or open, opaque to itself or transparent, the tension of existence remains, according to Voegelin, as the core of humanity. Because this tension is the ontological ground of longing or striving, and because longing and striving imply by their very nature a directional tendency, the human existence characterized by this tension has an essential structure defined by the directional tendency and its goal or goals. When the tension of inquiry is consciously unrestricted, it becomes clear that the goals it seeks not only correlate but ultimately coalesce; to seek unrestricted understanding is to seek the immediate enjoyment of all of being in a perfect luminosity that would constitute a fullness of truth. This is not to say that any human being could attain this goal. Voegelin is endlessly insistent on the limitedness of man. It is the desire, not the attainment, that is unrestricted.

The goal itself, if it could be reached, would be superhuman. Since the ancient traditional symbol for such superhuman comprehensiveness of being and knowledge is "God" or "the gods," Voegelin has termed the fundamental tension of human existence a "tension toward the divine ground." He uses the term "ground" because when the reaching is experienced as unrestricted, its goal is apprehended as one—an indefinable unity upon which all the lines of striving ultimately converge. "Divine" is used because the goal of unrestricted striving is absolute perfection in any order: the goal of an unrestricted desire to know is perfect knowledge, that of an unrestricted desire for the real is perfect being, and so on.

For the reader not yet familiar with Voegelin's thought and language there can be a pitfall at this point. One might assume that to speak in such terms is to presuppose or to assert dogmatically the existence of an entity or entities to which the terms refer. The same is true with regard to the term "transcendent," which Voegelin uses frequently; one might assume that it refers to a transcendent "place" or "state." To make such assumptions, however, would be to miss entirely the perspective from which he is speaking. This is not the perspective of a nominalist language and metaphysics but of symbolic exegesis of the experience of existence as it is undergone by an individual capable of reflection on the experience and its structure. The terms used in the exegesis are not the names of entities but symbols used to identify the poles of the experiential tension and to suggest their character in relation to the tension. Since the tension is unrestricted in its reaching, the pole toward which it tends must be symbolized as unlimited in its perfection, which is to say, at least in the traditional language of the West, divine. (A Buddhist, on the other hand, would use a quite different language, speaking of "supreme nothingness," "absolute emptiness," and so on.)

Far from wishing to make assumptions about the "existence" of a deity, Voegelin insists that in an analysis of the tension of existence as disclosed in human experience, "the poles of the tension must not be hypostatized into objects independent of the tension in which they are experienced as its poles" (Anam., p. 104). What is known through immediate experience and through the mediating reflective process in which the experience is articulated in symbols is only the tension itself, with its directional tendency and the poles that define its direction. The poles may be spoken of in the language of entities, and in fact these are the principal terms we have available with which to discuss it, but the language is used analogically.

There is a necessary reason for this. The experience is not an object, either external or intentional, and, a fortiori, neither are the directional tendencies in terms of which it is structured. Nor is this to say that it is subjective, for either assumption would presuppose a field of reality made up exclusively of subjects and objects, which would involve epistemological and metaphysical assumptions that would distort the essential nature of experience as such. "The subject-object dichotomy," says Voegelin, "which is modeled after the cognitive relation between man and things in the external world, does not apply to the event of an 'experience-articulating-itself'" (*OH*, 4:186). The first task of analysis, from Voegelin's point of view, is a description as faithful as possible to the character of the experience. But since there is no nonanalogical language to use for such descriptive purposes and there is no vantage point outside the experience itself from which it could be rendered an object of direct description, the only alternative is an indirect description using terms drawn from the language of subjects, objects, space, time, men, animals, nonanimate nature, the gods, and so on.

Many persons in history have speculated on the possible degrees of perfection or comprehensiveness of being that might lie beyond those known in human experience, and have developed concepts of superhuman beings with which to sketch them out, as far as this is possible within the limits of the human capacity to imagine and conceive. It is clear, moreover, that those who first used such symbolism were well aware of the limitations of the symbols and of their analogical character. As Voegelin says in the introduction to the first volume of *Order and History* (p. 7):

> If anything is characteristic of the early history of symbolization, it is the pluralism in expressing truth, the generous recognition and tolerance extended to rival symbolizations of the same truth. . . . The early tolerance reflects the awareness that the order of being can be represented analogically in more than one way. Every concrete symbol is true in so far as it envisages the truth, but none is completely true in so far as the truth about being is essentially beyond human reach.[17]

17. The phenomenon Voegelin refers to here is widely recognized among scholars of ancient religions. Rudolf Anthes, "Mythology in Ancient Egypt," in *Mythologies of the Ancient World*, ed. Samuel Noah Kramer (Chicago: Quadrangle Books; Garden City, N.Y.: Doubleday Anchor Books, 1961), pp. 21–22, speaking on the multiplicity of ways in ancient Egypt of symbolizing the sky as divine, says: "Nobody in Egypt was supposed to believe in one single concept of the sky,

The mythic language generated in this way remains, despite the possible misleading features intrinsic to the mythic mode, the most adequate language we have for articulating the directional tendency of the tension of existence insofar as this is a longing, an *eros*, for various possibilities of unlimited perfection. It is possible to develop terminology that is less colored by imagined circumstance than is the traditional language of mythology, but to the extent that it becomes abstracted from the sense of *eros* for the concretely desirable it loses its ability to suggest the experience, the actual *eros*, it is being used to explicate.

"Tension" itself is a somewhat more abstract term than *eros*, and, as Voegelin notes, it was a later coinage on the part of the Stoics (the Greek term is *tasis*) (*Anam.*, p. 97, and "Immortality," p. 274). The most abstract expression Voegelin uses for this experience is "tension toward the beyond," but even here the abstractness is largely apparent, since the term "the Beyond" (*epekeina*) was coined by Plato to refer to the divine, and the phrase retains its concreteness of reference when it is read in the light of this context.[18] In his discussion of the term in *Plato and Aristotle*, volume 3 of *Order and History*, Voegelin treats it as a synonym for "transcendent" (p. 113). It is a term, in other words, that refers in the simplest way possible to the pole of perfection that the tension is concretely a longing for.

---

since all the concepts were accepted to be valid by the same theologians. Furthermore, since the Egyptians had as much common sense as we have ourselves, we may conclude with certainty that no one, except perhaps a very unsophisticated mind, took the composite picture of the heavenly cow at its face value. This conclusion is supported by the fact that there exist, in the same royal tombs about 1300 B.C., other pictures of the sky, e.g., in the form of the human figure of Nut and with the sun disk in place of the sun boats. . . . There is no question that at the very beginning of their history, about 3000 B.C., the Egyptians were aware that the concept of the sky could not be understood directly by means of reason and sensual experience. They were conscious of the fact that they were employing symbols to make it understandable in human terms. As no symbol can possibly encompass the whole essence of what it stands for, an increase in the number of symbols might well have appeared enlightening rather than confusing."

18. See, for example, Plato's discussion of the Idea of the Good as the source of being and intelligibility in particular things while remaining "beyond" them, *Republic* 6. 508e–509a (references to the works of Plato will use the Stephanos numbers, which appear in the margins of most editions). See also *Anam.*, p. 96.

Robert B. Heilman, the literary critic, who helped Voegelin with the English of the first volume of *Order and History* (and to whom Voegelin expresses his gratitude in the acknowledgments of that volume) objected at that time, and still objects, to the linguistic construction "tension toward," and there will probably be others to whom it will sound strange. Heilman has wondered if perhaps some of Voegelin's constructions might sound more idiomatic in German. In fact *Spannung zu* is no more common in German than is "tension toward" in English, but the German language is more tolerant of neologisms, particularly in philosophical writing. Voegelin's problem is that he must work language hard in order to make it serve to express experiences that are usually articulated only in the most indirect way if at all. Unlike some philosophers, however, who in wrestling with the same problem proceed by the development of a new and unique technical vocabulary, Voegelin, characteristically historical in method, stays as close as possible to the vocabulary developed by earlier philosophers for the articulation of universal experiences. It is interesting to note that even the phrase "tension toward the beyond" has a traditional antecedent in Gregory of Nyssa's central concept of *epectasis*. Although Voegelin never refers to Gregory (having decided not to undertake a study of the rise of patristic Christian thought in *Order and History*), his own phrase is virtually an English equivalent for Gregory's and is used similarly, to refer to the experience of existence as a process of transcending or of movement into increasing participation in being.[19]

19. Gregory's term is composed of three Greek elements: *epi* (toward), *ek* (out), and *tasis* (tension). For Gregory's thought *epectasis* is the fundamental reality of the life of the soul as it is constituted by the process of increasing participation in the divine reality. See, for example, his *Life of Moses*: "And thus the soul moves ceaselessly upwards, always reviving its tension for its onward flight by means of the progress it has already realized." J.-P. Migne, *Patrologiae cursus completus, series graeca*, 162 vols. (Paris, 1857–66), 44:400D–401B, quoted in Jean Daniélou, *From Glory to Glory: Texts from Gregory of Nyssa's Mystical Writings*, ed. and trans. Herbert Musurillo (New York: Charles Scribner's Sons, 1961), p. 57. Voegelin's original plan for *Order and History* included volumes on "Empire and Christianity," "The Protestant Centuries," and "The Crisis of Western Civilization" (see *OH*, 1:x). Before the publication of *The Ecumenic Age*, however, the plan had been revised.

This brings us to the other major symbolism used in the ancient world to describe man's situation in reality as one tending between upper and lower limits of transcendence—between biological humanity and the gods, between earth and heaven, between darkness and light, between death and life. The symbolism of "participation in being" was developed in classical Greek philosophy, especially by Plato and Aristotle. It has now so widely fallen into disuse that many readers find it perplexing and uncomfortable. It may be helpful, therefore, if I offer a brief account of it.

The language of participation gained wide currency in the world influenced by Greek thought, and by the time of Gregory it had become virtually the universal language of patristic theology, especially among the Greek Fathers, but also among many Latin Fathers, such as Augustine, who learned it from the Neo-Platonists.[20] From the Fathers and from the Neo-Platonic tradition generally—including Plotinus, Porphyry, Proclus, Pseudo-Dionysus, Boethius, and Scotus Erigena—it was carried forward into the Middle Ages, where it continued to be widely used, among such thinkers as Aquinas and Bonaventure, for example, until it met major opposition from the nominalists.[21] Ockham, in particu-

20. For the influence of Plato, Porphyry, and Plotinus on Augustine, see Brown, *Augustine of Hippo*, pp. 91–100. For a general history of the participationist theme in philosophy and theology, see M. Annice, "Historical Sketch of the Theory of Participation," *The New Scholasticism*, 26 (1952): 47–79.

21. For the general history of the process of transmission, see Klaus Kremer, *Die Neuplatonische Seinsphilosophie und ihre Wirkung auf Thomas von Aquin* (Leiden: E. J. Brill, 1971), and Cornelio Fabro, "Platonism, Neo-Platonism and Thomism: Convergencies and Divergencies," *The New Scholasticism*, 48 (1974): 69–100. The interpretation of the participationist strain in the thought of Aquinas in particular has been a matter of considerable controversy among modern Thomists. See, for example, Cornelio Fabro, "The Intensive Hermeneutics of Thomistic Philosophy: The Notion of Participation," *Review of Metaphysics*, 27 (1974): 449–91, and an opposing article by Frederick D. Wilhelmsen, "Existence and Esse," *The New Scholasticism*, 50 (1976): 20–45. Bonaventure and Aquinas have often been interpreted as opposites (Bonaventure thinking in the tradition of the Neo-Platonists and Aquinas in that of Aristotle); for a discussion that sees their ways of thinking and speaking as fundamentally in harmony, see Thomas A. Fay, "Bonaventure and Aquinas on God's Existence: Points of Convergence," *The Thomist*, 41 (1977): 585–95.

lar, stands out in the history of medieval thought for his systematic opposition to the participationist framework of thought and language.[22]

The nominalist linguistic ideal—that of always using terms in such a way that they refer unambiguously to definite particulars and their relations—has since become widely influential, but it has never completely driven out the language of participation. Voegelin may well have seen it in its survival in Kierkegaard before he began his extensive explorations of its use in classical thinkers—as when Kierkegaard says that "the self is a synthesis in which the finite is the limiting factor, and the infinite is the expanding factor,"[23] or that "Existenz" is "between something and nothing, a mere perhaps."[24] This is not necessarily to imply that Kierkegaard had to get this way of speaking from the study of its historical manifestations, although he had plenty of opportunity to do so and perhaps did. Whether language is used against the background of earlier usage or not, where it is authentic it springs primarily from the intention of the speaker to reach an understanding of actual experience. Kierkegaard was aware, as his works in general show, of experience that is inherently ambiguous in character and that therefore requires an ambiguous, poetic use of language. Kenneth Burke, in his influential essay "The Philosophy of Literary Form," has defined poetic language as "strategic" in character and intent:

> Critical and imaginative works are answers to questions posed by the situation in which they arose. They are not merely answers, they are *strategic* answers, *stylized* answers. . . . So I should propose an initial working distinction between "strategies" and "situations," whereby we think of poetry (I here use the term to include any work

22. As Frederick Copleston has summarized his position, Ockham held that "being" is only an abstract concept that "signifies all beings, not something in which beings participate." See *A History of Philosophy*, vol. 3: *Late Medieval and Renaissance Philosophy*, part 1: *Ockham to the Speculative Mystics* (Garden City, N.Y.: Doubleday, 1963), p. 90.

23. *The Sickness Unto Death*, trans. Walter Lowrie (Garden City, N.Y.: Doubleday, 1954), p. 163.

24. *Gesammelte Werke*, 4:11, quoted in Jaspers, *Reason and Existenz*, p. 33.

of critical or imaginative cast) as the adopting of various strategies for the encompassing of situations. These strategies size up the situations, name their structure and outstanding ingredients, and name them in a way that contains an attitude towards them.

This point of view does not, by any means, vow us to personal or historical subjectivism. The situations are real; the strategies for handling them have public content; and in so far as situations overlap from individual to individual, or from one historical period to another, the strategies possess universal relevance.[25]

Voegelin would agree entirely. He would point out, moreover, that there is at least one situation in which all human beings are involved, along with the rest of what exists: "Whatever man may be, he knows himself a part of being. The great stream of being in which he flows while it flows through him, is the same stream to which belongs everything else that drifts into his perspective" (*OH*, 1:3). And this involvement has mysteries to which a nominalist language simply cannot do justice. The situation it cannot encompass is that of total immersion in a flow of reality that includes not only discernible objects of contemplation but also the contemplating itself. Limited to knowing both his own existence and external objects reflectively, through the mirror of symbolic models, man can never discern the precise boundaries either of his own reality or of what lies outside it. Human existence, which is the only reality man is able to know from within, he knows as a constant movement between poles of perfect luminosity and utter obscurity, and even between fidelity to truth and its betrayal.

The language of participation, explained briefly, sets up the metaphor of reality as a continuum of being ranging to a supreme pole designated sometimes in the language of divinity, such as the terms that speak of a "beyond" or of what is higher than the realm of the gods (Plato's *epekeina* and *hyperouranion*, for example), and sometimes in technical metaphysical language, as when Aquinas speaks

25. *The Philosophy of Literary Form: Studies in Symbolic Action* (Baton Rouge: Louisiana State University Press, 1941), p. 1.

of God as *Ipsum Esse*, Being Itself.[26] When the term "being" is used, so that one speaks of "participation in being," it is used in two ways. In one sense it refers to the whole of reality, on all its levels, as when Voegelin, in the preceding quotation, speaks of the "great stream of being"; in such a case the word "participate" means simply "to be a part of." The other use of the term refers not to any entity or collection of entities and not to the whole of reality but only to the supreme pole, by approximation or resemblance to which particular entities may be said to have the positive qualities or perfections that they exhibit. Thus Aquinas, for example, speaks of the "intellectual power of the creature" as a "participated likeness [*aliqua participata similitudo*] of Him who is the first intellect."[27] This participation, as thinkers like Aquinas and many others have conceived it, may admit of varying degrees, even to the point of virtual assimilation, at least in certain reaches of the creature's life, in the *apex animae* as the medieval mystics called it, to the character of the supreme pole itself: "For as man in his intellectual power participates in the Divine knowledge through the virtue of faith, and in his power of will participates in the Divine love through the virtue of charity, so also in the nature of the soul does he participate in the Divine Nature, after the manner of a likeness, through a certain regeneration or re-creation."[28] In this framework, the

26. For an example of Plato's symbolism of a supercelestial Beyond, see *Phaedrus* 247a–e. For Aquinas's interpretation of God as Being Itself, see *Summa Theologiae*, I, q. 3, a. 4; q. 13, a. 11. The latter work will subsequently be referred to as *ST*; unless otherwise indicated Latin references will be to the Marietti edition (3 vols.; Taurini, 1952–56) and translations will follow those of the Fathers of the English Dominican Province as reprinted in *Great Books of the Western World*, vols. 19 and 20.

27. *ST*, I, q. 12, a. 2. Aquinas goes on in the same article to turn to the metaphor of light ("Hence also the intellectual power of the creature is called an intelligible light, as though derived from the first light") and adds, "Therefore in order to see God, there must be some likeness of God on the part of the seeing power whereby the intellect is made capable of seeing God." For Biblical authority for this, he refers to Psalm 35:10, "In Thy Light we shall see light." As will eventually be explained, however, the type of "seeing" Aquinas is speaking of here is not what Voegelin terms *gnosis*; rather it takes place by way of love.

28. Ibid., Ia-IIae, q. 110, a. 4.

supreme pole (Aquinas's "God") is spoken of not as *a* being, not even the highest and best of beings, but as Being as such or "essential being," while individual entities are not essential being but "participated being" (*ens per participationem*).[29] They may be said "to be" to a greater or lesser extent according to the degree to which they participate (by analogy, not by composition or "being a part of" it) in the supreme pole, which alone truly deserves the name of Being.[30]

29. Ibid., I, q. 3, a. 4–5; see also q. 6, a. 4, for Aquinas's acceptance of Plato's treatment of "participation" to the extent that it applies not to separate forms but to universal or, in the medieval phrase, "transcendental" qualities, such as being and unity. It may surprise some readers not familiar with ancient and medieval Christian thought to hear God spoken of not as a particular being but as Being as such, but this was the standard pattern of thought among prenominalist Christian theologians, of whom Aquinas is, in this respect, actually quite typical. Ockham, in the fourteenth century, was unusual in denying the principle of participation (the *analogia entis*, or analogy of being) and in treating God as simply one more—although supremely powerful—entity among others. It was on the basis of this way of thinking—which became known at the time as the *via moderna*, the new or modern way of thinking—that Ockham was able to develop the other momentously important contribution of nominalist thought, the negation of the principle of the *summum bonum*, or the good as such. As Ockham interpreted it, the good was contingent upon the divine will; it was not what God had to will because of His nature. From this point of view there is no "natural law" or "order of being"; rather the good was whatever God arbitrarily commanded. See Copleston, *History of Philosophy*, vol. 3, part 1, pp. 115–22.

30. *ST*, I, q. 4, a. 3: "Therefore if there is an agent not contained in any genus [this is why Aquinas's God cannot be an entity or "substance"], its effects will still more distantly reproduce the form of the agent, not, that is, so as to participate in the likeness of the agent's form according to the same specific or generic aspect [in the unique case of God, the divine infinity], but only according to some sort of analogy; as being is common to all. In this way the things that are from God, so far as they are beings, are like God as the first and universal principle of all being." Put simply, this means that creatures do not resemble God by being more or less infinite (since infinity is characteristic of God alone) but by way of qualities that can vary in degree, such as clarity of intelligence, fidelity to the good as such, good will toward other beings, and so on. Modern readers sometimes react to the language of participation as though it suggested pantheism, but when this principle is understood it is clear that pantheism is not implied; pantheism would have to be based on the idea that the divine infinity was not peculiar to God. In fact the essence of the participationist way of thinking is that creatures are not Being as such, but are "participations,"

The illustrations from Aquinas here are very much to the point for an understanding of Voegelin's own thought and language. Although Voegelin has written critically of Aquinas's contribution to the dogmatizing of "metaphysics" as a "propositional science of principles, universals, and substances" (*Anam.*, p. 193), he has spoken frequently of the great achievement of thought that Aquinas's theory of the *analogia entis*, the analogy of being, represents—even referring to it as a high point of rational reflection in Western civilization.[31]

---

that is, finite analogues of Being as such. Participation is not identity but its opposite. For the purpose of clarity in the present study the word "being" is capitalized when used to refer specifically to the transcendental pole or "perfect Being" in which "finite" or "immanent" being (which will be left uncapitalized) is said to participate. One could also, as Voegelin tends to do, confine the word "existence" to immanent or participated being, so that one then would contrast "existence" and "Being." Speaking in this way, one would say that "Being" does not "exist" but stands as an index to be used in exploring the mystery of existence. The device of capitalizing one use of the term cannot, however, guarantee perfect clarity of denotation, because it is necessary sometimes to use the term "being" to include all of what may be said to be, either essentially or by participation. The phrase "participation in being," moreover, must *always* do double duty to refer both to involvement in the whole process of reality ("being a part of" being or reality as a whole) and to resemblance to that which is the standard of perfection or norm through reference to which the application of the term "to be" is controlled.

31. "Now history shows us . . . a progressive differentiation between the domain of transcendent Being and the domain of being that is immanent, but that participates in the *Lex aeterna*. In the writings of a Saint Thomas, this differentiation arrives at its maximum, and it is this that I consider the highest degree of reason. But it would seem that we are today on the descending slope, that of regression, in which we see reestablished the confusion between the two domains of Being." ["Or l'histoire nous montre . . . une différenciation progressive entre le domaine de l'Être transcendant et le domaine de l'être immanent, mais participant à la *Lex aeterna*. Chez un saint Thomas, cette différenciation aboutit à son maximum et c'est là ce que je considère comme le plus haut degré de la 'raison.' Mais il se pourrait bien que nous fussions aujourd'hui sur la pente descendante, celle de la régression, où nous verrions se rétablir la confusion entre les deux domaines de l'Être."] "Les perspectives d'avenir de la civilisation occidentale," in Raymond Aron, ed., *L'histoire et ses interprétations: Entretiens autour de Arnold Toynbee* (The Hague: Mouton, 1961), p. 136. For some other references to the *analogia entis*, see *From Enlightenment to Revolution*, p. 26; *Science, Politics,*

That one uses the same word for both the realm of participated being or immanent being and for the transcendent, perfect reality in which "beings" participate may seem ambiguous and confusing, but there is a reason this language has developed in this way. In fact, as Voegelin acknowledges, it *is* ambiguous, but necessarily so, since "the analysis of existence can express a certain phase of its process only through an ambiguous symbol" (*Anam.*, p. 164).[32] This is so because the "being" or "reality" man knows through his existential experience of involvement in it cannot be made "into an object of knowledge from a standpoint outside of reality," but can be known only from a perspective within it; to express the insight developed from that perspective he must use a symbol that points in several directions at once: "the noetic exegesis thus arrives at the point at which its insight [into] reality can be expressed adequately only through a symbol referring ambiguously to all dimensions and aspects of reality, in which the exegesis itself, knowing in perspective, really moves."

Such is the linguistic strategy that ancient and medieval thinkers found it necessary to develop over centuries to encompass what, at least from the point of view of the human perspective *within* existence, is an intrinsically ambiguous situation. It is a strategy that is useful, and for some purposes absolutely necessary, if one wishes to speak adequately about man and his situation in reality. The real problem that can develop when one is engaged in the attempt to speak of such matters does not derive from the inherent ambiguity of the language of participation but rather from the possibility, endemic to symbolism as such, that the symbol can be misinter-

---

and Gnosticism, p. 43; "The Gospel and Culture," p. 83. In *OH*, 3:368, Voegelin suggests that the symbolism of the *analogia entis* constitutes true metaphysics in contrast to the "immanentist metaphysics" of substances developed under Aristotelian influence. For a concise, if highly technical, discussion in Voegelin's own terms of the idea of participation in being, see *Anam.*, pp. 152–54.

32. The symbol he is speaking of specifically is the Greek *ousia*, which may be translated as "reality," "being," "entity," or "substance" (in the Aristotelian context he is referring to). For a discussion of the history of the word *ousia* and other terms for "being," see Christopher Stead, *Divine Substance* (Oxford: Clarendon Press, 1977).

preted through literalization. The functioning of analogical language of any sort, when one attempts to give a theoretical explanation of how it can take place, is one of the more difficult problems of philosophy.[33] Most of us, fortunately, are what Aristotle would call "men of experience," if not of "science," so that we have some sense, at least, of how such language works, and can apply it. The danger of slipping into literalism, however, is constant. The misinterpretation that proceeds from this may take two forms. It may take the form of the assumption that what is indicated by the analogy is simply "more of the same"; that is, one may assume that the analogy is too close, to the point that it may seem not analogy in the proper sense but a copy. Or—and nominalist habits of thought greatly encourage this—misinterpretation may take the form of the assumption that the terms referring to the supreme pole are the names of a thing or, as Voegelin frequently terms it, a "hypostasis": that "Being," for example, refers to a being named "Being."

To make clear the manner in which the symbols he uses function in the explication of the experience of existential tension, Voegelin has coined one of his few special terms, "index," meaning that which indicates the ultimate direction of some line of inquiry or striving. The poles of the tension of existence, as Voegelin discusses them, are not "things." They are no more than reference points that define a line of direction, the directional tendency of the tension as such, and the symbols that represent them function in an indexical manner: "We are compelled to speak in terms of objects because consciousness intends the form of objects, but the linguistic terms do not have the character of concepts or definitions relating to things. They have no meaning apart from the movement in the area of participation. In order to avoid misunderstandings, it is therefore preferable to call them linguistic indices of the meditative movement" (*Anam.*, p. 175; see also pp. 131–36 and 175–82).

33. For an excellent discussion of the problem of analogy, especially as represented in the thought of Plato, Aristotle, Aquinas, Scotus, Ockham, and Wittgenstein, see David Burrell, *Analogy and Philosophical Language* (New Haven: Yale University Press, 1973).

To clarify further how this analogical usage functions, not only as written or spoken language but also as an intention of the mind (what Aquinas called *verbum mentis*) in the movement of meditative experiential exegesis, it may be helpful to draw on Michael Polanyi's distinction between "focal" and "subsidiary" awareness.[34] Focal awareness, as Polanyi uses the term, is what one has when attending to something directly. Subsidiary awareness, on the other hand, is indirect, and what is known in this manner is usually not even noticed as such. He uses the example of the feelings in our palm and fingers when we are driving a nail with a hammer; our attention is focused on the goal of the activity and in particular on the nail, not on these feelings, although if we had no awareness of them at all, we could not do the job. He also gives the example of working with a probe: one's focal awareness is concentrated at the tip of the probe, while the feelings in the fingertips holding the probe, present as they are, remain subsidiary. Polanyi himself applies the principle to language, saying that "when we use words in speech or writing we are aware of them only in a subsidiary manner"; they function properly when they are transparent, as it were, and they cease to do so to the extent that they become opaque through the redirection of focal awareness to the words themselves rather than to what is intended by means of them (*Personal Knowledge*, p. 57). In Voegelin's terms, the symbols employed in the meditative exegesis of the experience of human existence as known from within—through the experience of existential tension—function properly when they do so indexically, to point beyond themselves in a direction that leads ultimately toward infinity.

34. For Aquinas's concept of the *verbum mentis* (word of the mind, or intelligent intention), see Bernard J. F. Lonergan, *Verbum: Word and Idea in Aquinas* (Notre Dame: University of Notre Dame Press, 1967), pp. 1–11. For Polanyi's discussion of focal and subsidiary awareness, see *Personal Knowledge* (Chicago: University of Chicago Press, 1962), pp. 55–57. Another interesting comparison would be with Maurice Merleau-Ponty's theory of the relation between consciousness and language; cf. his *Consciousness and the Acquisition of Language* (Evanston: Northwestern University Press, 1973), p. 6: "Language is neither thing nor mind, but is immanent and transcendent at the same time."

Voegelin did not begin to use the term "index" until the mid-1960s in his writings in German, and he has still not used it extensively in his English writings, but the basic concept has been present all along, as in his discussion of "man" and "being" at the beginning of the first volume of *Order and History* (p. 2):

> There is an experience of participation, a reflective tension in existence, radiating sense over the proposition: Man, in his existence, participates in being. This sense, however, will turn into nonsense if one forgets that subject and predicate in the proposition are terms which explicate a tension of existence, and are not concepts denoting objects. There is no such thing as a "man" who participates in "being" as if it were an enterprise that he could as well leave alone; there is, rather, a "something," a part of being, capable of experiencing itself as such, and furthermore capable of using language and calling this experiencing consciousness by the name of "man."

Voegelin insists constantly on the fundamental importance of the principle cited earlier that the poles of the tension, when viewed from a strictly experiential perspective, must not be hypostatized into objects independent of the tension. Of course they are not contentless points, because the tension itself has the character of a longing for a positive good; it is what Voegelin calls an "existential philia," or love (*Anam.*, p. 98). For the character of the tension to be made explicit it is necessary to elaborate the symbolic representation of the poles that define it by developing them, as has been explained, as hypothetical or mythic constructions proportionate to the tension. Nevertheless, to say that the tension is defined by the poles of "humanity" and "divinity" is not only not to make assumptions about the existence of a divine entity, it is not even to suppose the existence of man as an entity within the world. Man, in his experiential reality, according to Voegelin, is nothing other than the experienced tension itself in all of its concrete richness. "Man" considered as an indexical symbol with which to designate this experiential field and its possibilities of active reaching toward the divine pole of the tension is just as much a hypothetical construction or a mythic figure as are "Being" or the "divine ground." In the continuation of the passage above, in which Voegelin speaks of a "something" that calls the experiencing consciousness by the name of "man," he goes on to say that this calling by a name "is a fundamental act of evocation, of calling forth, of constituting that part of being as a distinguishable partner in the community of being," but "it is not itself an act of cognition" (1:2).[35] Man is not a mundane object to be examined and grasped within the confines of a concept; rather he is a process in which a center of mystery attempts to illuminate itself reflectively.

The reason human beings, while existing in individual concreteness, cannot be spoken of adequately as finite objects in the world, from Voegelin's point of view, is that man as such is constituted by a relation to infinity, a transcendental dimension within his very existence and without which he could not properly deserve the name of "man." He is man, in other words, by virtue of the presence within his experiential field of the divine pole that draws him, and by drawing him—insofar as it does so effectively—constitutes him as the being that tends toward the divine—toward the light of truth, toward beauty, toward love, toward all possible perfection of being. The issue is complex, but Voegelin has stated the essentials quite clearly in "What Is Political Reality?":

> In order to avoid misunderstandings, it should be noted that consciousness is real discretely but that the field of history does not for that reason dissolve into a field of persons of whom everyone has a private consciousness for himself, in the classical sense of *idiotes*. For consciousness is the existential tension toward the ground, and the ground is for all men the one and only divine ground of being. History becomes a structurally intelligible field of reality by virtue of the presence of the one ground in which all men participate, no matter how different may be their experiences of participation. [*Anam.*, pp. 179–80]

As the person constituted by this tension of participation explores and comes to know himself through the reflective symbolization of

35. For a discussion of "universal mankind" as an "eschatological index," see *OH*, 4:305.

the experience, he becomes aware, not of an object, but of a process of questioning. Voegelin's symbol of the "Question" was mentioned briefly in the preceding chapter. Voegelin develops it toward the end of the fourth volume of *Order and History* as an expression for the fundamental dynamic character of experienced human reality. It is not necessary, from the point of view of his analysis, to presuppose a thinker or questioner; one need only notice the reality of the Question itself as a reaching toward conscious participation in being. By its very nature as an unrestricted seeking it "presses toward the answer that is inherent to its own structure," which means that it "will not rest until the ground beyond the intracosmic grounds offered by the compact myth is found" (*OH*, 4:319). This does not mean, of course, that the ultimate is found in the sense that it becomes an object of direct experience; rather what is discovered, as the Question rises into full luminosity, is the unrestricted character of the Question itself. The myths are compact in that they do not reflect a differentiated awareness of the ultimately unrestricted reach of the Question. What they do is sketch out images of an intracosmic ultimate, that is, particular answers in the form of finite realities. These mythic answers are themselves "indices" of the type just discussed; they indicate a direction of inquiry, but do so with a partial opaqueness as well as a partial transparency. "The richly diversified field of the myth," says Voegelin, is to be understood as "a realm of equivalent answers to the same structure in reality experienced, that is to the Question" (p. 318). Their weight of meaning, however, he goes on to say, lies with the Question rather than with the answer. As the questioning consciousness becomes more differentiated and its mythic answers become more transparent, the indexical character of all answers becomes increasingly clear. Ultimately, as Voegelin puts it, "there is no answer to the Question other than the Mystery as it becomes luminous in the acts of questioning" (p. 330).

This is the mystery of a process of inquiry, an existential *eros*, a thirst for being and truth, that has no finite goal. Rather it is a reaching into a pure beyond. Because the one who reaches can possess truth only in the mirror of reflective, intentional conscious-ness, the reaching must take place at least in part through language, and language that can be used for this must function transparently to point into transcendence. The attempt to purify it of all ambiguity and to make it refer only to precisely defined objects would have the effect of rendering it opaque, stifling the dynamic Question, and condemning man the seeker to confinement in a closed universe of pure immanence. When, on the other hand, the experience of exis-tential tension is noticed, attended to, and raised into conscious-ness, this gives a vertical dimension to the language in which the experience takes on articulate form. In these circumstances a nominalistic language will break down under the pressure of the experience and the struggle for adequate expression.

In the writings of Voegelin's fellow Viennese, Ludwig Wittgen-stein, especially in the contrast between the *Tractatus Logico-Philosophicus* (1921) and the *Philosophical Investigations* (1953), one can see an attempt to overcome an excessively narrow conception of language. If space allowed, a detailed study of the similarities and differences between Voegelin and Wittgenstein would, in fact, be very interesting. Wittgenstein was Voegelin's elder by twelve years, but both grew up in basically the same philosophical milieu.[36] (Their political milieux were much altered by the results of the 1914–18 war, of course.) Both moved in circles where Schopenhauer, Nietzsche, and Kierkegaard were considered to rep-resent philosophy at its most significant, and both read them with great interest. Both also read Karl Kraus and Robert Musil. Both were confronted with a widespread assumption that there was a radical dichotomy between facts and values, and both were passion-ately concerned with maintaining the integrity of the realm of value and of the spiritual life that depends on it.

Wittgenstein, however, was trained as an engineer and was greatly influenced by the thought of mathematical physicists such as Heinrich Hertz and Ludwig Boltzmann, as well as by Bertrand

36. For a general treatment of Wittgenstein and his intellectual milieu, see Janik and Toulmin, *Wittgenstein's Vienna.*

Russell's symbolic logic and Fritz Mauthner's attempt to develop what Janik and Toulmin describe as a "complete and consistent nominalist theory of knowledge" (p. 121). With this background, Wittgenstein chose, instead of opposing the idea of the fact-value dichotomy, as Voegelin eventually did, to sharpen it by reducing language to the sphere of scientific knowledge in order to protect the transcendental realm of value and the spirit from distortion through the application to it of inappropriate language. By this means he hoped to leave the higher life of man free in the realm of silence. His *Tractatus* was an attempt to develop an absolutely pure language of facts that would leave in silence those matters—the entire transcendental realm—that could not be spoken of in that language.[37]

Wittgenstein's efforts in the direction of a purified, nominalistic language made him popular with positivist thinkers, both in England and Vienna. He felt, however, that they misunderstood him. The *Tractatus* was published under the sponsorship of Bertrand Russell and with an introduction by him, but while it was in press Wittgenstein wrote to his friend Paul Engelmann that he did not agree with Russell's interpretation; his depression over this failure of understanding grew to the point that he even considered withdrawing the book from publication.[38] The members of the Vienna Circle made much of Wittgenstein, but according to Engelmann he never felt at home with them, and he must have surprised them by defending such unscientific thinkers as Heidegger and Kierkegaard (p. 118). The way Wittgenstein was thinking during this period, between the *Tractatus* and the *Philosophical Investigations*, is nicely illustrated in Waismann's transcription of Wittgenstein's remarks at a meeting of the group at Schlick's house, December 30, 1929:

I can well imagine what Heidegger means by Being and Dread

37. *Tractatus Logico-Philosophicus*, trans. D. F. Pears and B. F. McGuinness (London: Routledge and Kegan Paul, 1961), pp. 3 and 74.
38. Letters of April 24 and May 8, 1920. Paul Engelmann, *Letters from Ludwig Wittgenstein, with a Memoir*, ed. B. F. McGuinness, trans. L. Furtmüller (New York: Horizon Press, 1967), pp. 30–31.

(*Angst*). Man has a drive to run up against the limits of language. Think, for example, of the astonishment that anything exists. The astonishment cannot be expressed in the form of a question, nor is there any answer. Anything that we might like to say would necessarily (*a priori*) be nonsense. But in spite of this we run up against the limits of language. Kierkegaard, too, saw this tendency and designated it quite similarly, as running up against paradox. This running up against the limits of language is *ethics*. I consider it extremely important that one put an end to all this talk about ethics—whether it is a form of knowledge, whether there are values, whether the good can be defined, and so on. . . . But the tendency to run up against the limits, that *signifies something.* St. Augustine knew that long ago when he said: "What, you filthy beast, you don't want to talk nonsense. Talk some nonsense, it doesn't matter."[39]

Voegelin remembers that in 1929 Jaspers discussed Wittgenstein and said that despite his popularity with positivist thinkers, he was not a positivist at all, but a mystic.[40] Paul Engelmann, on the basis of his long friendship with Wittgenstein dating back to the time of the writing of the *Tractatus,* has confirmed this judgment, saying that "Wittgenstein drew certain logical conclusions from his fundamental mystical attitude to life and the world" (*Letters,* p. 97). He

39. Friedrich Waismann, *Wittgenstein und der Wiener Kreis*, ed. B. F. McGuinness (Oxford: Basil Blackwell, 1967), p. 69 (my translation). The source of this "quotation" from Augustine has not been identified. McGuinness asked Peter Brown, who suggested as a possible source *Confessions* 1. 4: ". . . et vae tacentibus de te quoniam loquaces muti sunt" (". . . and woe to those who do not speak of You, since even the talkative fail in their powers of speech). It is interesting to compare this statement with Wittgenstein's remarks (about A. J. Ayer), ca. 1946–47: "It is very important in philosophy . . . not to be clever *all* the time. For the 'clever' philosopher risks losing touch with the grassroots problems on which his ideas are supposed to throw light, and becoming preoccupied with secondary problems of his own making. Only the occasional touch of honest stupidity will help us to see where the arguments of professional academic philosophy are failing to answer our true intellectual needs" (as summarized in Janik and Toulmin, *Wittgenstein's Vienna*, p. 260). Janik and Toulmin say in the same place that Wittgenstein continued to speak in praise of Augustine, Schopenhauer, and Kierkegaard in Britain in the 1940s and 1950s, when it was unfashionable to do so.

40. Conversation of April 27, 1978.

goes on to say that what Wittgenstein had in common with the positivists was that he drew a line between language and silence, but he concludes: "The difference is only that they have nothing to be silent about."

Wittgenstein never gave up his belief in the fact-value dichotomy, but the pressure of his experience of transcendence evidently did have something to do with his later rejection of the *Tractatus*'s theory of language and his attempts to sketch out a more adequate one in the *Philosophical Investigations,* where he said: "it is interesting to compare the multiplicity of the tools in language and of the ways they are used, the multiplicity of kinds of word and sentence, with what logicians have said about the structure of language. (Including the author of the *Tractatus Logico-Philosophicus.*)" [41] Wittgenstein begins the later work with a quota-

41. *Philosophical Investigations*, trans. G.E.M. Anscombe (New York: Macmillan, 1967), part 1, no. 23, p. 12. Janik and Toulmin, *Wittgenstein's Vienna*, pp. 235–36, speculate that Wittgenstein's retention of the fact-value dichotomy after the change in his thought about language may indicate that it had some personal importance to him apart from any philosophical grounding. It is interesting to note that the history of the idea of a fact-value dichotomy is traceable back through British empiricism (e.g., Hume, *Treatise of Human Nature*, 3. i. 1) to medieval nominalism and that Wittgenstein's affinity for nominalist thought regarding this question is clearly discernible. Where Aquinas, for example, had considered the good as such to be one with the very being of God (cf. note 29 above), so that God willed the Good by a necessity of his nature (*ST*, I, q. 6, a. 3; q. 19, a. 3, a. 10), Ockham argued that the moral law is based on God's arbitrary choice, not his essence, so that God could command fornication, hatred, theft, adultery, and so on, and if he did, such acts would be not only licit but meritorious: "By the very fact that God wills something, it is right for it to be done. . . . Hence if God were to cause hatred of Himself in anyone's will. . . neither would that man sin nor would God; for God is not under any obligation . . . ." (quoted in Copleston, *History of Philosophy*, vol. 3, part 1, p. 116). Cf. Wittgenstein's response to Schlick's suggestion that the idea that good is grounded in God's nature is more profound than the idea that it proceeds from the divine command. Wittgenstein argued that this would imply that value could be explained, and said finally, "Gut ist, was Gott befiehlt" (Good is whatever God commands). Waismann, *Wittgenstein*, p. 115. Cf. also the various conversations recorded in Waismann (pp. 116–18) to the effect that ethical theory is impossible and that the meaning of the word *soll* (should) is rooted in the reference to a power of reward or punishment.

tion from Augustine (*Confessions* 1. 8) describing Augustine's own early use of language, and it is significant that this language is not only one in which each word names a definite object but also that it was the language of a child for whom the world was constituted primarily of objects of appetite. (Wittgenstein does not mention it, but Augustine's own mature language was a highly versatile instrument for the expression of quite different experience.) He goes on both to say and to show that language is not limited to operating in this rudimentary manner, that one comes to understand the meaning of a word not by learning what it names but by seeing how it is used in the language (as one understands a move in a game), and that there are many, perhaps innumerable possible "language games."

Voegelin's own approach to the problem of breaking out of the confines of the prevailing language and the thought forms of the milieu he and Wittgenstein shared was quite different. His break with the belief in the fact-value dichotomy was described in the preceding chapter. With regard to the problem of language, his approach was, characteristically, more historical than Wittgenstein's.[42] Instead of considering the comparatively limited "language games" played in contemporary Cambridge or Vienna, Voegelin chose to look back to the ancient sources of language in order to discover what language could accomplish when it was stretching its resources to encompass richer experiences than the ordinary. Voegelin believes that the thinker has a responsibility to articulate his experience of the realm Wittgenstein would leave in silence. His attitude is that what remains inarticulate cannot be raised into the light of human, reflective consciousness and integrated into the moral life of the individual; the realm of silence—as much of Thomas Mann's work was an effort to show—tends to be defenseless against irrational forces arising from within.

Even apart from the pressures of transcendental experience seek-

42. Janik and Toulmin, *Wittgenstein's Vienna*, p. 243, describe Wittgenstein as a basically "ahistorical" thinker and quote him as saying, "What is history to me? Mine is the first and only world."

ing articulation, the inadequacy of nominalistic language becomes apparent to one who reflects on the real functioning of language and conceptual thought in relation to even the simplest realities they are used to express. The nominalist conception of language is based on what might seem at first to be a perfectly reasonable, indeed obvious assumption: that whatever is, simply is what it is. On closer examination, however, this assumption is not so obvious. To the attentive observer, reality, even considered only as a collection of mundane objects, turns out to be made up not of static entities, each with a fixed and precisely definable character, but of processes in continual change. These are not definable with reference to precisely "what they are," in the sense of their form at a given moment, but with reference to certain tendencies or possibilities that seem implicit in the process. One describes an object such as a "man," a "dog," or a "circle," for example, by developing an idea based on the indicating tendencies, then comparing this with the individual instance to see how it measures up to the standard and whether it does so sufficiently to be placed in the category so established. Various instances conform in varying degrees at various times in their history to the criteria we use for categorization. In the light of an awareness of this way of applying linguistic categories, it becomes clear that rather than simply saying a thing "is what it is," one can more adequately say that realities in process are understood in terms of what they may be construed as being on their way to being.[43]

43. Despite the reputation that classical and medieval thought now has for a supposed belief in static objects, a recognition of the processual character of reality (the realm of "being," in this case, rather than of "Being") seems to have been generally present even then. Plato's theory of ideal forms was designed to take account of just this sort of discrepancy between instances and types. Cf. also Maurer's commentary on Aquinas's discussion of a quiddity as *quod quid erat esse*, his term for Aristotle's *to ti en einai* (what a thing was to be), in St. Thomas Aquinas, *On Being and Essence*, trans. Armand Maurer (Toronto: Pontifical Institute of Medieval Studies, 1949), p. 27: "When we ask the question,—What is this thing?—the complete answer is the statement of its definition, or that which the nature tends to fulfill. . . . The definition thus expresses what a thing is, its *whatness* or the *what a thing was to be*. The past tense of the verb (*was*) does not express past time. It expresses absolutely the direction of the tendency of a being's nature."

This need not involve the supposition that the individual instance will ever fully attain the status defined by the categorial concept. It may, but need not from a strictly logical point of view, involve assumptions about the immanent dynamics of the process. The criteria used in setting up categories can serve one way or the other to organize the field of experience cognitively in terms of the possibilities of development that might be present in it, and this can give one a basis both for understanding and for comparative evaluations.

If one attends in this way to how language actually operates, even on the most basic level, one must acknowledge that just as reality is always changing, so language is always reaching after it, as well as after the possibilities of perfection it points toward. And just as reality may be said to involve levels of participation, so language tries to identify the levels and situate its objects properly among them. As Gadamer has said, "We can learn from the sensitive student of language that language, in its life and occurrence, must not be thought of as merely changing, but rather as something that has a teleology operating within it." [44]

The ideal of an unambiguous, univocal language will probably always have appeal, but ultimately it is the appeal of *gnosis*. It would be attainable if man and reality itself, as known by man, were unambiguous, which would be the case: (1) if reality were made up entirely of entities with precise and stable limits, so that there could be no question of their exemplifying their characteristic qualities to a greater or lesser degree (human consciousness, for example, would have no degrees of clarity and obscurity and there would be no need to speak of the unconscious or of degrees of consciousness); (2) if the entities known were known, as Ockham claimed, by immediate intuition of each in its singularity and in such a way that the concept of the thing (Ockham's *terminus conceptus*) were the natural product of that intuitive apprehension;[45] and (3) if existence, as

44. Hans-Georg Gadamer, *Philosophical Hermeneutics*, trans. David E. Linge (Berkeley and Los Angeles: University of California Press, 1976), p. 13.
45. Ockham, Prologue to *Expositio super viii libros Physicorum*, in William of

Ockham also claimed, were a single, uniform property possessed always in the same way by each entity possessing it, from God to the least of his creatures.[46]

The nominalist ideal of language applies best within the artificial—not false, but only humanly conceived—framework of hypothetical knowing, where what is known, as in the natural sciences, is known from without as a possible reality to which actuality is attributed on the basis of evidence and reasoning. It is no accident that nominalistic patterns of thinking—without necessarily a realization of all their implications—have had greatest appeal among scientistic thinkers. Hypothetical knowing has its uses, and Voegelin has no quarrel with the natural sciences, only with scientism.[47] The question is: is this, as scientism would claim, the only kind of knowing? Voegelin maintains, along with by far the greater part of the mainstream of philosophical thinkers over the centuries, that it is not. Hypothetical knowing and attributed actuality do not exhaust, either as knowledge or as reality, the situation man must attempt to find linguistic strategies to encompass. Man is also inextricably involved in existential knowing and experienced actuality—existence as known from within.

From the point of view of man's concrete experience of existence and the mode of knowledge proper to its perspective, reality is not an assemblage of "things"—even if that perspective opens out upon the world of things as well—but a stream of mingled possibility and actuality that the knower is himself immersed in. His physical reality may be constant as long as he is in existence at all, but on the

Ockham, *Philosophical Writings*, ed. and trans. Philotheus Boehner (Edinburgh: Thomas Nelson, 1957), pp. 23, 28–30. Ockham developed this way of thinking on the basis of the epistemology of John Duns Scotus; cf. Burrell, *Analogy*, pp. 185–93. See also the comment by Bernard J. F. Lonergan, *Insight: A Study of Human Understanding*, 3d ed. (New York: Philosophical Library, 1970), p. 372: "Five hundred years separate Hegel from Scotus. . . . that notable interval of time was largely devoted to the working out in a variety of manners the possibilities of the assumption that knowing consists in taking a look."

46. *Reportatio* III, q. 8, in *Philosophical Writings*, p. 111. Ockham did not, however, claim that God is intuitively knowable (see p. 110).

47. See *Anam.*, pp. 177–78, and "The Origins of Scientism."

higher levels—moral, intellectual, and spiritual—he may be said to exist to a greater or lesser degree to the extent that he yields and gives himself to the call of transcendence. As Vogelin and the classical philosophers to whom he appeals understand it, being is not an object, external and inert, to be known by a look. It is a life, to be lived and known in one's commitment to it. In the words of Gabriel Marcel: being is the "place of fidelity." [48]

48. "De l'être comme lieu de la fidélité" (*Être et avoir* [Paris: Aubier, 1935], p. 55).

CHAPTER 3

Philosophical Knowing as an Existential Process

"PHILOSOPHY," says Voegelin in the most pregnant of his definitions of it, "is the love of being through love of divine Being as the source of its order" (*OH*, 1:ix).[1] This definition is likely to sound strange to the modern ear, especially since philosophical discourse in our period usually tries to maintain both a dispassionate attitude and a clear distinction between its language and that of theology. Voegelin's own effort, however, is an attempt to recover the original import of the symbol as it was used by the early Greeks who first coined the term to express precisely the experience he describes.[2] His emphasis, as the preceding discussion has indicated, is on the experiential perspective from which the enterprise of philosophy stems: in the center of philosophy, he says, stands the experience of existential tension, with its "ordering truth" (*Anam.*, p. 136). The exposition of Voegelin's thought will have to take the form of a spiral, returning again and again, as here, to its center in the experienced tension of existence, the existential *philia* or love for perfection of being, in order to draw out its implications for an understanding of man, philosophy, and history.

Philosophy, as Voegelin conceives it, is not a subject matter, or a collection of propositions, opinions, and arguments, but an existen-

1. The term "Being" in this quotation refers, in the manner discussed in the last chapter, note 30, to the supreme ontological ground, while the uncapitalized form of the word refers to the entire complex of the experienced tension of existence and its supreme pole.

2. See, for example, *OH*, 2:165–83, and "Reason: The Classic Experience," in *Anam.*, especially pp. 89–97.

tial event, a *Seinsereignis,* in which the principle of order in the experiential tension is raised into consciousness and freely affirmed (*Anam.*, p. 136, German, p. 276).[3] What philosophy becomes, when viewed in this way, is a process in which the philosopher seeks to enter into more adequate and comprehensive participation in the possibilities that existence holds open to him—to enact, in other words, the love of being and of Being just referred to. But in the case of man this participation takes, in addition to its bodily form, the form of consciousness (p. 163). And this in turn means that philosophy, seeking consciousness, seeks knowledge—not just any knowledge, however, but the knowledge that is the self-reflective clarity of consciousness itself. "In historical reality," says Voegelin, "a philosopher's truth is the exegesis of his experience."[4] There is a constant structure, according to Voegelin's way of thinking, to be found universally in human experience as such. This is the structure given in the experience of existential tension: it is a process of consciousness (either more or less clear and well developed) ordered through its orientation toward a supreme pole of perfection (comprising truth as such, the good, wisdom, and so on)—the ultimate pole that Voegelin refers to as the "divine ground." This is in fact one way Voegelin defines the term "consciousness," as when he says, "Consciousness is the experience of participation, participation of man in his ground of being," or "we can speak of consciousness as the sensorium of participation" (*Anam.*, pp. 175, 163). Consciousness as he conceives it is not simple awareness, abstracted from the concrete experience of the tensional pull toward the supreme pole in which luminosity, reality, and the ultimate object of love coalesce. To the extent that it is consciousness at all, it has the structure constituted by this pull, even if it may vary in clarity and fullness, as aspects of its structure may go unnoticed or be deliberately buried in obscurity.

Thus, although as Voegelin put it in one place, "The range of

3. For a discussion of the way Kierkegaard and Karl Kraus conceived of ethics as event, see Janik and Toulmin, *Wittgenstein's Vienna*, p. 179.
4. "On Hegel: A Study in Sorcery," *Studium Generale*, 24 (1971): 344.

human experience is always present in the fullness of its dimensions," its clarity and explicitness, by which it is constituted as *conscious experience,* may vary considerably depending on the extent to which the implicit fullness of experience always present on the level of immediacy is allowed to unfold its dimensions in the symbolizations that mediate their presence on the level of consciousness (*OH*, 1:60). According to Voegelin's understanding of man, the tension of existence with its proper structure is always present in immediate experience, and it is this constant presence that constitutes the universality of human nature. But it is not on the level of immediacy that the philosopher, or any person, begins to think. Every human being finds himself first on the mediated level, where he lives amid his interpretations of reality in general, including that reality that is the immediate experience of existential tension. In the new introductory chapter of the English *Anamnesis* Voegelin speaks of the "horizon of consciousness" and says that "the quality of the horizon will depend on the analyst's willingness to reach out into all the dimensions of the reality in which his conscious existence is an event, it will depend on his desire to know" (p. 4).

Although Voegelin does not say so there, it will also depend on a few other things, among them the symbols available in his culture, or discoverable through historical memory, that can mediate and thereby help to raise into consciousness the fullness of structure already present and "known" preanalytically and dimly in the depths of immediate experience.[5] It may also depend on the intensity of the tensional pull. This may vary in different places and periods depending on cultural factors, and perhaps also for reasons that will remain ultimately mysterious. To speak of "tension toward the divine ground" is, after all, to speak of what has for thousands of years been called the love of God, and many generations of thinkers have noticed its variability and have attributed this to divine causality, the "grace of God."

If a philosopher wishes, as Voegelin has, to pursue the implica-

5. Cf. *Anam.*, p. 134, and "On Debate and Existence," *Intercollegiate Review*, 3 (1967): 150.

tions of this conception of philosophy, it will follow that he must turn for the experience and its symbols to thinkers who have reflected on this at times that were propitious to the task and whose thought suggests and evokes an appropriate richness of conscious experience. It is to find such experiential fullness and the symbols engendered by it that Voegelin has gravitated toward the study of ancient sources. There he has found, he believes, symbols more closely in touch with the depths of experience, less fossilized and reified, than may easily be found among modern thinkers. This is also why so much of Voegelin's discussion of fundamental issues is couched in Greek and Latin terminology. The rediscovery of philosophy, for Voegelin, must involve the recovery of the kinds of motivating experience represented in such ancient symbols and largely lost in their modern versions. What has become obscured in particular is the fundamental experiential tension, the existential *philia* or love in which one both seeks and is drawn toward the light of truth, the good, the divine ground.

Philosophy, as Voegelin conceives it, is not simply an action on the part of the philosopher. It is as much a *pathos*, to use the Greek term, something that is undergone, as it is an action. The classical symbols for these active and passive aspects of the event of philosophy, says Voegelin, were *zetein* (to seek after, inquire into) and *helkein* (to pull or drag). The element of *zetesis* (seeking) is present already in the experiential core as the directional tendency of the tension, but so also is the pull (*helkein*) toward the pole that defines the direction of the tension. The two symbols are ways of expressing two aspects of one and the same "movement," the tension itself: "The terms seeking (*zetein*) and drawing (*helkein*) do not denote two different movements but symbolize the dynamics in the tension of existence between its human and divine poles. In the one movement there is experienced a seeking from the human, a being drawn from the divine pole" ("The Gospel and Culture," p. 71).[6]

6. Cf. *OH* 1:10: "The conversion [toward the source of order] is experienced, not as the result of human action, but as a passion, as a response to a revelation of divine being, to an act of grace, to a selection for emphatic partnership with God."

The poles, it must be remembered, are not entities, and the terms that designate them are not the names of "things" but indices used in the explication of the structure of the tension. Depending on which of them is emphasized in discussion, the language used will tend toward the symbolism either of philosophy or of revelation. In either case the basic structure is the same. The seeking is moved throughout by the appeal of the truth that is sought, and it is the presence, in a nonspecific form, of the intended pole that gives direction to the inquiry. The questioning unrest is not a blind thrashing about but a directional movement; it already has a knowledge sufficient to generate the question, though not knowledge of a sort that would answer it. The seeking, as Voegelin puts it, is both a knowing questioning and a questioning knowledge (*Anam.*, p. 148).[7]

It may help to clarify this point to draw on a terminology other than Voegelin's for a moment. Bernard Lonergan speaks in a similar way—though in slightly different language—of the same experience. He developed his own concepts of horizon and of the distinction between the "known," the "unknown," and the "known unknown" to take account of the partial knowledge and partial ignorance that characterize inquiry. What is known is no longer to be sought, but what is totally unknown is also beyond inquiry in the sense that without at least some notion of it one could never ask about it. The "known unknown" is that area of human experience in which questions can arise and answers be sought. This in turn may be analyzed into "categorial" and "transcendental" dimensions.[8] Categories have limited denotation; that is, they apply to particulars of one sort or another. What Lonergan, following scholastic usage, calls the "transcendentals," on the other hand, are unrestricted in their scope. They are the content of what is intended in any line of inquiry and they carry a dynamic potential:

7. Voegelin is referring here to Aristotle's discussion of *zetesis* as involving both desire and a sense of the meaning of the question or the direction the question reaches in.

8. See Bernard J. F. Lonergan, *Method in Theology* (New York: Herder and Herder, 1972), pp. 10–12 and 23–25.

While categories are needed to put determinate questions and give determinate answers, the transcendentals are contained in questions prior to the answers. They are the radical intending that moves us from ignorance to knowledge. They are *a priori* because they go beyond what we know to seek what we do not know yet. They are unrestricted because answers are never complete and so only give rise to still further questions. They are comprehensive because they intend the unknown whole or totality of which our answers reveal only part. . . . So if we objectify the content of intelligent intending, we form the transcendental concept of the intelligible. If we objectify the content of reasonable intending, we form the transcendental concepts of the true and the real. If we objectify the content of responsible intending, we get the transcendental concept of value, of the truly good. But quite distinct from such transcendental concepts, which can be misconceived and often are, there are the prior transcendental notions that constitute the very dynamism of our conscious intending, promoting us from mere experiencing towards understanding, from mere understanding towards truth and reality, from factual knowledge to responsible action.[9]

The term "transcendental" here means cutting across or passing beyond the confines of particular categories.

The fundamental congruence between Voegelin's analysis of the structure and dynamics of consciousness and Lonergan's should be obvious.[10] The "questioning unrest" of inquiry is stimulated by the

9. Ibid., pp. 11–12.

10. This is not a matter of influence in either direction; rather both Voegelin and Lonergan draw their basic insights from classical Greek philosophy, especially Plato. For Lonergan's descriptions of the influence of Plato on his thought see "Insight Revisited," in *A Second Collection*, ed. William F. J. Ryan and Bernard J. Tyrell (Philadelphia: Westminster Press, 1974), pp. 264–65, where he describes how a new and more adequate approach to Plato was opened up to him by J. A. Stewart's *Plato's Doctrine of Ideas* (Oxford: Clarendon Press, 1909): "From Stewart I learned that Plato was a methodologist, that his ideas were what the scientist seeks to discover, that the scientific or philosophic process towards discovery was one of question and answer." Voegelin also holds Stewart's book in high regard. Voegelin and Lonergan recognize the affinities in one another's thought. For a discussion of Voegelin by Lonergan, see Bernard Lonergan, "Theology and Praxis," Catholic Theological Society of America, *Proceedings of the Thirty-Second Annual Convention*, Toronto, 1977, pp. 6–14.

pole toward which it moves and which is simultaneously present and absent, empty of particular content but filled with a dynamism that reaches toward all possible content. Voegelin's language, on the other hand, derives more from ancient sources than from medieval ones and consequently tends more toward mythic than technical vocabulary.

This is deliberate on Voegelin's part: by keeping as close as possible to the point at which both philosophy and theology branch out from the compact symbolism of mythology, Voegelin is able to retain through its more richly connotative vocabulary a sense of the complexity and mysteriousness of the wonder that engenders all three. Thus he speaks of man being "moved to his search by the divine ground of which he is in search" and of how in this process "the wondering and questioning is sensed as the beginning of a theophanic event that can become fully luminous to itself if it finds the proper response in the psyche of concrete human beings—as it does in the classic philosophers" (*Anam.*, pp. 95–96).

A term like *psyche*, for example, has a concrete experiential reference in much of Greek thought that can easily become obscured by the frequent modern tendency to think of the "soul" as something that one "has"—a kind of detachable "thing." Still more difficult to duplicate are the implications of the Greek term *nous*, which for Plato and Aristotle involved the idea of the pull of a powerfully attractive goal, particularly the light of truth.[11] The nearest modern English equivalent, the word "mind," has all sorts of quite different associations—from the Cartesian "ghost in a machine" through Hume's empty theater to more recent models based on cybernetics.

Psyche and *nous*, according to Voegelin's analysis, were symbols developed by Greek philosophers to explicate the central experience

11. This sense of the term may go back much earlier than Plato and Aristotle. Voegelin's interpretation of the Greek concept (and existential event) of *nous* receives support from the recent study by Douglas Frame, *The Myth of Return in Early Greek Epic* (New Haven: Yale University Press, 1978). According to Frame, the term *nous* derived from the Indo-European root *nes-*, the root of *neomai* ("to return home"), which had an early sacred meaning, to return to light and life from darkness and death.

of the ordered, directional quality of the tension of existence as known from within with varying degrees of clarity.[12] *Psyche*, in this analysis, is not a "thing" that a human being "has" but a symbol of a process of conscious existence; it represents that area of experience in which the pull toward the pole of transcendence is sensed and begins to emerge into consciousness: "the psyche . . . is found as a new center in man at which he experiences himself as open toward transcendental reality" (*The New Science of Politics*, p. 67). This is not, says Voegelin, the discovery of an object that had always existed; rather the *psyche* is constituted by the experiential process in which it is discovered. The tension is always present, of course, on the level of immediacy, but it may remain unnoticed, merely implicit. When it begins to emerge into conscious presence, then that, according to Voegelin, is *psyche*.

Consciousness, however, has degrees of clarity and articulateness. The symbol *psyche*, in Greek use, referred to an experiential continuum ranging from a maximum of self-reflective clarity to obscure depths in which the tensional pull only barely begins to emerge from the darkness of pure immediacy. The symbol *nous*, says Voegelin, was developed to refer to the upper range of this continuum, though *nous* also may involve degrees of reflectiveness and explicitness of articulation.

In the Greek conception, *nous* is never, as the modern conception of "mind" would have it, a detached, neutral contemplation or a

12. Far from offering unique interpretations of classical material, Voegelin bases his account on those of recognized specialists. For a discussion of the development of these symbols in early Greek thought by classical scholars to whom Voegelin refers, see, for example, Werner Jaeger, *Paideia: The Ideals of Greek Culture*, 3 vols. (New York: Oxford University Press, 1939–44), and *The Theology of the Early Greek Philosophers* (Oxford: Clarendon Press, 1947), and Bruno Snell, *The Discovery of the Mind: The Greek Origins of European Thought* (Cambridge, Mass.: Harvard University Press, 1953). Snell discusses the evolution of the symbols *psyche* and *nous* from Homer to Heraclitus in his chapter 1, "Homer's View of Man," pp. 1–22. On p. 19 Snell discusses the emergence of a notion of a "tension within the soul." The discussion by E. R. Dodds in *The Greeks and the Irrational* (Berkeley and Los Angeles: University of California Press, 1951) also accords with those of Jaeger and Snell.

dispassionate calculative process. Another modern scholar, David
Starr, in a study that relates Aristotle's *nous* to Heidegger's *Dasein*,
lends support to Voegelin's analysis on this point. Referring to the
use of the term *nous* on the part of Homer, Hesiod, and some other
early Greek thinkers, Starr says: "Such instances and examples,
whether applied to gods or men, make it perfectly clear that *nous*
was generally understood and accepted as a function, perhaps the
most important function, of personal care, residing in the heart of
the body, grasping the import of things, and responding heedfully
with plans, words, deeds."[13] He also points out the significance of
the fact that both Parmenides and Heraclitus used forms of the word
phroneo rather than *noeo* to describe the activity of *nous* (p. 239).
Phroneo (to think, ponder, deliberate) is formed from the word *phren*
(diaphragm), which is virtually equivalent to the term "heart" when
used to refer to one's center of deepest concerns. As Voegelin stated
the principle in "What Is Political Reality?" *noesis*, the activity of
nous, is a struggle to illuminate a movement of the soul in which one
is passionately caught up: "The noetic exegesis lifts the logos [the
intelligible structure] of participation into the light of consciousness
by interpreting the noetic experience of participation. Noetic
knowledge, therefore, is not abstract knowledge obtained by gather-
ing cases of participation and examining them for general characteristics. Rather, it is concrete knowledge of participation in which
a man's desire for knowledge is experienced as a movement toward
the ground that is being moved by the ground" (*Anam.*, p. 183).

It is easy to see that from this point of view *nous*, as a symbol, is
virtually equivalent to "philosophy" as Voegelin considers its Greek
originators to have understood it. Both symbols were born of and
represent the same experientially grounded process in which reflective consciousness emerges from the womb of mythic thought: "For
philosophy as a symbolic form is distinguished from myth and
history by its reflective self-consciousness. What philosophy is, need
not be ascertained by talking *about* philosophy discursively; it can,

13. David E. Starr, *Entity and Existence: An Ontological Investigation of Aristotle
and Heidegger* (New York: Burt Franklin and Co., 1975), p. 86.

and must, be determined by entering *into* the speculative process in which the thinker explicates his experience of order. The philosophers' conscious break with the form of the myth occurred about 500 B.C. The individual steps taken toward a differentiated experience of the psyche, during the two centuries after Hesiod, had the cumulative result of letting the self-conscious soul emerge as the tentative source of order in competition with the myth, as well as with the aristocratic culture of the archaic polis" (*OH*, 2:170).

Voegelin's most concise treatment of the historical process in which this emergence took place may be found in his essay of 1974, "Reason: The Classic Experience." There he describes it as proceeding from what is at first only "man's existence in a state of unrest" due to his "experience of his life in precarious existence within the limits of birth and death," the awareness that he is not a divine *causa sui*, not the source of his own being (*Anam.*, p. 92). This experience of unrest, the most primitive form in which the tension of existence expresses itself, becomes a questioning unrest as it gives rise to "the wondering question about the ultimate ground, the *aitia* [cause] or *prote arche* [first beginning], of all reality and specifically his own." "The question," says Voegelin, "is inherent in the experience from which it rises": the experience of precarious existence without an explanation is virtually a living question mark to the person who undergoes it.[14] The questioning unrest can take various forms in actual expression. Philosophy is born of wonder, but so is myth; and it is the same wonder, for it is always the same existential mystery that gives rise to it: "Though this questioning is inherent in man's experience of himself at all times, the adequate articulation and symbolization of the questioning consciousness as the constituent of humanity is . . . the epochal feat of the philosophers. . . . Everyone's existence is potentially disturbed by the *thaumazein*, but some express their wondering in the more compact medium of the myth, others through philosophy. By the side of the *philosophos*, therefore, stands the figure of the *philomythos* and 'the *philomythos* is in a sense *philosophos*' (*Met.* 982b18 ss). When Homer and Hesiod

14. Cf. Heidegger, *Being and Time*, p. 174.

trace the origin of the gods and all things back to Ouranos, Gaia, and Okeanos, they express themselves in the medium of theogonic speculation, but they are engaged in the same search of the ground as Aristotle himself (*Met.* 983b28 ss). The place on the scale of compactness and differentiation does not affect the fundamental identity of structure in man's humanity" (p. 93).

The initial experience of wonder is, as Voegelin puts it, "the infrastructure for the noetic insights proper" (p. 94). The noetic insights in turn are constituted by the self-reflective apperception and symbolization of the process of questioning consciousness as it notices, for example, what has been spoken of already as *psyche* and as it notices also the features that became symbolized in the language of "divine-human encounter": "In the Platonic-Aristotelian experience, the questioning unrest carries the assuaging answer within itself inasmuch as man is moved to his search of the ground by the divine ground of which he is in search. The ground is not a spatially distant thing but a divine presence that becomes manifest in the experience of unrest and the desire to know. The wondering and questioning is sensed as the beginning of a theophanic event that can become fully luminous to itself if it finds the proper response in the psyche of concrete human beings—as it does in the classic philosophers" (pp. 95–96).

Voegelin goes on to explain that this implies, as these philosophers realized, that philosophy is not a body of ideas or opinions, "but a man's responsive pursuit of his questioning unrest to the divine source that has aroused it." This takes place as a process of experience and symbolization that together constitute the characteristic activity of *nous* and its mode of knowing, *episteme.* "This pursuit . . . ," says Voegelin, "if it is to be responsive indeed to the divine mover, requires the effort of articulating the experience through appropriate language symbols."

The process by which these language symbols themselves develop is a continuous one running throughout the process of meditative exegesis or self-discovery, through its mythic phases as well as its noetic or philosophical ones. Paul Ricoeur, in his discussion of the various levels of language used to describe "sin" or self-loss, "the experience of being oneself but alienated from oneself," has made basically the same observation: "the consciousness of self seems to constitute itself at its lowest level by means of symbolism and to work out an abstract language only subsequently, by means of a spontaneous hermeneutics of its primary symbols" (*Symbolism of Evil*, pp. 8–9). Ricoeur's terminology here ("symbolism" versus "abstract language") might make it seem as if two quite different languages are involved, but actually, for both Ricoeur and Voegelin, there is a gradual process, a continuum of symbolization, by which one renders increasingly articulate and explicit a meaning already compactly present as a whole on the earliest, most compactly suggestive level of symbolism. It is precisely for this reason that both consider it possible and important to trace back through the layers of symbolization to the basic experiences that engender the whole series of layers.

This principle carries with it the corollary, which may be unwelcome to some who seek perfect definiteness of reference, that there is no sharp line that can separate mythic from noetic symbols. At a certain point one begins to recognize that thought has become explicit and critically reflective and one indicates this by the use of the term "noetic." Insofar as *nous* is an expression, however, of the same tensional pull, the same "homing instinct," one might call it, that characterizes human experience on all its levels of differentiation or compactness, it remains within the experiential continuum that is the *psyche* as a whole.

Since discussion of these issues may seem highly abstract when it is cast entirely in verbal form, it may be helpful to depart from Voegelin's analysis for a moment and consider a way of representing the matter in visual symbols. If we consider that human existence is constituted as a tension of longing or striving toward conscious participation in reality and that this striving proceeds through reflective mediation in consciousness, we might diagram the total pattern in the following way:

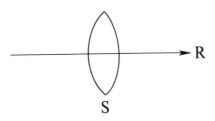

The line with the arrowhead in this picture represents the tension of existence both as experienced on the level of immediacy and as articulated in consciousness through the medium of symbolization. "R" stands for reality, in which the inquirer is immediately involved through his participation in existence and which he also comes to know reflectively. As such it is intended to embrace all that is, including the entire process represented in the diagram. The figure in the middle marked with "S" is in the shape of a lens. "S" stands for symbol; this may take the specific form of visual symbols, myths, ideas, philosophical propositions, and so on. It could even take the form of dance or liturgy. Whatever its form, it functions to represent some aspect of the reality attended to through it and to direct inquiry toward that. This is why it is represented in the diagram as a lens; it is not, when it is functioning properly, an object of attention in its own right, but serves as a focusing device to direct attention beyond itself toward the object of interest. It is only through that lens or medium that human existence can attain consciousness and reflective knowledge of the real, even when what is inquired into is human existence.

Between S and R there is a constant interplay: the immediacy of experience stimulates the wondering question that seeks knowledge, and it also engenders the symbols that make possible that knowledge. It is only by way of the symbolic representation that one can attend to the experiential field, and only those features of it may be consciously discerned that are articulated in the symbol. Experience, however, always contains the full range of features that call for attention, and these exert a constant pressure on consciousness, seeking adequate symbolization. It is paradoxical, perhaps, that we can notice only what we can symbolize, while we are called by the reality in which we are involved to develop symbols for all of what is available to be noticed. This is what it means, however, to be human: paradoxically both to be involved immediately in reality on the most basic level of experience and to know that immediate reality consciously only through the mediating process of symbolic articulation. What makes for paradox is our attempt to find an adequate symbol that can do full justice to all the dimensions of the experience of human existence on its levels of both immediacy and mediation. What resolves the paradox for us in practice is our experience itself of experience as a continuum of varying degrees of relative consciousness and obscurity. We are not perfectly luminous Cartesian egos whose existence must be fully expressible with logical precision. Rather we are participants, Voegelin would say, in what the Greeks called *psyche*.

It is the diagram as a whole that depicts *psyche*. The symbol *psyche* refers to the entire process of participation in reality, its symbolization, and the tension that moves and guides the process.

Nous also is constituted by the entire pattern represented in the diagram. *Nous*, as Voegelin interprets it, is not a part of the *psyche*; it is *psyche* raised to self-reflective clarity. This clarity in which the nature of the mediating process of articulation becomes conscious to itself opens up the possibility of conscious and deliberate critical reflection on the adequacy of symbols. It also makes possible the realization of their irreducibly analogical character when they attempt to give expression to what is inherently mysterious: the soul in its depths, the mystery of existence, the eminent reality of the gods, and so on. It makes both careful knowing possible and the limits of human knowing visible.

The classical term, as was mentioned above, for the characteristic mode of knowing of *nous* is *episteme*, and Voegelin has made this a central term in his own analysis of philosophical knowing as an existential process. This is not, of course, the only way to conceive of the nature of knowing, nor is it much regarded in the modern setting. There is also the type of knowledge now usually referred to as "scientific," but which could perhaps be more accurately described as "hypothetical," since the term "science," derived as it is from the medieval Latin *scientia*, itself a translation of the Greek *episteme*, is a name that could as reasonably be claimed on historical grounds for Voegelin's *noesis* as for modern science's investigations into external nature (cf. *Anam.*, p. 177). This history of terminology is worth mentioning, because it indicates the fundamental confusion that has developed regarding what constitutes knowledge as such and what type of knowledge can best lay claim to the name— the question of which, in the terms of the preceding chapter's discussion, is the controlling sense of the word, through analogy to which other uses derive their meaningfulness.

An underlying problem is that one may speak of knowledge in at least two fundamentally different ways: knowledge of existence from within and knowledge of existence from without. In the classical setting these two ways were sometimes designated by such terms as *episteme, aletheia,* and *theoria,* on the one hand—all of them terms for the experientially rooted mode of knowing of *nous*—and the term *doxa* (opinion) on the other. Much of Voegelin's treatment of the basic issue is to be found in his historical studies of the use of these terms. This historical approach is complicated, however, by the fact that the terms were used in different ways over time by different philosophers—in ways that also reflected the same conceptual confusion as does the modern term "science."[15]

15. For a general account of the historical range of meanings, see "Episteme," F. E. Peters, *Greek Philosophical Terms* (New York: New York University Press, 1967), and "Science," André Lalande, *Vocabulaire technique et critique de la philosophie* (Paris: Presses universitaires de France, 1956). One of the main complications of the issue came from the association of *episteme* quite early with scientific certainty, as when Plato, *Republic* 533–34, speaks of geometry as an *episteme*. Eventually the emphasis on certainty became the major association of the term, which led to the development of the ideal of a speculative system giving certain knowledge even of contingent reality. Mortimer Adler, "Little Errors in the Beginning," *The Thomist*, 38 (1974): 33–35, says that although the ancients (he has in mind especially Aristotle) and medievals developed this way of conceiving of *episteme*, they did not in practice proceed in accord with it; Descartes and

The question of the distinctions and relations between *episteme*, *doxa*, and *gnosis* is of central importance for Voegelin, but unfortunately his treatment of it is not one of the clearer aspects of his thought. There is no single place in his writings where he spells out in perfect detail his analysis of the types of knowledge and cognitive claim that these terms have come to designate for him. In part this is probably because he assumes the reader's prior familiarity with the use of the terms in classical sources. But the fact that these sources are sometimes ambiguous can lead to confusion.

Spinoza, he says, were the first to try to do so. Actually, however, the seeds of the seventeenth-century developments may be seen already in the tendency of the concepts of *episteme, theoria*, and *scientia* to take on different meanings in the Middle Ages when used in different contexts; cf. M.-D. Chenu, *Nature, Man, and Society in the Twelfth Century*, ed. and trans. Jerome Taylor and Lester K. Little (Chicago: University of Chicago Press, 1968), pp. 83–84: "The Greek idea of *episteme* (certain knowledge), as typically happened in Neoplatonic tradition, was realized through the cathartic and mystical operation of a *theoria* (contemplation), a term which Latin spiritual writers, though not the scholastics, took over bodily and contrasted to *scientia* (scientific or demonstrable knowledge), which for them usually retained a secular meaning." For a treatment of the theme of *episteme* by Plato that is more in keeping with Voegelin's emphasis on participatory knowledge through love, see *Republic* 475–80, a section that begins by distinguishing the love of beauty as such from that of particular beautiful objects, then compares the love of beauty with philosophy and *episteme* and concludes by distinguishing philosophy (as the love of transcendental truth, the Idea of the Good) from philodoxy (the love of opinions), a distinction that will be discussed in more detail shortly. *Doxa* in this passage is described as a fallible faculty, because its opinions regarding particular truth may or may not be true, whereas *episteme* is infallible. It is clear from the comparison with the love of beauty that Plato's conception of epistemic certainty is at least not limited to the certainty of logical proof or scientific demonstration but includes also the philosopher's immediate sense that whatever the truth of a particular opinion or doxic construction of the field of reality may be, the love that motivates his inquiry and leads him to weigh and assess the truth of *doxai* is a radical love not of any *doxa* but of truth as such. The certainty of *episteme* is the certainty of knowledge grounded in immediate experience.

Plato has various, and varying, treatments of *episteme* and *doxa*. It is interesting to compare this section of the *Republic* with *Meno* 97a–98b, where *episteme* is treated as the anamnetic experience which serves to give stability to *doxai*, which may be perfectly true and adequate to guide conduct, but which without experiential roots would tend to wander about. See also *Phaedrus* 247c.

Voegelin is certainly subject to criticism on this point, and it is the principal area in which the limits of his method of discussion manifest themselves. Because it is a matter of principle with him to concentrate on historical experience and its symbolization, Voegelin prefers always to maintain as consistently as possible a historical approach. Therefore, when he discusses various ways of conceiving of the nature of human knowledge, he proceeds by referring to the language symbols of *episteme*, *doxa*, and *gnosis* as the terms developed by the classical thinkers who first experienced the process of self-reflective critical inquiry and developed these as symbols with which to designate its modes—or purported modes. This can be an effective strategy where sufficiently clear symbols have been developed and have acquired normative status so that one may know with a fair degree of precision what the terms refer to. The source of difficulty in the present case is that a fully clear and adequate analysis is not available, in either ancient or modern sources, and that no single way of using the terms has become normative.

There are the rudiments of such analysis, but a modern thinker like Voegelin is in the position of having to develop that analysis further to render it clear enough for its terms to serve as analytic tools for the discussion of the fundamental political and philosophical questions he believes demand our attention. Voegelin does this, but he does it indirectly—in diverse places, and often as though in passing. Both to understand Voegelin himself and to join in penetrating to the core of the central issues with which he is concerned, it will be necessary, while following him as closely as possible, to analyze the possible ways of knowing—and of going astray—more explicitly and systematically than he has.

The present discussion can be simplified by concentrating first on this basic issue: existence can be known from within in a way that is the explication or symbolic articulation of the concrete experience of the existing knower, or it can be known as the external reality of a hypothetical entity other than the knower himself. Voegelin used just this terminology in his 1943 essay, "On the Theory of Consciousness," in which he said: "The thing-in-itself is a symbol through which Kant sought to grasp the correctly seen fact that our experience of nature is an experience 'from without,' while the 'within' of matter remains inaccessible for us: our experience of natural being is, strictly speaking, phenomenal. Kant furthermore has seen correctly that consciousness, under the title *Vernunft*, is a special case, inasmuch as in consciousness we have experience of a process 'from within'" (*Anam.*, p. 32). (It is worth noting that the experiential reality referred to here as *Vernunft*, usually translated "reason," is not essentially different from that referred to in the classical setting as *nous*, in spite of changes in emphasis deriving from their historical contexts.) He also used this way of speaking more recently in "What Is Political Reality?" where he says that "noetic knowledge . . . is not the type of knowledge of the natural sciences, observing things 'from without,' but the experience of a relation 'from within'" (p. 175).

Another way to put the distinction between the two modes of knowledge would be to speak of the epistemic mode or that "from within" as "existential knowing" and of the doxic mode or that "from without" as "hypothetical knowing." Voegelin does not use this terminology, but Jaspers, dealing with the same problem, comes close to it when he speaks of "existential elucidation" (*Existenzerhellung*) as the illumination of *Existenz* from within and contrasts this with the investigation of "empirical existence" in the natural sciences (see, for example, *Philosophy*, 2:3–46). What is characteristic of knowing in the hypothetical or doxic mode ("doxic" is a term that Voegelin has come to use extensively to refer to this) is that it speculates regarding the external existence, apart from the knower, of a reality sketched out in an hypothesis or speculative model (*doxa*). For example, one catches a glimpse of a strange object ("What is that over there?"), then develops a concept or speculative schema (*doxa*) that may fit it ("Is it a chair?"), and finally confirms the fit by closer observation ("It *is* a chair!"). Epistemic or existential knowledge, on the other hand, which for Voegelin is the proper sphere of philosophy, is the knowledge in which the tension of existence, the love of the divine ground, becomes conscious to itself and commits itself to live in fidelity to its love; for this kind of knowledge is not a matter of mere observation of fact but of clarifying, opening up, and rendering conscious and available the possibilities implicit in existence in its fullness.

As should be clear already, the term "existence" is used in two different though analogous ways in connection with the two kinds of knowledge. In epistemic, existential knowledge it refers to an experience in which one is wholly involved. From this point of view, existence has fullness, density, texture; it is a life of drama, a wager in which the stake is life itself, and in which the possible prize is heightened or eminent life. From the doxic point of view, in contrast, existence is narrowed to what in experiential terms is absolutely minimal: the bare opposite of nonbeing. It is a kind of logical counter used to indicate no more than the truth of a proposition—not the lived truth of *aletheia*, or true being in its luminous self-disclosure.[16]

For Voegelin it is the epistemic meaning of the term "existence" that is the controlling norm for any other analogical uses. He does not consider the doxic use entirely illegitimate, as long as its relation to the controlling sense is kept clear. "In fact," says Voegelin in his commentary in *The World of the Polis* on Parmenides's discussion of *aletheia* ("Truth") and *doxa* ("Delusion"), "the Delusion is quite as true as the Truth, if by truth we mean an adequate and consistent articulation of an experience. . . . Being and Delusion are not two different worlds; they are two aspects of one world that is given in two kinds of cognitive experiences of the same human being" (*OH*, 2:216–17).[17] Both are knowledge in the sense that they are ways of construing reality; the distinction is between levels or degrees of reality: "Truth is the philosophy of the realissimum that we experience if we follow the way of immortalization in the soul;

16. This last point, of course, suggests a comparison with Heidegger, who has made *aletheia*, or the "unhiddenness of being," one of the major themes of his thought. See *Being and Time*, p. 265. Another interesting comparison is with Gabriel Marcel's discussion of the human experience of existence as mystery in *The Mystery of Being*, 2 vols. (Chicago: Henry Regnery, 1951).

17. Cf. Heidegger, *Being and Time*, p. 265, also on Parmenides.

Delusion is the philosophy of the reality that we experience as men who live and die in a world that itself is distended in time with a beginning and an end. The characterization of this philosophy of reality as a Delusion derives its justification from the experience of a superior reality, of an immortal ground of the mortal world" (p. 216). There is mundane reality, the reality of finite objects in the world, and there is eminent reality, the reality known in the experience of a movement of transcendence that reaches beyond the world.

Episteme and *theoria* were the terms used by certain classical philosophers, as discussed by Voegelin, for the reflective illumination of this experienced movement of transcendence. Since the former term has disappeared and its Latin equivalent, *scientia*, has been preempted in modern usage to describe the natural sciences, it is the word "theory," as Voegelin uses it at least, that carries the classical meaning forward. It does so, that is, as best it can under the circumstances, since "theory," too, has largely been preempted in the doxically oriented modern setting to serve as a term for speculative hypotheses.[18] The ambiguity produced by the possibility of both epistemic and doxic uses of the term has led to perplexity even among long-time readers of Voegelin. William Havard, for example, has written recently of the difficulty of abstracting from the totality of Voegelin's writings a firmly fixed concept of theory:

> He uses the terms "theory," "theoretical," and "retheorization" as familiar language symbols which connote neither a logically coherent, but inadequately tested, explanation to be used as a framework for directing experimental inquiry, nor a synthesized explanation of the results of empirical analysis, nor a union of these two cognitive functions to form a paradigm according to which science proceeds. . . . one might say that theory, for Voegelin is more a process than a logical construct abstracted from the whole experiential activity which produced it.[19]

18. The doxic use of the term "theory" is not exclusively modern, however, but may be traced back to the classical period itself. For Jaspers's use of the term in a sense similar to Voegelin's as the explication of experience through analogical language, see "Philosophical Autobiography," p. 19.

19. "Notes on Voegelin's Contributions to Political Theory," *Polity*, 10 (1977): 36.

The possibility of confusion comes from the fact that even Voegelin, writing as he does in modern languages, is forced to use the term in both doxic or hypothetical and epistemic or existential senses. Whenever Voegelin makes "theory" as such an explicit theme for discussion, however, he is concerned with the epistemic sense, as in *The New Science of Politics*, where he defines it as "an attempt at formulating the meaning of existence by explicating the content of a definite class of experiences," which he specifies as "the differentiating experiences of transcendence" (pp. 64, 80).

"Theory," as Voegelin primarily uses the term, refers to knowledge that is the conscious expression of immediate experience and that has become explicit through adequate symbolization. The mediating symbols, of course, function analogically, and fully developed theoretical understanding involves recognition of this. Also, precisely because theory involves mediation by means of symbols, it casts in an objectifying mold an experience that in itself does not have the structure of division into subject and object; but again this is recognized, or at least it is when theoretical reflection attains maximum lucidity. It is not the use of interpretive models that differentiates theory in Voegelin's sense from *doxa*, since all reflective understanding on the level of articulate consciousness takes place in the medium of symbolizations.[20] Rather the difference lies in the relation of the model to experience.

This, however, introduces another aspect of the distinction between *episteme* and *doxa* in addition to that which can best be discussed in terms of knowledge from within or from without. To

20. Cf. Aristotle *De Anima* (trans. J. A. Smith in *Basic Works*, ed. McKeon) 413a14–20: "To the thinking soul [*dianoetike psyche*] images [*phantasmata*] serve as if they were contents of perception. . . . That is why the soul never thinks without an image." See also 432a7–8: ". . . when the mind is actively aware of anything it is necessarily aware of it along with an image." It should be noted, however, that the mental images or interpretive models used in theoretical reflection need not take the form of sensual imaginations. All sorts of confusion can follow from the assumption that they do. Cf. Janik and Toulmin's discussion in *Wittgenstein's Vienna*, pp. 182–86, of the misinterpretation of Wittgenstein's concept of *Bilder* (lit. "pictures") on the part of English-speaking readers who assumed he was speaking of visual images.

return to the model of knowledge represented in the earlier diagram, the interpretive model functions as a medium or lens through and by means of which one attends to reality, which is also present on the level of immediate experience, but which cannot become explicitly conscious except by way of the mediating symbolic representation. To describe the process in Polanyi's terms of focal and subsidiary awareness, what should be attended to focally is reality in its fullness and intrinsic mysteriousness. The idea or interpretive model is not a cognitive object, but only a *means* of attending, and its place is in subsidiary awareness. Epistemic knowing has this structure and realizes it. The philosophical theorist in Voegelin's sense, one who seeks truth in the epistemic mode, uses his concepts in the manner of a reflecting device or lens to direct his attention into a reality which they open up for exploration, but which they never precisely capture.

It is always tempting, however, to avoid acknowledging the relative and limited character of interpretive models and to claim absolute knowledge. There are two ways one may do this. One is by claiming an ineffable intuition of ultimate reality. The other is by claiming that one's articulated understanding captures the real perfectly. Both are versions of what Voegelin calls *gnosis*, a term that had shifting meanings in antiquity but which Voegelin uses to designate what is claimed as absolute knowledge.[21] The former could be called transcendentalizing *gnosis* and the latter immanentizing; this is a distinction that Voegelin does not himself state explicitly, but it is implicit in his treatment of the subject. Both deny the essential structure of human knowing as a process involving levels of both immediacy and reflective mediation. The transcendentalizing form of *gnosis* is a sort of inflated mysticism that

21. In the classical period of Greek philosophy, *gnosis* was the common term for knowledge generally. Aristotle *Posterior Analytics* 2. 99b–100b, uses it to include *episteme* as well as sense perception, experience in the broader sense, and memory. In the early Christian era it was used in a more special sense, to refer to a secret higher knowledge accessible only to a spiritual elite. As will subsequently be explained in more detail, it is this later meaning that lies behind Voegelin's use of the term. Cf. Peters, *Greek Philosophical Terms*, p. 74.

exalts the status of the gnostic visionary, but by the very nature of its claim has little actually to say. Voegelin has been more concerned, on the whole, with the immanentizing variety, which tends to say a great deal about man, the world, history, and the divine and to claim absolute authority for its pronouncements.

It is this immanentizing pattern of gnostic thought that Voegelin refers to as "doxic," because of the emphasis it places on the perfect truth of the *doxa* or speculative idea. Doxic thinking focuses on the interpretive model and tends to assume that this is not merely a representation but a direct view of the real as it is in itself. The result is that the model, which should remain subsidiary and retain its transparency for the reality beyond it, becomes focal and thereby opaque. The proper cognitive relation of reflection to experience is consequently broken and the structure of inquiry distorted.

This is what makes for the emphasis of doxic thought on externality. The epistemic, which is founded on self-reflective clarity about the relation of limited and analogical understanding to a mysterious reality in which one is oneself involved, takes the conscious form of an explication of experience from within a total complex of immediacy and reflective articulation. Epistemic theory is the articulation on the level of reflective consciousness of experience that is already present in its wholeness ("in the fullness of its dimensions" as was said earlier) on the level of immediacy. Doxic speculation, on the other hand, looks toward what presumably lies outside experience, and insofar as it does articulate experience, the experience is minimal and fragmentary—the experience of "sense data" or perhaps of "psychological" data.

Knowing reality only as though from an external perspective, *doxai*, according to Voegelin, never penetrate to the essential substance, the ultimate experiential concreteness of the reality they attempt to explore.[22] This applies, it may be noted, even to knowledge of oneself when this is in the doxic mode, as when a person attempts to understand himself not through insight into his own actual experience, but in terms of an ideology that would reduce

22. See, for example, *OH*, 3:73, and *From Enlightenment to Revolution*, p. 115.

him to a mode of behavior, or a center of exclusively economic interests or of sexual appetites, and so on.

The substantial reality to which episteme can penetrate, and which the *doxai* do not reach, is the experience of "participation in being." The bedrock of reality, which the philosophical theorist comes to know epistemically, is nothing other than the tension of existence. To know this with full theoretical clarity is both to experience it and to recognize its directional character and its transcendental goal. This is why in another place Voegelin defines *episteme* as "transcendental cognition" and says, in the language of the myth of the Last Judgment in Plato's *Gorgias*, that it is "in reality existential knowledge of the fulfillment of human destiny in eternal life."[23] The substance of reality is the luminous tension of existence, and the luminosity of this tension is what constitutes *episteme* or *theoria.* The direction of the tension is toward the maximum of luminosity. To pursue this faithfully and to dwell in it maximally, at least as far as this is possible to man, is to participate in the eternal life represented by the symbol of the "divine ground."[24]

It is a necessary corollary of this analysis that theoretical understanding, in Voegelin's sense of the term, makes existential demands of the inquirer. In the accustomed modern usage, theory should be intelligible to any investigator who uses properly objective scientific methodology; the demands are not on the observer but only on the method, and the observer is supposed to be personally disengaged from the subject matter under study.[25] From this point

23. "On Readiness to Rational Discussion," in Albert Hunold, ed., *Freedom and Serfdom* (Dordrecht: D. Reidel, 1961), pp. 227–28.

24. Cf. Voegelin's comment on Plato's *Phaedrus* 245, in *OH* 3:137: "In the state of the erotic *mania* [the love for the good as such] man lives in the dynamic substance of the cosmos and the substance lives in him; and since this substance is the 'order,' the Idea itself, we immerse ourselves in *mania* in the Agathon [the Good] and, reversely, in *mania* the Agathon fills the soul."

25. For another recent philosopher, however, who also discusses the role of personal existential involvement in theoretical understanding, see Hans-Georg Gadamer, *Truth and Method,* p. 111: "Perhaps we may remind the reader of the idea of sacral communion which lies behind the original Greek idea of theoria. . . . In the same way, Greek metaphysics still conceives the nature of

of view, any two investigators should arrive at mutually confirming observations provided their methodology and the "theory" itself—in this case a form of *doxa*—is sound. For Voegelin on the other hand, again following classical thought, the theorist must be what Aristotle called a *spoudaios* or mature man, one whose character has been formed by the aggregate of experiences which theory inquires into: "theory cannot be developed under all conditions by everybody. The theorist . . . must, at least, be capable of imaginative re-enactment of the experiences of which theory is an explication. . . . theory as an explication of certain experiences is intelligible only to those in whom the explication will stir up parallel experiences as the empirical basis for testing the truth of theory" (*The New Science of Politics*, p. 64).[26]

The theorist in Voegelin's sense—which is to say, the philosopher—must be one who dwells consciously and freely in the tension of existence, and this means that he must experience the tension and be willing to acknowledge it and the demands it makes on his existence. This, according to Voegelin, is why Heraclitus attacked the polyhistoric collector of facts and considered that "the soul of man is a source of truth only when it is oriented toward god through the love of wisdom" (*OH*, 2:227). It is also why Plato has Socrates spend so much time in the dialogues on the question whether *episteme* can be taught: "For the kind of vision (*opsis*) that

theoria and of nous as pure presence to what is truly real, and also the capacity to be able to act theoretically is defined for us by the fact that in attending to something it is possible to forget one's own purposes. . . . Theoria is a true sharing, not something active, but something passive (pathos), namely being totally involved in and carried away by what one sees."

26. In the early part of his career Voegelin could have found this way of thinking about ethical theory in his immediate milieu in the thought of Kierkegaard and Karl Kraus even before finding it in Aristotle. Cf. Janik and Toulmin, *Wittgenstein's Vienna*, p. 179: "Kraus further agreed with Kierkegaard that the unity of form and content in a work of art was absolutely essential. Aesthetic form and ethical content are two faces of the same coin. Only the good man knows what values are, and only he can communicate them. No amount of scientific knowledge can ever make a man good." For Aristotle's discussion of the *spoudaios*, see *Nic. Ethics* 1098a and 1113a29–35.

enables a man to see the Agathon [the transcendental pole of the "Good" as such] must exist in a soul, as a man must have eyes to see" (3:115, commenting on *Republic* 518c).

What confers this ability to discern the *agathon* is the directional character of the universal tension of existence. There may be persons in whom the tension is inactive, at least in the sense that it lacks intensity and remains below a certain threshold of noticeability, and in such a case the vision it could give rise to becomes obscured or eclipsed. "Es gibt entspannte Menschen," says Voegelin: "There are easy-going people like the couple whom Doderer describes in his *Merowinger*: 'They belonged to the multitude of the happy-without-history endowed with the well-being of born atheists, who do not necessarily conduct themselves without piety, and mostly go to church'" (*Anam.*, p. 168).[27] In such cases there is neither the vague restlessness that leads most of us either to questioning or to a quest for distractions or something to put us to sleep, nor is there the more acute sort of anxiety that led the Athenians to condemn Socrates to death. Where the tension is consciously present, on the other hand, it can become the means of vision. By reading the directional pull in the tension carefully and following it toward its goal, one discovers what Plato called the "vision of the Good." This is a knowing by means of love, in which love itself becomes the medium of knowledge and what is known is the loveliness of what is loved. Voegelin makes Plato the center of his discussion of this mode of knowing, but it has been noticed and given expression by others as well. Aquinas, for example, who considered no concept to be adequate to God, spoke of love replacing concepts so that God is known not conceptually, or even through analogies, but by "connaturality" (since God is Love), and Saint John of the Cross followed him on this and made it the basis of his mystical theology.[28]

27. *Anamnesis* (German), p. 309. The quotation is from Heimito von Doderer, *Die Merowinger* (Munich: Biederstein, 1962), p. 353.

28. See Jacques Maritain, *The Degrees of Knowledge* (New York: Charles Scribner's Sons, 1959), pp. 260–65, 320–25. For Aquinas on this subject, see, for example, *ST*, IIa–IIae, q. 45, a. 2.

This way of conceiving of philosophy and of the nature of theoretical understanding conflicts most profoundly with common modern approaches in the role it gives to love as a source of knowledge and, in fact, of true objectivity. For Voegelin's "philosophy" is to be understood in the original Greek sense of the term as the "love of wisdom." It is born not of disengagement but of the ordering event of *philia*, love for the true good. One of Voegelin's major criticisms of much of modern thought is its tendency to identify knowledge as such only with the upper reaches of the experiential continuum, or what is usually called "reason." Reason, says Voegelin, is only one of a rich spectrum of modes of knowledge which also includes faith, love, and hope as ways in which the tension of the soul and its orientation toward transcendent perfection emerge gradually into conscious clarity. As he stated the principle in "What Is Political Reality?": "Historically considered, the reality of participating knowledge manifests itself as a fullness so rich that it goes far beyond *ratio* alone. I am thinking particularly about the experience of faith, love, and hope, which Heraclitus had already recognized and distinguished as sources of knowledge. One may therefore speak not only of *cognitio rationis* [knowledge by way of reason] but also of *cognitiones fidei, amoris, et spei* [knowledge by way of faith, love, and hope]. Furthermore, the *cognitiones* in the reality of knowledge are woven together into a complex that is knowledge only as a whole. Neither is there a *ratio* independent of the other modes of knowledge nor can they be independent of it."[29]

This is to say that faith, love, and hope are ways in which the tension of existence becomes enacted in man's search for true being, and that they lead necessarily, when one is faithful to their intrinsic dynamics, to attempts to develop adequate, critically reflected symbolizations. It is also to say that no matter how far reason progresses into conscious clarity, it remains rooted in the whole of experience,

29. *Anamnesis* (German), p. 324 (my translation). Cf. Niemeyer's rendering in *Anam.*, p. 184. For a discussion of Heraclitus's thought on the cognitive roles of faith, hope, and love, see *OH*, 2:228. For the carryover of this way of thinking about knowledge from the pre-Socratics into Plato and Aristotle, see *Anam.*, p. 97.

which is informed throughout by the direction-giving tension. Reason, the power of self-reflective, critically methodical inquiry, could never begin its seeking without the preliminary, fundamental sense of a truth and good to be sought and without a basic trust in the intelligibility of the real and the possibility of its disclosure in the experience that the Greeks termed *aletheia* or truth, literally the "unhiddenness" of the real. Faith, love, and hope, therefore, are central ways in which the tension expresses itself and begins to emerge into luminosity, and because the mystery of being can never be reduced to simply the answer to a question, there is no way that reason can ever pass entirely beyond them. Both before and after the development of *noesis*, faith, love, and hope are and remain man's most fundamental relation to mystery. "To face the Mystery of Reality," says Voegelin, "means to live in the faith that is the substance of things hoped for and the proof of things unseen (Heb. 11:1)" (*OH*, 4:329).

There are several reasons for the modern tendency to distrust the idea that faith, love, and hope can be basic modes of orientation toward reality. One is that, as Voegelin frequently points out, the term "philosophy" has largely lost its original meaning and has come to be used to refer to what Plato called "philodoxy," the love of opinions.[30] When one asks about a person's "philosophy," one is usually inquiring not about the manner in which he enacts his love for truth but about the doctrinal statements he holds to be true and about the arguments he believes validate them. As a result one also tends to interpret "faith" as the holding of opinions—in fact of ungrounded, even unreasonable opinions. Hope is similarly assimilated into the doxic framework as a sort of expectation of that which faith holds opinions about. Given such a matrix of interpretation, no reasonable person could help but be distrustful of the idea that faith could be a form of knowledge. Since the classical sources of philosophical language are readily available, however, Voegelin

---

30. See, for example, *OH*, 3:82, on how philosophy and philodoxy were originally a pair of contrasting terms in Plato's thought and how the latter term eventually dropped out of use as its meaning was absorbed into the former.

would also say that a reasonable person has little excuse for continuing to operate within so inadequate a framework.

Another reason for the rejection of the classical *cognitiones* is that philodoxic thinkers, modern or ancient, are motivated mainly by a desire for certainty—not by the love of wisdom as a consciously accepted tension toward a truth that must always remain transcendent, but by a desire to possess the wisdom that Plato's Socrates had said could belong only to a god (*Phaedrus* 278d).

If knowledge of this sort regarding actual existence were possible to man, it would amount to what has been described already as *gnosis*. As was explained, the claimant to *gnosis* seeks the certainty of a direct and immediate vision of reality as it is in itself. He is basically a naïve (as opposed to critical) realist who assumes that reality is known not through reflection but by a direct look. The natural scientist is often interpreted as thinking doxically, but if he does so, it is not naïvely but critically.[31] The philodoxer, on the other hand, tends to be a naïve realist in flight from the tension of uncertainty.

Faith is not certainty but trust under conditions of uncertainty.[32] Faith and hope, although their content may be described obliquely through doxic formulations, are not acts of opining but of trust—the trust that what is longed for is forthcoming.[33] Similarly, love is not possession but longing, and all the knowledge love gives is the knowledge of what it is one loves. The philodoxer seeks the security in possession that will put an end to longing; the philosopher has only the continuing pain and insecurity that are the essential correlates of love.

31. It is the tendency of "scientism," at least, to interpret the natural sciences and their methods in doxic terms. Michael Polanyi's major purpose in his writings on the philosophy of science has been to argue that in actual practice the scientist operates in a manner essentially the same as that which Voegelin considers the term *episteme* to designate. See Voegelin, "The Origins of Scientism" (1948), and Polanyi, *Personal Knowledge* and *The Tacit Dimension* (Garden City, N.Y.: Doubleday, 1966).

32. Cf. Aquinas, *ST*, Ia–IIae, q. 67, a. 3.

33. On hope as means of knowledge, see Augustine *City of God* 19. 1. 6; 19. 11. 26–33; 19. 20. 11. Cf. Brown, *Augustine of Hippo*, p. 327.

The philodoxer also suspects that the love of the lover is "merely subjective." To the philosopher, on the other hand, the love is experienced as objectively real; he does not make it up arbitrarily, but suffers it as a passion. It is the pull (*helkein*) which initiates his own philosophical seeking (*zetesis*). In Plato's *Republic* the pull by which the man in the cave of shadows is dragged upward to the light in which he sees the "vision of the Good," like the pull of the cords that work man the puppet in the *Laws*, is a *pathos*, a fate inflicted.[34] One could not create it if one tried; one can only submit to it.

Or one can resist it. The tension of longing may feel too painful; one may prefer an illusion of certainty to the challenge of epistemic existence in truth, which Voegelin has defined as "the awareness of the fundamental structure of existence together with the willingness to accept it as the *condicio humana*" ("On Debate and Existence," p. 151). Where this willingness is lacking, one may avert one's gaze from the mysteriousness of reality and seek refuge in opinions. Voegelin has borrowed Lonergan's term, *scotosis* (darkening), for this voluntary closure against reality, and has interpreted it as a major source of philodoxic thinking.[35]

"The history of philosophy," says Voegelin, "is in the largest part the history of its derailment," of its degeneration, that is, into philodoxy (*OH*, 3:277). What is philosophy in its authentic form? Probably the clearest example, Voegelin believes, may be seen in Plato. The common modern interpretation of Plato is in the philodoxic mode; it represents his thought as a body of "Platonic" doctrines and arguments designed to support them. In Voegelin's analysis this is a radical misreading of Plato, for whom "truth is not a body of propositions about a world-immanent object; it is the world-transcendent *summum bonum*, experienced as an orienting force in the soul, about which we can speak only in analogical symbols" (p. 363). Plato's philosophy, says Voegelin, "is not *a* philosophy [in

34. *Republic* 7. 515e; *Laws* 1. 644e–645a.
35. Voegelin first used the term *scotosis* in "What Is Political Reality?" *Anam.* p. 201, citing Lonergan's *Insight*, pp. 191–203. See also *OH*, 4:267.

the philodoxic sense], but *the* symbolic form in which a Dionysiac soul expresses its ascent to God" (p. 70). The substance of philosophy is not to be found in the philosopher's ideas but in the ascent that he enacts, in response to divine calling and grace.

An understanding of the principles outlined in this way can illuminate the relationship, as Voegelin conceives it, between the sorts of knowledge and experience that have traditionally been designated as "Reason" and "Revelation" or "Philosophy" and "Revelation." Voegelin himself used the latter pair of terms frequently in the first three volumes of *Order and History*. In his more recent writings, such as "Reason: The Classic Experience" and *The Ecumenic Age*, he has tended to replace these with "noetic differentiation" and "pneumatic differentiation." His reason for this is that the traditional pairing has tended historically to be associated with the idea of contrast between the two, whereas his own emphasis is on their fundamental continuity. *Pneuma* is the Greek term for wind or breath. As a symbol it became associated, especially in Septuagint and Christian usage, with the vital principle of a living being, with the life of the *psyche* as well as that of the body. It came therefore to mean "life," "spirit," and "inspiration." Voegelin's term "pneumatic" is based on this last set of meanings and refers specifically to the sense of the pull from the transcendental or divine pole in the experience of existential tension.[36] The "pneumatic differentiation" Voegelin speaks of is the awakening of the soul both by and to the experience of the tensional pull and its sense of the unrestricted character of the reaching that this pull elicits. To put it another way, it is a falling in love with transcendental perfection and a realization that what is loved and sought lies beyond all finite manifestations. It is, in the simplest and most richly connotative words, a matter of falling in love with God and realizing that God is

36. For some places in which Voegelin discusses "pneumatic differentiation" or the symbol of *pneuma*, see "The Gospel and Culture," pp. 79–80; "The Growth of the Race Idea," *Review of Politics*, 2 (1940): 290–93; "Configurations of History," p. 39; *From Enlightenment to Revolution*, p. 96; *OH*, 1:194, 240; *OH*, 4:56, 228, 244, 250–51, 258, 303. The Hebrew term *ruach* (as discussed in *OH*, vol. 1), it should be noted, is an equivalent term for the Greek *pneuma*.

not a being in the world but a supreme, creative fullness—perfect Life, Truth, Love, Joy, and so on—beyond the world. Augustine's "Our heart is restless until it rests in you" is an expression of what Voegelin means by pneumatic differentiation.

It should be clear already why for Voegelin noetic experience and pneumatic experience are in continuity, so that Reason or Philosophy does not stand opposed to Revelation: every experience of noetic striving, the critically conscious seeking after truth and its articulate expression, is motivated by the same love of the divine fullness that is central to pneumatic experience, and in fact it is the pneumatic experience of falling in love with the goal that generates the noetic striving toward it. This is why Voegelin speaks of "the constitution of reason through revelation" and says that "the structure of a theophanic experience reaches from a pneumatic center to a noetic periphery" (*OH*, 4:228, 244).

Another way to state the principle is to say that according to Voegelin's analysis of the experience in question, the divine *helkein* or tensional pull and the human *zetesis* or seeking after the ultimate Being or Reality toward which one is pulled are, as was mentioned earlier, not two different movements but one and the same movement of the soul. The underlying issue is the unavoidably paradoxical character of the experience of existential tension. Looked at one way, the tension is an experience of being pulled; looked at another way, it is an experience of reaching toward. The two ways of viewing it are expressed in two different, mutually exclusive interpretive models: seeking and being drawn. This is paradox in the most proper sense of the word: two parallel, contradictory *doxai* (opinions or hypotheses), both equally applicable.

The term "differentiation" as Voegelin uses it in speaking of noetic or pneumatic differentiation refers to the process by which one notices and develops an articulated, explicit consciousness of a previously "compact" (comparatively implicit, unarticulated) field of experience. In noetic differentiation the field is the tension of inquiry and the process of questioning to which it gives rise, and the differentiation is the conscious realization of its structure and of the demands this structure makes on the seeker, who by his faithful response (insofar as it *is* faithful) grows into and appropriates his potential humanity (*Anam.*, pp. 92–93; see also *OH*, 4:177). What made both the noetic differentiation in classical Greece and the pneumatic in Israel and early Christianity epochal events is that they involved a distinctly new realization of the difference between the transcendental pole of the tension of existence and the entire field of immanent reality. The substance of the noetic breakthrough was the clear realization that human conceptions of truth and goodness were grounded in a reference beyond themselves to the True and the Good as such. The substance of the pneumatic breakthrough was the realization that the object of transcendental love and obedience was not one more figure within the cosmos but a supreme reality beyond all created beings.

It was to emphasize the decisiveness of this step that Voegelin coined his well-known phrase, "leap in being." This experience of "conversion," the Platonic *periagoge*, of turning around to seek consciously the true source of order, "results," says Voegelin, "in more than an increase of knowledge concerning the order of being. . . . The more perfect attunement to being through conversion is not an increase on the same scale but a qualitative leap" (*OH*, 1:10). What opens up that is radically new through this realization of the essential structure of existence is the possibility of free, deliberate loyalty to the normative order implicit within it.

Because this "leap" or movement of the soul into heightened participation in being is constituted of both a seeking (*zetein*) from the side of the human pole and a drawing (*helkein*) from that of the divine pole, either one or the other of the poles may be apprehended as more prominent in the experience. Where the emphasis is on the human struggle for truth, and on the conceptual illumination of the movement by which it is sought, there is the possibility of critical reflection, which can result in more careful and controlled thinking and the preservation of psychic balance. What was referred to a moment ago as the "noetic periphery" of the movement constitutes the area that was spoken of in the preceding chapter as the level of mediated, explicit consciousness, and it is the awareness of the process of mediation that makes for enhanced possibilities of critical control. Where the emphasis is on the *mysterium tremendum et fascinans*, the awesomeness of its presence, the forcefulness of its pull on the soul, and the transcendent majesty of the source of the pull, this is experienced as a moral and spiritual regeneration, but dangers of noetic distortion abound.[37] The reason is that pneumatic experience is concentrated primarily on the level of immediacy—at the point of irruption (the "pneumatic center") of the pull toward the transcendent goal. It is constituted, that is, of the immediate experience of existential tension and the initial, comparatively spontaneous and uncritical symbolizations of the tension and its structure. The latter may take such forms, for example, as the image of man as servant or slave of an enthroned, majestic deity issuing arbitrary demands— seemingly arbitrary, that is, but deeply felt within the soul for their intrinsic force.

Centered as it is on the level of immediate experience, the pneumatic differentiation tends to involve considerably less reflective self-awareness on the human side than does the noetic, and it may leave the structure of questioning consciousness almost completely inarticulate. It can have a powerful effect on the lives of individuals who experience it, and through them on their societies, but the comparative lack of human self-understanding in the experience may leave it with a rather precarious noetic hold on reality. This may lead to a tendency to claim excessive "certainty" for the symbolizations of the experience, a claim to *gnosis*, as though one's symbolizations were not that but direct intuitions of a reality having precisely the form of the symbol. This is a basic denial not only of the analogical character of the mediating symbols but also of the nature of human knowing as structured, in its finitude, of a combination of immediacy and mediation. Such a gnostic claim, even if not fully explicit, is what lies at the base of a tendency to literalize both religious and philosophical symbols.

37. For a discussion of what Voegelin calls the "unbalancing dynamics of theophany," see *OH*, 4:239–40.

The literalizing of symbols is the destruction, according to Voegelin, of both religion and philosophy, in that neither is a simple description of objects but an existential ascent or movement into luminosity of existence, to heightened participation in being. The convergence of the two can be seen in Plato's conception of the philosopher's *zetema*. The nearest English equivalent for this key term in Plato's thought is "inquiry." It is not the type of inquiry, however, in which one seeks information; rather it is a process in which human existence articulates itself to itself (*OH*, 3:83).

The language in which the *zetema* of philosophy expresses itself, even when it is refined to conceptual precision—which is a matter of terminological explicitness—never ceases to be analogical, for analogy is the only language that can be used for mystery, and existence is intrinsically mysterious. The philosopher does not examine and describe an object, nor even ideas about an object; rather his own existence, in which he is totally immersed, becomes luminous from within as it emerges into the luminosity of being: "the concepts of the inquiry do not refer to an external object, but are symbols evolved by the soul when it engages in the exegesis of its depth. . . . the concepts and propositions do not primarily tender information about an object, but are the very building blocks of the substantive stature into which the soul grows through its inquiry" (p. 84). In the historical development of Greek philosophy there was first a realization of the inadequacy of the traditional myths of the poets as representations of truth, then a subsequent separation between those who wished to find a nonmythic, nonanalogical language and those who, like Plato, recognized the misleadingness of the earlier myth but at the same time realized that the self-expression of the philosophical *zetema* can never transcend analogy. Voegelin has said, in his analysis of the modern controversy over the validity of mythic forms of expression, that only "when symbols and dogmas are seen in a 'literal,' disenchanted opaqueness from the outside, do they acquire the 'irrationality' which brings them into conflict with logic, with biology, history, etc."; in its original use "mythical language was . . . the precise instrument for expressing the irruption of transcendental reality, its incarnation and its operation in man" (*From Enlightenment to Revolution*, p. 21). Plato was critical of the myths of the poets, but in his own philosophical myths, which he used increasingly in his later works, he regained, says Voegelin, "the truth of the myth on the new level of the differentiated consciousness of the mystic" (*OH*, 3:188).

As an illustration of Plato's use of philosophical myth and of the extent to which he was reflectively aware of its character as both philosophy and myth Voegelin cites the *Timaeus* and its story of the Demiurge's creation of the cosmos as "a living creature truly endowed with soul and intelligence by the providence of God" (30c): "Now when the creator had framed the soul according to his will, he formed within her the corporal universe, and brought the two together and united them center to center. The soul, interfused everywhere from the center to the circumference of heaven, of which also she is the external envelopment, herself turning in herself, began a divine beginning of never-ceasing and rational life enduring throughout all time" (36d–e).[38] This is described in the dialogue as a "likely myth" (*eikos mythos*), which is not final truth, but which should be acceptable to the reasonable inquirer because, as Timaeus says, "we must remember that I who am the speaker and you who are the judges are only mortal men, and we ought to accept the tale which is probable and inquire no further" (29d). "As being is to becoming," he says, "so is truth to belief." It is worth noting here that the Greek for the last word is *pistis*, which can be rendered as "faith" or "trust." Plato was well aware, says Voegelin, that the symbolism of this myth does not give expression to a direct experience of its purported object: "The *anima mundi* is a philosopher's myth: It articulates neither the experience of the primordial field [the realm of particular reality including the gods], nor the experience of the *psyche*, but achieves the imaginative fusion of insights gained by the two types of experience" ("Equivalences of Experience

38. Trans. Benjamin Jowett, in *The Collected Dialogues of Plato*, ed. Edith Hamilton and Huntington Cairns (Princeton, N.J: Princeton University Press, 1961).

and Symbolization," p. 228). This is not to say, however, that it is merely speculative in the philodoxic manner. The myth of the ensouled cosmos, to which the *psyche* of man is linked at its innermost center, is, says Voegelin, an expression of the hope and trust without which there could be no philosophic *zetema*:

> It is true we have no experience of the depth of the Cosmos as *psyche*; and Plato himself is careful enough to claim for the *psyche* and *logos* of man no more than to be kindred (*syngenes*) to the divine *psyche* and *logos* of the Cosmos. Still, the imaginative play has its hard core of reality as it is motivated by man's trust (*pistis*) in reality as intelligibly ordered, as a Cosmos. Our perspectival experiences of reality in process may render no more than fragments of insight, the fragmentary elements may be heterogeneous, and they may look even incommensurable, but the trust in the underlying oneness of reality, its coherence, lastingness, constancy of structure, order and intelligibility will inspire the creation of images which express the ordered wholeness sensed in the depth. . . . The result is the *eikos mythos* whose degree of likeness will depend on the amount of disparate experiences it has achieved to unify persuasively in its imagery. [Pp. 228–29]

The reason it is not a philodoxic speculation is that although it expresses itself in objectifying language, the experiences it gives expression to are those of the soul as it moves into increasingly conscious participation in the deepest, substantial level of reality, the tension of existence. When viewed in this perspective, myth is not a function that can be falsified or superseded by "science," because they are not in competition; their attention is turned in different directions. Science, both natural and social, explores the realm of particular phenomena, Parmenides's realm of *doxa*, which has its own degree of reality and of truth. Myth is the symbolic language by means of which the soul explores and articulates as conscious experience its participation in the tension of existence. Moreover, says Voegelin, "without the ordering of the whole personality by the truth of the myth the secondary intellectual and moral powers would lose their direction"; without the trust that there is a substantial truth with which we are linked through the "cosmic *omphalos* [navel] of the soul," there could be no ordered seeking after truth (*OH*, 3:186, 184). Nor would there be a soul either to do the seeking or to be sought through it; the soul, as was said earlier, is not a "thing" in the realm of phenomena, but is constituted by the very ordering that takes place through trust in the myth. "There is no knowledge of order in the soul," says Voegelin, "except through the *zetema* in which the soul discovers it by growing into it" (p. 95).

This, then, is why Voegelin insists on the emergence of reason from within the more fundamental experiential complex of faith, love, and hope. Reality, at its deepest level, is not a "thing" or a "fact," but an existential tension which is structured, through the poles of "world" and "Beyond," as a pull toward the perfect fullness and luminosity of being that is symbolized in the language of myth by the realm of the divine. The substance of reality, in other words, at least as far as it can be known by man in epistemic experience, is nothing other than the love of God. This is, again, to speak mythically; but to articulate in all of its experiential richness a philosophical penetration into the living depths of existence no other language can be fully effective. Existential reality is not known through an objectifying "look" which could subject it to cognitive mastery in the philodoxic mode, but only through the involvement of the whole person surrendering, entrusting, and committing himself to it. To one who places his faith in the philosophic myth of the *Timaeus*, mythic language has authority because it emerges into the *psyche* from the depths in which the soul is united with the living, ensouled cosmos—which is to say, from the point in experience at which man enters into participation in the luminosity and love that are the substance of reality itself. There are many mythic symbols, but where they express the concrete experience of involvement in the tension of existence, they cannot be in radical conflict, but cluster, supplement, and support one another: "A myth can never be 'untrue' because it would not exist unless it had its experiential basis in the movements of the soul which it symbolizes" (p. 184).

This is not a dogmatic assertion. Voegelin makes no claim to certainty, nor did Plato. It is a matter of trust in the structuredness of reality, that existence is a drama with a meaning. At the beginning of *Order and History* Voegelin says that "man is not a self-contained spectator. He is an actor, playing a part in the drama of being and, through the brute fact of his existence, committed to play it without knowing what it is" (1:1). His knowledge of it can never be certain; the playing is an act of trust, hope, and love. Without the willingness to risk himself for the love of what he can never reduce to precise and certain knowledge, he could never play his part, nor could there be a drama. The philosopher, unlike the philodoxer, cannot claim to replace mystery with concept, faith with certainty. His mode of persuasion is not argument but invitation. The most he can offer is a myth, which, as in the case of Plato's, can serve to invite us to take part in the drama of existence: "The most intimate truth of reality, the truth about the meaning of the cosmic play in which man must act his role with his life as the stake, is a mythopoetic play linking the psyche of man in trust with the depth of the Cosmos" ("Equivalences of Experience and Symbolization," p. 229).[39]

39. It is perhaps worth mentioning that although Voegelin concentrates mainly on Plato's use of philosophical myth, other examples could be cited. Even a thinker so seemingly unpoetic or mythopoeic as Aquinas can be seen to contain the basic outline of a philosophical myth, with a meaning moreover that closely parallels Plato's in that he represents all of reality, from its lowest to its highest manifestations, as caught up in a movement of return to the Creator. This movement, as Aquinas represents it, manifests itself as a series of levels of love, from the *inclinatio* by which even inanimate nature moves toward the supreme perfection, through the increasingly conscious *appetitus* and *amor* of the vegetative and animal levels of life, to the supernatural *dilectio* or *caritas* into which the saints may become increasingly assimilated. For a full treatment of this theme in Aquinas, see Albert Ilien, *Wesen und Funktion der Liebe im Denken des Thomas von Aquin* (Freiburg: Herder, 1975). Ilien's language even suggests Voegelin's, as when he speaks (p. 31) of Aquinas's analysis of the relation between matter and form as implying a sort of "tension" in the being of the material entity ("eine merkwürdige Spannung im Sein des materialen Seienden selbst"). Cf. also Janik and Toulmin, *Wittgenstein's Vienna*, p. 190, on Wittgenstein's *Tractatus* as a philosophical myth: "In a manner of speaking, therefore, the whole *Tractatus* had been (as he acknowledged later) a kind of Platonic myth."

The role the philosopher is called to play, in the drama to which only faith can give him entry, is his *zetema*. The essence of philosophy is not doctrine and argument but the existential movement in which the soul ascends toward increasingly full and luminous participation in the love of God. What the philosopher leaves for those who read him and accept his invitation is not a set of doxic formulae, "*a* philosophy," but symbols that may be used in the conscious articulation of the movement of ascent. Their meaning cannot be learned and appropriated on the level of ideas. This takes place only when one works with them in the struggle for clear and adequate expression of one's own philosophical experience.

CHAPTER 4

Reality and Consciousness

EARLY in his discussion of Plato in *Plato and Aristotle*, referring to the difficulty Socrates has in engaging his Sophistic opponents in genuine dialogue, Voegelin says that the "dialogue is the symbolic form of the order of wisdom, in opposition to the oration as the symbolic form of the disordered society. It restores the common order of the spirit that has been destroyed through the privatization of rhetoric" (*OH*, 3:12). The oration is the natural form for the expression of opinions (*doxai*), which each opiner asserts against all others. The philodoxic opiner is not interested in exploring truth; he claims to possess it already and only wishes to tell what it is and defend his claim to it. The dialogue, on the other hand, is the form of discourse in which claims to final possession of truth are relinquished and the partners engage together in its exploration. The philosophic dialogue requires a delicate balance between a real seeking after knowledge and the renunciation of claims to its final and complete possession. As soon as one of the partners adopts a fixed doctrinal position claiming exclusive and exhaustive truth he steps out of the community of philosophy into the isolation of the philodoxer. Philodoxy, like the hells described by such writers as Dante or Milton, may be peopled by many, "thick as Autumnal leaves that strow the Brooks/In Vallombrosa," who give the appearance of forming a great company, but in reality the only interest each has in the others is as allies in the defense of his own position.

The essential quality of philodoxy is to be found in the way it hardens and renders opaque the symbols that must remain transparent to function in the philosophical exploration of the mystery, adventure, and pain of human existence. The fundamental motivation behind this is the desire for the certainty and finality of *gnosis*. But, as the last chapter explained, the claim to *gnosis*, as Voegelin analyzes it, is a denial of the nature of human knowing as such. In reality there *is* no *gnosis*, only its pretense: although where the will to *gnosis* is strong, the pretense can generate a powerful delusion that can pass, sometimes indefinitely, for reality. Kierkegaard was driving at essentially this point when he said: "If Hegel had written the whole of his logic and then said, in the preface, that it was merely an experiment in thought in which he had even begged the question in many places, then he would certainly have been the greatest thinker who had ever lived. As it is he is merely comic." [1]

What enables one to seek insight into truth and articulate that insight while avoiding a fall into the comedy and isolation of philodoxy is, as the last chapter indicated, the *eikos mythos*, the likely myth, of the philosopher. Myth, of course, can always be literalized and gnosticized into a quasi-theoretical, speculative "explanation" that tries to reduce mystery to problem, but then it ceases to be myth in what Voegelin considers the proper sense and ceases to fulfill its function in the existential inquiry, the *zetema* of the philosopher. As Ricoeur has put it, "in losing its explanatory pretensions the myth reveals its exploratory significance and its contribution to understanding . . . its symbolic function—that is to say, its power of discovering and revealing the bond between man and what he considers sacred" (*Symbolism of Evil*, p. 5). Philosophy, for Voegelin, is such an exploration, taking place in the medium of symbolism that must always remain mythic in its ultimate reaches.

This is why Voegelin speaks so critically of immanentizing schemes of metaphysics: he sees them as attempts to reduce existence, a mystery in which we are overwhelmingly involved, to the object of a doxic science, as though the standard of reality were to be found not in the soul seeking fullness of participation in being but in entities clearly defined and external. To recognize that the ultimate expression of philosophical insight, of *episteme*, as described

1. *The Journals of Søren Kierkegaard: A Selection*, trans. Alexander Dru (London: Oxford University Press, 1961), p. 497.

in the last chapter, can never completely transcend myth is to recognize that existence is an irreducible mystery and that whatever the philosopher may say about it, what he says remains a tentative formulation based on the philosopher's perspective, which will vary with the extent and quality of his experience, and, of course, with his willingness to admit a full range of experience into consciousness.

The variability of perspectives must not only permit but demand a corresponding variety of ways of construing and symbolizing the universal reality known from those perspectives. Voegelin's theory that philosophy cannot finally transcend myth, despite the denial of all claim to give a final and exclusive account of reality, is not a relativism in the sense of denying that there is reality and that it can be known. The philosopher's mythic construction is empirically testable because it is a construing—not a fabrication—of actually discernible features of the experiential field. The criterion of the adequacy of the construing is its ability to include, in a comprehensive and maximally differentiated view, the full range of such features without omission, addition, or distortion, either of them or of the field as a whole. And if no single construction can capture reality exhaustively on all the levels on which it may be experienced, then more than one will be needed. In no case is the interpretive construction more than a "cognitive resting point," as Voegelin has phrased it, in a journey that is endless.[2] What the philosopher sees in the experiential field, moreover, will change steadily depending on the existential level he reaches in the course of his own philosophical quest. This implies, of course, the principle spoken of earlier, that philosophy in the proper sense, the sense of a *zetema*, is an activity for the mature human being, and it also implies the corollary that the truth of a philosopher's representation of reality will be either more or less clear to others depending on their own progress in the same *zetema*.

The principle that representations of reality may vary without

2. See "Toynbee's History as a Search for Truth," in Edward T. Gargan, ed., *The Intent of Toynbee's History* (Chicago: Loyola University Press, 1961), pp. 183–84.

loss of truth Voegelin refers to as the "equivalence of symbolic forms."[3] It is parallel to the similar principle known in the science of physics as "relativity." Voegelin purchased a copy of Einstein's "The Foundation of the General Theory of Relativity" in 1917, the year after its publication, and even at that time was impressed by its thesis, and he has continued over the years to interest himself in the problems it deals with. His 1948 essay, "The Origins of Scientism," traced the problem of relativity in physics back to the point at which it was initially broached in the controversy between Newton and Leibniz over the question of absolute spatial location of astronomic bodies. According to Voegelin's historical investigation of the issue, the problematic character of the idea of absolute space was recognized already by Copernicus, Bodin, and Bruno, and Leibniz formulated the principle involved as what he termed the "general law of equivalence" (p. 467). Newton and his followers in England were so intent on tying the absolute character of space to the absoluteness of God, and attaining certainty regarding spatial location, that they never really listened to what Leibniz was saying and dismissed it as unintelligible. The claim to absolute knowledge has generally shown itself historically to have strong appeal, and in this case it prevailed until Einstein.

In philosophical inquiry the problem is broader in scope and it has been an explicit issue a great deal longer. Voegelin traces it back as far as the time of Xenophanes's attack on the "anthropomorphism" of myth in its representation of the gods: Homer and Hesiod, he said, ascribed shameful actions, such as "stealing, adultery, and cheating each other," to the gods and did so because of the same naïveté which led them to suppose that gods have "clothes, voices, and bodily forms like theirs," and which would lead horses and oxen to imagine their gods as horselike and oxenlike.[4] In place of this,

3. For Voegelin's most extensive discussion of this subject, see "Equivalences of Experience and Symbolization."
4. Quotations from Xenophanes are from Voegelin's translations, *OH*, 2:172. See also p. 224, on how the apparent anthropomorphism of myth may also be interpreted as a theomorphic symbolization of areas and forces of the soul.

Xenophanes suggested a more "seemly" symbolism by which the divine would be represented as incorporeal consciousness—"all through it sees, all through it thinks, all through it hears" (B 24)—that remains ever unchanging while moving all things through thought. As is true of most advances in symbolization, this claimed to oppose a "true" representation to a "false" one. As Voegelin has traced the history of this development in Greek thought, it was Aristotle who "discovered the relation of equivalence between symbolic forms" when he recognized that both myth and philosophy arise from the experience of wonder and both are "engaged in the same search of the ground" (*OH*, 4:188, 191). In Aristotle's words, the "*philomythos* is in a sense a *philosophos*, for the myth is composed of wonders (*thaumasion*)."[5] Voegelin's own formulation of the principle is: "Two symbolisms are equivalent in spite of their phenotypical differences [differences in individual manifestation], if they refer recognizably to the same structures in reality" (p. 188). Or to put it another way, they "express the same reality in various modes of compactness and differentiation" (p. 191).

These considerations provide a necessary background for understanding why Voegelin, despite his many references to "Being" and "existence," does not found his philosophical thought on what is usually called an ontology.[6] In Voegelin's case, instead of an ontol-

5. *Metaphysics* 982b18, quoted in *OH*, 4:191 (see also 3:292).

6. In the early stages of my study of his works I was naïve enough to suggest to Voegelin that he should "make more explicit the implicit ontology of his thought." He answered that "ontology" was a language symbol developed in the seventeenth century for the enterprise of attempting to reduce being to the object of a doxic science. Historically the term was used as early as 1613 (R. Goclenius, *Lexicon Philosophicum*) as well as J. Clauberg (1646) and Jean-Baptiste Duhamel (1678). It was established in general philosophical use by Christian Wolff through his *Philosophia prima seu ontologia* (1729). Ontology as a subfield of metaphysics is generally thought to derive from Francisco Suárez's distinction between "general metaphysics," as the science of all *possible* reality, and "special metaphysics," the science of what actually is. The term "metaphysics" itself as a name for a field of study derives from Aquinas, who based it on the traditional name for the section of Aristotle's writings coming after the *Physics*. Voegelin

ogy one finds a theory of consciousness—with emphasis on the process by which consciousness can move from compactness to differentiation as it notices and articulates the implicit contents of universal human experience. Some of Voegelin's discussion of this subject has taken the form of direct theoretical exposition, as in the essay on "Equivalences" and in most of those reprinted in the English *Anamnesis*.[7] His characteristic approach, however, is primarily historical, studying the process by which the consciousness of individual thinkers has explicated itself over time. The present discussion will follow Voegelin's historical approach.

According to Voegelin's appraisal of the history of experience and symbolization, there have been "at least two historical modes of experience": on the first level, that of the "primary experience of the cosmos," and on a more advanced level, that of "differentiated consciousness" or the "differentiated experience of existence" ("Immortality," p. 272). The terms used here may need some explaining. It is necessary always to remember that as Voegelin uses the term "experience" it does not mean mere data, but, as the first chapter explained, a more or less compact combination of data and interpretation. Therefore the primary level of experience that becomes articulated as the "primary experience of the cosmos" is not

---

considers Aquinas to have played the leading role in the development of a fully articulated metaphysical speculation in the Middle Ages. For Voegelin's strongly negative criticism of Aquinas in respect to this, see *Anam.*, pp. 193–94. This way of reading Aquinas is well established, especially among those "neo-Thomists" who read him in a manner influenced by Scotus. It is possible to read Aquinas quite differently, however, and some of his more recent commentators have begun to do so; see, for example, Burrell, *Analogy*, pp. 119–70 and 197–99. For Voegelin's discussion of the manner in which Aristotle was already beginning to veer from genuine *noesis* or *episteme* toward an immanentist doxic construction of reality in terms of a "metaphysic of substances," see *OH*, 3:363–66. In *OH*, 4:148, Voegelin speaks of "the immanentist derailment of a philosophy of being in the transition from the Parmenidean vision of *Is!* to the immanentist speculation of the Sophists."

7. Gerhart Niemeyer, in his editor's preface to the English *Anamnesis*, has explained how he selected for inclusion those essays which would give the volume thematic unity as an exposition of Voegelin's philosophy of consciousness.

primary in the sense of most fundamental or that which underlies interpretation; rather it is the level of interpretation that first manifested itself historically. It is the experience of existence as it was known, for example, by the ancient Mesopotamians and Egyptians. There is every reason to suppose—and some of Voegelin's current research has to do with this—that basically the same experiential pattern was shared by people of the Stone Age, and it is still to be found among some peoples at the present time, though it may express itself in superficially different symbols. This primary level of experience is not a level of experiential immediacy but of comparatively naïve mediation.

The term "cosmos" is one that could be easily misinterpreted. In Voegelin's discussion it does not refer, as it frequently does in modern usage, to what is sometimes called the "astrophysical universe." The latter tends to be a purely physical, basically materializing conception based on the assumption that reality as a whole is made up of world-immanent entities. Voegelin's own use of the term refers to its ancient use to designate a much larger conception of the wholeness of reality, including spiritual as well as physical dimensions.

According to Voegelin's analysis, the experiential field of the primary experience of the cosmos is construed as made up of individual entities which tend to be grouped into four categories: God or the gods, man, the world, and society. As symbolized in the ancient cosmologically conceived societies, these entities are not usually thought of as entirely discrete but as participating, on a hierarchy of levels, in an underlying continuum of reality, a "primordial community of being," which as a whole constitutes the "cosmos" that embraces all the partners (see especially *OH*, 1:1–16). This is an experience, that is, both of "consubstantiality" and of "separateness of substances." (It is in fact, according to Voegelin, through a sort of pseudotheorization on the basis of this experiential perspective that a metaphysics of substances is generated.) The differentiated experience of existence, on the other hand, is the experience of existential tension structured through the indexical poles that divide it into the areas of immanence and transcendence, "world" and "Beyond" (*Anam*., p. 159).

It is important to remember that, as Voegelin says, "the two experiences do not pertain to different realities but to the same reality in different modes. The experience of cosmic reality includes in its compactness the existential tension; and the differentiated consciousness of existence has no reality without the cosmos in which it occurs" ("Immortality," p. 278). There is, in other words, a constant core of human experience which, whether it is consciously recognized or not, is always characterized by involvement in the tension of existence. In the cosmological symbolization of the primary experience, this tension expresses itself in the hierarchical relation of the four intracosmic partners; in the differentiated consciousness of existence it expresses itself in the symbols associated with the Beyond, such as that of a world-transcendent divine ground as the pole of the longing for perfection of being. In this manner the two serve as equivalent symbolisms; the experiences they express involve different degrees of clarity and conscious articulation, but the existential structure represented in them remains the same.

The important difference between the two patterns of symbolism lies in the clear awareness that develops, in differentiated consciousness, of the world-transcendent character of the Beyond. In the compact vision of the primary experience, world and Beyond remain confused—in spite of the distinction between men and the gods:

> The cosmos of the primary experience is neither the external world of objects given to a subject of cognition, nor is it the world that has been created by a world-transcendent God. Rather, it is the whole, *to pan*, of an earth below and a heaven above—of celestial bodies and their movements; of seasonal changes; of fertility rhythms in plant and animal life; of human life, birth and death; and above all, as Thales still knew, it is a cosmos full of gods. This last point, that the gods are intracosmic, cannot be stressed strongly enough, because it is almost eclipsed today by such facile categorizations as polytheism and monotheism. The numbers are not important, but rather the

consciousness of divine reality as intracosmic or transmundane. [*OH*, 4:68]

The cosmological style of truth can long persist as an adequate expression of the experience of existence, since in its hierarchical ordering of intracosmic "things" it does at least partial justice to the underlying structural tension; but it is nevertheless "fundamentally unstable," because the tension keeps up a constant pressure on consciousness to have the element of radical discontinuity—the full Beyondness—in its directional tendency recognized (p. 76). When the intensity of the pressure reaches a certain point, or when for one reason or another the intracosmic realm no longer seems to contain within it elements of sufficiently numinous character simultaneously to represent and to mask the absolute perfection of the Beyond—as when in the modern experience since Galileo the astrophysical universe becomes too merely material and spatial for its planets and stars to be divinized—then the cosmological style will crack as "the cosmos dissociates into a dedivinized external world and a world-transcendent God" (p. 77).[8] Or to phrase it in ontological language, "The leap in being differentiates world-transcendent Being as the source of all being, and correspondingly attaches to the 'world' the character of immanence" (*OH*, 3:277).

To some readers this phrasing may sound at least slightly preferable to the theological language that derives more directly from ancient myth—"cleaner" and more "modern." Nevertheless, as Voegelin makes clear, antisepsis has a price. When the ontic link between world and God is lost sight of through the suppression of its symbolism, the world ceases even to be experienced as a "world" in the full sense, implying unity and order, but dissolves into a set of discrete particulars. And when the *Vollgott* (the full God), as

8. For a discussion of the steps by which modern thought and sensibility became disengaged from the traditional cosmological symbolism, see Marjorie Nicolson, *The Breaking of the Circle*, rev. ed. (New York: Columbia University Press, 1960). In the modern case, as Nicolson shows, the break with the traditional cosmology has also led frequently to a disruption of the symbolism of divine transcendence.

Voegelin puts it in "What Is Nature?" (1965) is reduced to *Seinsgott* (the God of Being), a new tension develops between the fullness of the compact symbol and the thinned-out truth of the new (*Anam.*, p. 79).[9] Of course not all will sense this loss and feel this tension, any more than all have any clear realization of the fundamental tension of existence; but those who do, says Voegelin, will find in themselves an echo of Pascal's cry: "Dieu d'Abraham, Dieu d'Isaac, Dieu de Jacob, non des philosophes et des savants" (p. 79). The "compact truth of reality does not become obsolete," he says, "when later thinkers explore the structure of the process in the several realms of being; on the contrary, it supplies the context in which alone the specific insights make sense. . . . the later specific insights connote the earlier wholeness as the context in which the differentiating work is conducted" (*OH*, 4:175). The differentiation of consciousness is not a movement from an archaic to a modern cosmos but "the Movement in which man's consciousness of existence emerges from the primary experience of the cosmos," and in which "consciousness becomes luminous to itself as the site of the revelatory process, of the seeking and being drawn" ("The Gospel and Culture," p. 96). A symbolism will be fully adequate only when it can do justice to the depths of longing in the existential tension—"the seeking and being drawn"—that the differentiating consciousness brings to light. Only when the symbol "Being" is read against the background of the symbolism of divinity can it serve to indicate a tensional pole fully proportioned to the existential *eros* to which it correlates.

It is probably for all of these reasons that Voegelin's own favorite symbolism for the experience of human existence as participation in

9. See also *OH*, 3:276, on Aristotle's "intellectual thinning-out" of the experience of transcendence that had become clear in Heraclitus, Parmenides, Xenophanes, and Plato: "The fullness of experience which Plato expressed in the richness of his myth is in Aristotle reduced to the conception of God as the prime mover, as the *noesis noeseos*, the 'thinking on thinking.'" The diminution of experiential fullness involved in the shift from mythic to ontological language in medieval theology will be a theme of *The Beginning and the Beyond*, on which Voegelin is currently at work.

being is that of Plato's *metaxy*, or "Between," as developed in the *Symposium* and *Philebus*.[10] This is a symbol of rich complexity and depth, drawing on the language of divinity and of spirits as well as of man and *psyche*:

> Man experiences himself as tending beyond his human imperfection toward the perfection of the divine ground that moves him. The spiritual man, the *daimonios aner*, as he is moved in his quest of the ground, moves somewhere between knowledge and ignorance (*metaxy sophias kai amathias*). "The whole realm of the spiritual (*daimonion*) is halfway indeed between (*metaxy*) god and man" (*Symp.* 202a). Thus, the in-between—the *metaxy*—is not an empty space between the poles of the tension but the "realm of the spiritual"; it is the reality of "man's converse with the gods" (202–203), the mutual participation (*methexis, metalepsis*) of human in divine, and divine in human, reality. [*Anam.*, p. 103][11]

It may render the symbolism somewhat clearer to point out that it draws on symbols from the primary experience of the cosmos in order to represent analogically the experience of existence as it is known in the perspective of differentiated consciousness. So, the "spiritual man" (*daimonios aner*) who moves in the realm "between" god and man is a symbol of differentiated consciousness, whereas the "man" of the pair "god and man" is man conceived of as one of the "things" within the cosmos; the "spiritual man" is not a "thing"

10. Paul Ricoeur is another who has drawn on Plato's symbol of the *metaxy* for the explication of the experience of human existence. See *Fallible Man*, trans. Charles Kelbley (Chicago: Henry Regnery, 1965), pp. 12–25. Ricoeur describes the soul as "tendency and tension" (p. 13).

11. "Equivalences of Experience and Symbolization," p. 220, offers an extensive list of poles of the tension: "Existence has the structure of the In-Between, of the Platonic *metaxy*, and if anything is constant in the history of mankind it is the language of tension between life and death, immortality and mortality, perfection and imperfection, time and timelessness; between order and disorder, truth and untruth, sense and senselessness of existence; between *amor Dei* and *amor sui*, *l'âme ouverte* and *l'âme close*; between the virtues of openness toward the ground of being such as faith, love, and hope, and the vices of infolding closure such as hybris and revolt; between the moods of joy and despair; and between alienation in its double meaning of alienation from the world and alienation from God."

at all but the act and experience of self-luminous participation in the tension of existence. Both are Man, one might say, but in two different existential modes. Let us call the "spiritual man" man$_1$ and the other man$_2$.[12] Man$_1$ is the human being as he transacts his existence in the field of tensions between the divine pole, symbolizing perfect luminosity and life, on the one hand, and the pole of inert, self-opaque "thinghood" on the other (mortality and immortality are another pair of symbols that Plato uses to express this opposition). Man$_2$ is less a reality than an index defining the negative or lower pole of the tension in which man is drawn positively toward the realm of the divine. The reality of human existence, when it realizes its true character as a conscious "seeking and being drawn," occurs in the mode of man$_1$. When a person fails and lapses into a state of comparative existential complacency, then he is tending toward the mode of existence symbolized by man$_2$, inert thinghood. In practice, of course, it is just as impossible to escape from the *metaxy* in the direction of man$_2$ as it is to become God; there always seems to remain a certain minimal level of tension, at least in the form of a residual restlessness or anxiety, to remind us that our existence is incomplete, that we are more than animals and less than gods.

Just as "man" is a necessarily ambiguous term in the symbolism of the *metaxy* as the realm of divine-human participation, so is "consciousness":

> As far as consciousness is the site of participation, its reality partakes of both the divine and the human without being wholly the one or the other; as far as it is the sensorium of participation, it is definitely man's own, located in his body in spatio-temporal existence. Consciousness, thus, is both the time pole of the tension (sensorium) and the whole tension including its pole of the timeless (site). Our participation in the divine remains bound to the perspective of man. If the distinction between the two meanings of con-

---

12. Voegelin does not use such terms, but for a closely parallel discussion of the same idea, see *Anam.*, p. 176.

sciousness be neglected, there arises the danger of derailing into the
divinization of man or the humanization of God. ["Immortality,"
p. 275]

Again it is a matter of the paradox that human existence is
genuinely between the extremes; man's consciousness is not simple
unconsciousness, but at the same time it is not the perfect luminosity of being that lies in the direction of the Beyond. In fact, consciousness at its most perfect lies so clearly beyond man's position in
the Between that its application to man's actual cognitive participation in being is analogical, just as is any other term relating to
participation, including "existence."

The hypostatizing metaphysics of immanent entities has become
so habitual a form of thought for the modern mind, especially since
the rise of nominalism, that to speak of reality in any other way can
seem strange or paradoxical. One tends to say that a given entity
must either exist or not exist and that if it does, it exists completely.
As was previously explained, "existence" when used in such a context serves as a kind of logical counter, a true-false switch, that
applies either wholly or not at all. From the point of view of the
participationist way of thinking, a different use of the language of
"existence" is called for: existence does not have this simple, factual
character at all, but has fluctuating meanings as it represents different levels between perfect Being and nothingness. As Voegelin
stated the issue in "The Gospel and Culture" (p. 63):

> Well, existence is not a fact. If anything, existence is the non-fact of
> a disturbing movement in the In-Between of ignorance and knowl-
> edge, of time and timelessness, of imperfection and perfection, of
> hope and fulfillment, and ultimately of life and death. From the
> experience of this movement, from the anxiety of losing the right
> direction in this In-Between of darkness and light, arises the enquiry
> concerning the meaning of life. But it does arise . . . because life is
> experienced as man's participation in a movement with a direction to
> be found or missed; if man's existence were not a movement but a
> fact, it not only would have no meaning but the question of meaning
> could not even arise.

Voegelin considers it to be with reference to the constituents of the experiential field known in the primary experience of the cosmos that a metaphysic of purely immanent entities develops. Even then, however, it can develop into a fully and explicitly immanentist form only when, as for many in the modern period, the transcendental dimension of the primary experience is forgotten. The rise of a metaphysic of this sort is commonly associated with Aristotle, but in fact, says Voegelin, Aristotle's own discussion of *ousiai* (usually translated as "substances" or "entities") was still firmly rooted in the primary experience: "This background is so much alive for Aristotle that the one term *ousia* suffices him for all modes of being; his glance always passes through the *ousiai* correctly to the 'things' of the primary experience. . . . It does not make sense to translate *ousia* . . . with 'substance,' as is conventionally done, for one would thereby only get involved, anachronistically, in the problems of later dogmatic metaphysics" (*Anam.*, p. 160). What Aristotle contributed to the development of such a metaphysic was some terminology and a focus on the individual mundane "things" that Parmenides had referred to as collectively constituting the realm of *doxa*. Combined, over centuries, with a developing tendency to interpret the world, not as constituted by its participation in an eminent reality beyond it but as having an independent mode of existence of its own, this heritage has produced the various immanentizing constructions of reality that have become familiar. Voegelin has described the process: "Under the pressure of the noetic experience, which dissociates the cosmos into the world and its ground, all 'things' that Aristotle calls *ousia* are then objectivized according to the model of things in the world, composed as they are of form and matter in space and time" (p. 161).

The long-range result has been that "the residual mode of world-immanent existence alone still carries the title being and *ousia*," and this means ultimately, says Voegelin, that "the reality of reality, about the truth of which man historically is concerned, is simply denied." The doxic reduction of reality to purely immanent, external objects in a world without transcendence leads to the denial of the transcendental dimension of man and his history and of the very possibility of the epistemic knowledge of existence from within. In fact, the very idea of a "within" of existence is dismissed as a subjectivistic notion. Man is conceived of as an external object like any other and equally limited to a finite, intramundane existence.

Voegelin has described the process by which such a way of thinking develops as "grotesque" (p. 161). In fact it is one of the great ironies of history that a mode of existence which is actually highly speculative—that of existence as known purely from without—has become widely accepted as the standard of reality, while that mode of existence man actually experiences in consciousness is treated as unreal. Voegelin's own approach is to retain both levels of reality but to recognize which of them is speculative and which is experienced concretely. As he stated the basic issue in his 1943 essay, "On the Theory of Consciousness":

> We have experience of our consciousness only qua consciousness, only as the process experienced from within, which is neither bodily nor material. The substantive unity of human existence, which must be accepted as [an] ontological hypothesis for the understanding of consciousness's basis in body and matter, is objectively inexperienceable. That does not mean, however, that there is no such thing. At any rate, the hypothesis is indispensable for grasping the "ensemble" of consciousness and bodily process in the total process of human existence. We cannot descriptively grasp "pure" consciousness as process; rather we can only interpretatively grasp a "human" consciousness as consciousness in the body and the world. [*Anam.*, p. 31]

Both the experience of consciousness itself, in other words, and the experience of objects make up the reality of human experience, but there is a difference in level between them, with that of existence as known from within constituting the higher level, both in its experiential fullness and in the standard of reality that it sets.

The implication of this way of thinking is that man must be recognized as living always on two levels of experience. There is the level represented symbolically in the primary experience of the cosmos, in which reality, even if not a high degree of reality, is attributed to the world of "things." In addition, there is the level of reality known in the differentiated consciousness of existence. Besides the two levels on which man lives, there is also the higher, eminent reality in which both his bodily and spiritual levels in their respective ways participate and through participation in which they derive whatever reality they have: "There is no In-Between of existence as a self-contained object but only existence experienced as part of a reality which extends beyond the In-Between" ("The Gospel and Culture," p. 76).[13] The hypostatizing imagination that would interpret man as a self-enclosed entity in the world is a residue of the primary level of articulated consciousness; to complete successfully the advance to the differentiated level, this imagination must be left behind. When this happens and the differentiated consciousness of existence develops fully, then the hierarchy of degrees or strata of reality becomes clear.

13. It is with regard to this point—that man cannot be adequately construed as an intramundane entity—that the difference between Voegelin's way of thinking about *psyche* and that of C. G. Jung becomes clear: Jung tends toward an immanentizing conception of *psyche* as an entity or a closed system of intramundane psychic forces. Gregor Sebba, in "Prelude and Variations on the Theme of Eric Voegelin," has described the difference aptly: "On the Voegelinian scale, Jung represents a European form of regression to myth, the return to the archetypal womb. Jung's case is not that of a 'gnostic' but of a genuine shamanic visionary in a scientific society, a tribal seer without a tribe. Unable to make his visions socially effective by ritual enactment, yet feeling himself to be representative of his society and responsible for it, he develops the symbol of the 'European personality,' the fully 'individuated' self that encloses the outer and inner world within itself, expressed in the only form possible in that society, the incongruous form of a 'scientific' analytical theory of the psyche. His efforts to save this society from itself can only consist in healing individuals who suffer from the suppression of myth and are cut off from transcendent understanding and participation, as he is himself" (p. 671). See also Victor Frankl on Jung's tendency to reduce religion to a matter of impersonal drives and instincts, *The Unconscious God: Psychotherapy and Theology* (New York: Simon and Schuster, 1975), pp. 63–65. Kierkegaard's way of putting the idea that man was not a simply intramundane entity was to speak of his involving both finite and infinite dimensions: "Existence is a synthesis of infinite and finite, and the existing individual is both infinite and finite" (*Concluding Unscientific Postscript*, p. 350).

The fact that these levels of participation may be spoken of as having degrees of reality, depending on their nearness or distance from the divine pole in which they analogically participate, throws a further light on the implications of Voegelin's discussion of myth as a mode of knowledge that can never be transcended. As was mentioned at the beginning of this study, Voegelin has a high regard for the philosophy of history offered by Thomas Mann in his *Joseph* tetralogy, especially the way in which Mann represents reality as a tale told by God which man is called to enter responsively. From this point of view, it is the divine ground that is ultimately real, while all created reality may be described as a myth—a myth not in the sense that it is false but in the sense that its truth is an analogical imaging forth of the eminent reality of the ground. Seen in this light, time and history are mythic representations of the eternal presence that is the ultimate standard of reality. As Mann himself put it: "the essence of life is presentness, and only in a mythical sense does its mystery appear in the time-forms of past and future. . . . For it *is*, always *is*, however much we may say It was. Thus speaks the myth, which is only the garment of the mystery." [14]

Myth, then, can never be transcended cognitively, because it can never be transcended existentially. The problem of representation is not to find a description of reality that will not be mythic but to find a myth that will be adequate for the exploration of reality on all its levels.

Plato's *metaxy*, suggests Voegelin, is an example of such a myth. Through the complexity and even ambiguity of its symbols it does justice to the manifold mystery of consciousness. Moreover, by providing an adequate symbolic language for its articulation it makes the specifically human experience of consciousness possible. The impossibility "of separating language and experience as separate entities" was one of Voegelin's first discoveries in his early studies of the nature of consciousness: "There was no engendering experience

14. *Joseph and His Brothers*, pp. 32–33. Cf. *OH*, 4:333. See also Jaspers, *Philosophy*, 1:57, 2:43.

as an autonomous entity but only the experience as articulated by symbols" (*Anam.*, p. 12). Without this or an equivalent symbolism, there could be consciousness—in a more limited form—but not the experience of consciousness in its self-reflective, human fullness. It would lack what Voegelin calls "luminosity": "Cognition of participation, as it is not directed toward an object of the external world, becomes a luminosity in reality itself and, consequently, the knower and the known move into the position of tensional poles in a consciousness that we call luminous as far as it engenders the symbols which express the experience of its own structure" ("Equivalences," p. 221).

Reality, as a whole, however, is more comprehensive than the *psyche* which becomes luminous within it. Human existence in the *metaxy* is a mystery embedded in mystery. Above it is the divine Beyond, and below it are the depths which lie beneath articulate experience, but from which meaning can emerge as it becomes the experience that engenders the analogical symbols that make it consciously present. Aeschylus, says Voegelin, noticed this continuity between depth and consciousness and represented it as a means to saving truth in *The Suppliants* when he had King Pelasgus, perplexed over a question of justice, say, "There is need of deep and saving counsel, like a diver's, descending to the depth, with keen eye and not too much perturbed." Voegelin points out the likely derivation of this image from "the Heraclitean 'deep-knowing' of the soul whose border cannot be measured because its Logos is too deep" (*OH*, 2:249). Plato noticed this experiential continuum as well. When in the *Timaeus* he developed the philosophical myth that extended *psyche* into the depths of the cosmos, Plato was culminating, says Voegelin, the process in which Hellenic thinkers from Heraclitus to himself had expanded the earlier symbol of *psyche* into one that through its paradoxical linking of luminosity with the depth beneath experience became an equivalent to Plato's other major symbol, the *metaxy* (see *OH*, 3:84, and "Equivalences," pp. 224–34).

What is most mysterious of all about man's participation in being is that it is something he can refuse. Man's existence, as was said earlier, is not a fact, but a movement in the *metaxy*, a struggle between light and darkness, between open participation and closure against reality. This does not mean, of course, that, short of suicide, man can ever step completely out of reality. The most he can succeed in doing through a determined revolt is the deforming of his mode of existence from the luminosity and well-orderedness (*eunomia*) of what Voegelin calls "existence in truth" into disorder and semiopacity. This does, however, have existential import. The *scotosis*, or turning toward darkness, which was discussed in the preceding chapter is more than a merely cognitive disorder. Because, as Voegelin says, consciousness is "the specifically human mode of participation in reality," the rejection of luminosity is the choice of a reduced level of participation in being (*Anam.*, p. ix).[15] And this reduction is not simply a letting go of something that one may take or leave according to taste. Because the core of man's existence always remains a tension that reaches toward the Beyond, the attempt to withdraw from it must necessarily take the form of a distortion of consciousness whereby one seeks to mask the transcendental dimension of experience by an effort to misconstrue it in an immanentizing manner:

> If a man lives in openness toward God, Bergson's *l'âme ouverte*, his consciousness of his existential tension will be the cognitive core in his experience of reality. If a man deforms his existence by closing it toward the divine ground, the cognitive core in his experience of reality will change, because he must replace the divine pole of the tension by one or the other world-immanent phenomenon. The deformed cognitive core, then, entails a deformed style of cognition by which the First Reality experienced in open existence is transformed

15. In *Anam.*, p. 168, Voegelin says, "The intentionality of consciousness as such would not conduce to the fallacious images of reality if man's participation were an automatism that produced in consciousness infallibly correct pictures of reality and nothing but correct pictures. Consciousness, however, has a dimension of freedom in the design of images of reality."

into a Second [imaginary] Reality imagined in closed existence. ["On Hegel," p. 354][16]

Similarly, the person experiencing, man in the *metaxy*, must be correspondingly interpreted as a world-immanent entity, a process that Voegelin speaks of as "the contraction of his humanity to a self imprisoned in its selfhood," and which he says has become especially prominent since the eighteenth century, "when man begins to refer to himself, not as Man, but as a Self, an Ego, an I, an Individual, a Subject, a Transcendental Subject, a Transcendental Consciousness, and so forth" ("Eclipse of Reality," p. 185).

Despite such contortions, the deformed existence can never escape from reality. The man who "engages in deforming himself to a self," says Voegelin, does not cease to be a man, nor does the surrounding reality in which he is embedded change its structure (p. 185).[17] The development of an imagined Second Reality can only mask, not displace, the primary reality of existence, in which man must live whether he wishes to recognize it or not. Imagination can "eclipse" reality, in Voegelin's phrase, but not abolish it, and the reality that is eclipsed remains and continually exerts pressure to

16. Bergson's symbol of the "open soul" is developed in his *Two Sources of Morality and Religion* (1932). Voegelin was already speaking of "das offene Ich" and "das geschlossene Ich," however, in *Über die Form des amerikanischen Geistes*, pp. 7 and 50–51. Voegelin says he derived the term Second Reality from the Viennese novelist Robert Musil. It is perhaps worth mentioning that this term was also used by the Viennese psychoanalyst Otto Rank in his discussion of the psychology of self-deception. See *Will Therapy and Truth and Reality*, trans. Jessie Taft (New York: Alfred A. Knopf, 1945), p. 195. Cf. "The Eclipse of Reality," in Maurice Natanson, ed., *Phenomenology and Social Reality* (The Hague: Martinus Nijhoff, 1970), pp. 187–88; "Imagination, it appears, can cut loose from reality and produce the sets of images that we call Second Reality because they pretend to refer to reality though in fact they do not; and, setting aside the phenomena of error or of imperfectly articulated experience, imagination will cut loose in this manner, when the imagining man has developed centers of resistance to participating in reality, including his own, so that his imagery will no longer be true [will no longer give expression to real experience] but express reality in terms of his resistance to it."

17. This is the surrounding reality that on the level of cosmological symbolism is articulated as the quarternarian structure of man, the divine, the world, and society.

emerge into consciousness (p. 188). The result is that "frictions between the shrunken self and reality" and between Second Reality and First Reality inevitably develop, and as they do so they generate the anxiety that is so widely recognized as a feature of modern experience (pp. 185, 190–91). They also produce the cognitive and emotional twistings that have been studied by psychologists from Pascal and Hegel to Freud and Jung:

> The major thinkers who suffer from the compulsion to deform their humanity to a self are never quite unaware of what they are doing. From the eighteenth to the twentieth century, the stream of Second Realities is paralleled, therefore, by a stream of self-analysis. . . . Self-analysis is so much the accompaniment of imaginative projections that the age of Second Realities has become the great age of Psychology. A peculiar compound of insight and intellectual dishonesty has become an enduring twilight mode of existence, replacing the clear existential rhythms of degenerative fall and regenerative repentance. [P. 188]

Interesting as such explorations may be—for a while—unfortunately the man who deforms himself does not live in a vacuum, or in a laboratory for the study of abnormal psychology, but in society, where his Second Reality wages a quite real war on the First Reality and those who would dwell in it. What Voegelin calls "this game of transforming reality in the image of deformed existence" on the part of a "humanity contracted to its libidinous self" leads not merely to private madness but to an attempt to force the remainder of human beings to accept the dream as true and to scale down their own level of conscious participation in being to that of the dreamer (OH, 4:182). Existence, again, is not a fact. It is something that must be fought for—against hostile forces both within and without—through the struggle for truth. History is a battlefield—but not one on which victory can be won by opposing force with force, either physical or intellectual, as Socrates and Jesus taught and demonstrated. Argument will not work, if only because "behind the appearance of rational debate" there lurks "the difference between two modes of existence, of existence in truth and existence in untruth" ("On Debate and Existence," p. 143).[18] But still more important, it will not work because what is needed is not an attack on the dream but a return to reality, and this is something that is as much a matter of grace as of effort, of *helkein* as of *zetesis*. The process of history, says Voegelin, "will reveal its meaning only where men are open toward the mystery in which they participate by their existence and allow the reality of the process to become luminous in their consciousness. After the crippling of the truth through existential closure, it becomes the philosopher's task to heal and restore it by opening his existence to the divine ground of reality" (*OH*, 4:184).

The true battlefield of history is within, where the struggle for truth and for existence attuned to transcendental reality takes place in the soul of man. This chapter began with a reference to Voegelin's statement that the philosopher's dialogue is the symbolic form of the order of wisdom, whereas the sophist's oration is the expression of the disordered society. It is the style of the sophist, the philodoxic thinker, to deliver opinions with arguments intended to coerce assent. The sophistic battle is between opinion and opinion and between man and man. The orator's victory is a conquest of minds. The philosopher, in contrast, as Voegelin interprets him, does not seek to conquer but to explore truth and ultimately to surrender to it. What he delivers is not opinions but an invitation. He invites the hearer to join him in seeking a truth that transcends all *doxai* and that calls all men to its exploration. This must take place through analogical, imperfect symbols, and it requires that one partner's experience and perspective supplement that of another. The battle is not between speaker and hearer but between forces present within each. These are the conflicting pulls of truth as such and its relative and limited formulations, of pride and humility regarding claims to knowledge, of the longing for transcendental perfection and of distracting desires for limited goods, of fidelity and infidelity to the call of the divine Beyond. The invitation into

18. See also "On Readiness to Rational Discussion," especially pp. 268 and 282.

the dialectic exploration, moreover, must be responded to in freedom. It is only in a relative sense that one can speak of any individual as issuing the invitation. It comes ultimately from the universal goal that draws each soul into the search and struggle. Assent might be coerced, but inquiry cannot; inquiry is the active expression of the soul's own love of the real. When the philosopher invites one to it, he is only giving voice to a love in which both speaker and hearer are involved, the universal tension of existence.

To engage in this, the real struggle of history, the human partners need each other, and the loss of any one is a loss to the whole community of dialogue. An effort to coerce, however well intended, would threaten the very life of that community, which comes to it not from any strictly human wisdom or intention but from the divine drawing that quickens each seeker in his love and freedom.

At the end of the exposition of the theoretical principles of Voegelin's thought, we are brought around once again to its fundamental political thrust. Voegelin's thought began its own historical course in his struggle to free himself from the destructive war of ideological and physical coercion that has been waged with increasing ferocity during this century. What may seem at times like abstract theory is in fact the expression of an effort to understand human concreteness and to offer an interpretation of man and his life in society that may help him to find a way to live less murderously with his fellows. For only when man is interpreted as having a dimension of transcendence can his freedom be acknowledged and valued. If social peace is sought for its own sake, it will lead to renewed efforts of coercion. Only when human beings, accepting their finitude, hear and respond to the call of unlimited perfection beyond them, can they enter into genuine community. The next chapter, "The Discovery of Reality," will trace in brief outline Voegelin's study of the historical process in which the transcendental calling of humanity emerged into consciousness and developed symbolisms with which to speak its invitation.

PART 2

ANAMNESIS

The Study of History and the Struggle for Truth

CHAPTER 5

The Discovery of Reality

THE crux of intellectual history as a discipline is the question whether it is to be conceived of as the study of opinions or ideas linked together in a temporal chain of influences or whether it is to be conceived of philosophically as the study of a struggle to enter into conscious participation in the same truth of existence with which the historian himself is fundamentally concerned. It is possible to go to either of two extremes. One may assume there is no substantive truth, but only discrete *doxai* that are related not through a reference to reality but merely through the fact that each of a series of thinkers has read and adopted, with basically arbitrary or fortuitous modifications, the ideas of predecessors. This extreme might be termed that of historicistic reductionism. It is a subjectivistic conception in that it assumes that what any given thinker actually intends is not reality but ideas—whether he realizes it or not.

The other extreme tends to deny the relevance of historical development altogether, assuming that all valid thought develops through a simple "look" at reality; what is said may differ to some extent because of differences in language and in clarity of vision, but the source of meaning and the criterion of intention is the objective essence of the particular reality under consideration, and this is known directly. This is sometimes referred to as a "confrontational" theory of knowledge. The principle on which it is founded was stated with unusual boldness and simplicity by Auguste Comte in 1851: "If we could place ourselves always under the most favorable circumstances for research, we would have no use for intelligence,

155

and we could appreciate things by simple inspection."[1] This objectivism is also reductionistic, but what is left out in this case is a critical awareness of the role of interpretive models, whether the scientist's hypotheses or the philosopher's concepts and myths, in mediating an apprehension of the real. It is consequently a denial of the relevance of the history of interpretation for an understanding of thought.

It is not necessary, however, to go to either extreme, and only a position that takes account of the different facets of truth defended by the proponents of each can do justice to the full dimensions of the experience of inquiry in the philosopher's search for understanding of the real. Nor, of course, is it only the philosopher who seeks adequate interpretation of reality. The process of inquiry is essentially the same for the scientist and for the artist as well. The principle in question can be illustrated from the history of visual representation. The art historian Sir Ernst Gombrich speaks of it as the "rhythms of schema and correction."[2] In his chapter, "Truth and Stereotype," in *Art and Illusion*, he shows a drawing from approximately 1235 by Villard de Honnecourt depicting, in what now seems a rather fancifully heraldic manner, a lion. The picture is based on standard schematic designs, of which many examples survive. What is interesting about this particular image, however, is that in the upper right corner the artist wrote a claim to realistic accuracy:

> To us, it looks like an ornamental or heraldic image, but Villard's caption tells us that he regarded it in a different light: *"Et sacies bien,"* he says, *"qu'il fu contrefais al vif."* "Know well that it is drawn from life." These words obviously had a very different meaning for Villard than they have for us. He can have meant only that he had drawn his schema in the presence of a real lion. How much of his

1. *Système de politique positive*, 4 vols. (Paris: L. Mathias, 1851–54), 1:408–9, quoted by Voegelin, in his own trans., *From Enlightenment to Revolution*, p. 162.
2. E. H. Gombrich, *Art and Illusion: A Study in the Psychology of Pictorial Representation*, 2d ed. (New York: Pantheon Books, 1961), p. 74.

visual observation he allowed to enter into the formula is a different matter.[3]

The artist was imitating both the real lion and the schema that had been worked out by previous artists over centuries as a solution to the technical problem of how to represent with line on paper the head of a large feline. Gombrich further illustrated the nature of this interplay between interpretive model and reality during a lecture at the University of Washington in the spring of 1977, by juxtaposing the Villard lion with a slide of a lion by Rembrandt, which seemed perfectly realistic by comparison. Then he showed a close-up of the Rembrandt image which made clear that the schema Rembrandt was working with was that of a human face with a somewhat blunted nose. Finally he showed a photograph of a real lion, which seemed only somewhat less remote from Rembrandt's version than from Villard's.

It would be naïve to say either that an artist with realistic intentions does not attend to the reality he is concerned with or that his way of perceiving and representing reality is not influenced by the tradition of interpretation within which he works. The same applies to any thinker who seeks to find adequate formulas for the representation of the real. Historically it is a fairly recent development that anyone would attempt seriously to deny that there is a genuine interplay in which both reality and traditional schemata play their roles. It is significant that the person who seems to have been the first to advocate a total break from tradition in this respect was Jean-Jacques Rousseau, who in his *Émile* in 1762 attacked the traditional way of teaching drawing by the imitation of the work of other artists; he insisted that Émile should copy only nature. "This is one of those programs," says Gombrich, "which may be said to be charged with explosive ignorance" (p. 174).

The skeptical counterpart to this approach, on the other hand, usually gives the appearance of choking on its own learnedness. This

3. Ibid., p. 79. The picture is reproduced on p. 78.

takes various forms. It may, for example, be based on theories that claim to explain the development of ideas not through the thinker's cognitive involvement with reality but through the influence of economic, sociological, psychological, or other determinants. Or it may be based on an acute awareness of the "burden of the past," as well as on despair in the face of the conflicting opinions to which the thinkers under study have given expression.

Voegelin's own approach to intellectual history rejects such distortions. His basic assumption is that the philosophical thinker, to the extent that his thought is an expression of open existence, is directly involved in the reality he seeks to understand and knows it in a pretheoretical manner on the level of immediate experience. Theoretical reflection is the elucidation of this experience through its self-explication as it seeks language that will analogically represent its discernible features and essential structure and so bring them into focus. This is the process by which the thinker moves from compact experience to the differentiated consciousness of existence. To the extent that he is motivated by a radical desire for conscious participation in reality, he is engaged in a struggle for truth—not the truth of an opinion but the truth of existence; not the truth that consists of accurate correspondence between ideas and external reality but the truth that is the self-luminosity of the reality in which the philosopher's entire existence is a participation. This is what the Hellenic thinkers called *aletheia*, the "unhiddenness" or self-disclosure of being. It is a reality that can become luminous if one is willing to accept and enter into it. What is required is fidelity to the order of being. This is the price of its "unhiddenness." The opposite of truth in this existential sense is not falsehood or inaccuracy, as in the case of an opinion, but eclipse, the darkening of reality through existential closure.

Voegelin has analyzed this "truth of existence" as having four basic aspects. In the first place, it is an experience "of finiteness and creatureliness," of having come into being and of awaiting the time when one will go out of it again; we are not the makers of reality, but find ourselves involved in it through a process we neither generate nor control ("On Debate and Existence," p. 146). It is also an experience "of dissatisfaction with a state experienced as imperfect, of apprehension of a perfection that is not of this world but is the privilege of the gods, of possible fulfillment in a state beyond this world, the Platonic *epekeina* [the Beyond]" (p. 146). The "tension of existence," in other words, is the fundamental structural feature of the order of being that becomes luminous as *aletheia*. The luminosity itself is the third aspect of the truth of existence; the existence that becomes open in the "unhiddenness" of existential truth is conscious existence: "Human existence, it appears, is not opaque to itself, but illuminated by intellect (Aquinas) or *nous* (Aristotle). This intellect is as much part of human existence as it is the instrument of its interpretation. In the exegesis of existence intellect discovers itself in the structure of existence; ontologically speaking, human existence has noetic structure" (pp. 146–147). Finally, the conscious existence that lays itself open in man is intrinsically self-transcending as the Question that seeks conscious participation in reality by reaching out to know both the things of the external world and human actions and their meanings: "The intellect discovers itself, furthermore, as a force transcending its own existence; by virtue of the intellect, existence not only is not opaque, but actually reaches out beyond itself in various directions in search of knowledge" (p. 147). Existential truth is not a static correspondence between interpretive model and reality but a dynamic movement into increasingly conscious participation in the process of reality.

The movement into truth is a process by which one both submits to and appropriates the order constituted by the existential tension that animates the Question. This order is constantly threatened, in human experience, by forces both from within and from without. Truth is not the only pull that acts upon the questioner. He is also drawn by a variety of other attractions that disrupt true order by tempting one toward existential closure and the darkening of intelligence. Consequently the quest for existential truth always has, to some degree, the character of a resistance to disorder.

In intellectual history this applies both to the historical thinker under study and to the historian who studies him, both to history as subject matter and to history as discipline. The thinker studied was himself involved in the project of human existence, whether he played his role well or poorly. He may, through his own entry into existential truth and the record he has left of that process, have become a source of luminosity for subsequent thinkers, or he may have become an example of existential closure and disorder. The philosophical historian who studies him must be more than a chronicler or a doxographer. To fulfill his own obligation to truth, he must seek not only correct opinions about what the thinker of the past meant or did not mean, said or did not say, but also the same truth of existence to which every human being in history has been called. What he must locate is not merely the way of thinking represented in texts but the existential Question that has manifested itself in both thinker and text to the extent that the thinker has opened himself to it. And he locates that Question not by forming an opinion about it but by entering into it himself and engaging in the struggle to which it calls him. [4]

This means that to understand his historical subject matter as it actually existed, he must struggle either with it or against it. Scholarly analysis, says Voegelin, "is concerned with the therapy of order"—because it goes beyond the validity of propositions to the truth of existence: "The opinions for the clarification of which the analysis is undertaken are not merely false: they are symptoms of spiritual disorder in the men who hold them. And the purpose of the analysis is to persuade—to have its own insights, if possible, supplant the opinions in social reality" (*Science, Politics, and Gnosticism*, p. 19). No person, past or present, stands outside the struggle,

---

4. Voegelin's approach to intellectual history as a recovery of the motivating experiential question has much in common with that of Hans-Georg Gadamer. Cf. Gadamer, *Truth and Method*, pp. 337–38, where he says that the interpretation of a text does not aim at taking one back inside the mind of the author to reconstruct his private experience or intention, as Dilthey had claimed; rather it seeks to recover the question that the text expresses and in which both author and reader are caught up. "To understand a question," says Gadamer, "means to ask it" (p. 338).

because no person stands outside reality and its tensional structure. One who claims neutrality is actually engaged in resistance, attempting to withdraw from the tension. Either one resists the reality in which one is immersed, or, resisting the resistance, one seeks existence in truth, which is conscious and willing participation in the order of being as constituted by the divine drawing: "To separate the 'truth' of insight from the effort of resistance would make nonsense of the insight into the in-between structure of existence. The life of reason is not a treasure of information to be stored away, it is the struggle in the *metaxy* for the immortalizing order of the psyche in resistance to the mortalizing forces of the apeirontic lust of being in time" (*Anam.*, p. 112).

The project of intellectual history that Voegelin has undertaken in his historical studies, particularly *Order and History* and *From Enlightenment to Revolution*, has been an effort of responsible participation in the discovery of reality that it studies and of opposition to the loss of reality that it also studies. This has required a broad temporal coverage, because the process of discovery and loss has never ended, and its earliest beginnings fade off into obscurity. As Voegelin said in the first volume of *Order and History*: "history creates mankind as the community of men who, through the ages, approach the true order of being that has its origin in God; but at the same time, mankind creates this history through its real approach to existence under God. It is an intricate dialectical process whose beginnings . . . reach deep into the cosmological civilizations—and even deeper into a human past beyond the scope of the present study" (p. 128).

Much of the process of the discovery of reality, the emergence of human existence into luminosity through the experience and symbolization of its tensional structure, has already been traced indirectly in the exposition of the theoretical principles of Voegelin's thought. Even though it will involve some repetition of material touched on in the first part, it may be helpful to the reader who has followed the exposition of theory to see how Voegelin applies his principles historiographically in his study of civilizational development. The following will summarize in broad outline the major steps he sees in the historical process by which existential reality opened itself up to men over a period of some five thousand years, since the beginning of recorded history. Although the same fundamental dynamics have been at work in all civilizations, Voegelin has chosen to concentrate primarily on the history of the Western and ancient Near Eastern developments both for reasons of economy and because he believes that in the Western case the fundamental issues have been rendered more explicit.

First came the cosmological symbolism by which man represented himself as one entity among many, ordered hierarchically in the four general categories of man, society, the world, and the gods—in ascending order of enduringness and therefore of eminence in being. This is, as far as it goes, an adequate symbolization of the structure of the reality in which man participates: it is a schema in which he is represented as standing between the primeval chaos and the various degrees of perfection of formed reality that extend beyond him. Historically there have been a number of versions or styles of cosmological symbolism: in Mesopotamia, Egypt, Iran, and China, to name only a few. Voegelin goes into the Mesopotamian and Egyptian examples in some detail.

In both cases the cosmological myth is the symbolic form through which a society interprets and thereby constitutes itself. The creation of a political order is seen as a participation in the creative activity of the gods, who are in turn represented as constituting a political order in the heavenly realm. This makes for a sense of consubstantiality linking the divine and human levels; the patterns of order correspond analogously, and there is thought to be a single creative energy working in both. In Mesopotamia, the creation epic known as the Enuma Elish, for example, represents the development of imperial power centered in Babylon as a parallel to the heavenly order that was the product of Marduk's victory over Tiamat. The gods themselves, under Marduk's direction, built the temple of Marduk in the center of Babylon, the "gate of the gods," which serves as the sacred center, the navel of the cosmos, at which the divine and human orders are linked, both through the imperial order seated there and through the festival of renewal, the Akitû, annually reenacted there. The laws of the empire, as in the case of the Code of Hammurabi, are interpreted as an extension of the imperial rule of Marduk, authorized by the gods.

The Egyptian version of the cosmological symbolism is different in style but similar in import. In this case the monarch is not, as in the Mesopotamian example, an earthly representative of the divine order but its manifestation in human form. The divinity—which may be symbolized variously as Horus, Re, and so on—extends his divine substance into the person of the Pharaoh and of his successors so that they become the channel through which the divine ordering force of Maat radiates into the empire. Maat, symbolized theomorphically as the daughter of Re, represents the order of being, in all of its manifestations: "The symbol is too compact to be translated by a single word in a modern language. As the Maat of the cosmos it would have to be rendered as order; as the Maat of society, as good government and justice; as the Maat of true understanding of ordered reality, as truth" (OH, 1:79). This force was embodied not only in the Pharaoh himself but in every official acting with his authority.

Where, as in the Mesopotamian and Egyptian cases, the political order is interpreted as grounded in cosmic-divine order, in turn symbolized as political in character, the two symbolizations of order, cosmic and political, tend to reinforce each other and thereby to impede a further breakthrough to the differentiated consciousness of existence. The latter requires a sense of separation between the world of immanence on the one hand and a world-transcendent divine ground on the other (p. 40).[5] Voegelin has made the same observation regarding the manner in which the Hellenic movement

5. See ibid., p. 84, for the idea that since it did not involve a differentiation between immanent and transcendent realms of being, the Egyptian sense of consubstantiality cannot be interpreted as a theory of divine immanence. To so interpret it would be to read later experiences and patterns of conceptualization back into a more primitive mode of apprehending the structure of existence.

of differentiation stopped at a certain point still within the compact cosmological symbolism, for example in Plato's treatment of the cosmos as the image of the Eternal rather than man, as in the Israelite and Christian cases.[6] He has also noted that there can be good reason for such hesitation: the symbolism of a de-divinized world may lead not to loyalty to a differentiated transcendent pole of truth and supreme good beyond the values of the political order consecrated by the tradition but to agnostic directionlessness and the loss of the experience of consubstantiality—divine-human partnership—altogether (OH, 1:84).

If the movement from compact to differentiated consciousness is fraught with perils, however, so also is compactness itself. The too simple identification of a mundane order with cosmic law may easily serve, as history has abundantly shown, to reinforce injustices rooted in the appetitive existence of rulers and to inhibit efforts of attunement to true order. It also tends to produce a situation in which the breakdown or perversion of political order in a society will lead not to efforts of reform but a crisis of faith: disorder on earth may lead to doubts about the reality of the divine order itself. Ancient Egypt during the Intermediate Periods offers a number of texts reflecting such despair, including the "Dispute of a Man, Who Contemplates Suicide, with His Soul" discussed in Voegelin's "Immortality: Experience and Symbol."

Cosmologically symbolized orders tend to fail. To put it more

6. "The Gospel and Culture," pp. 82–83: "The obstacle to further differentiation is not some disability peculiar to the Classic movement, such as the limitation of natural reason unaided by revelation, a topic still favored by theologians who ought to know better, but the cosmological mode of experience and symbolisation dominant in the culture in which the movement occurs. For the experience of the movement tends to dissociate the cosmic-divine reality of the primary experience into the contingent being of things and the necessary being of the world-transcendent God; and a culture in which the sacrality of order, both personal and social, is symbolized by intra-cosmic gods, will not easily give way to the *theotes* [the Godhead] of the movement whose victory entails the desacralization of traditional order." This is a reference to the *Timaeus*. The same residual compactness shows up in the *Phaedrus's* treatment of "soul" as the idea or form of the cosmos articulated into nobler and lesser souls.

precisely, they tend to manifest, sometimes more and sometimes less clearly, a weakness inherent in their structure: they are never in concrete reality what they represent themselves as being. Their symbolization of cosmic-divine order on the level of society is not a description of a fact but an evocation; it is an invitation and a command to enter into the order so symbolized. The cosmological symbolism may take account of this, as in the recognition in Mesopotamia of a need for annual renewal of order, but its compactness makes it difficult to differentiate between the earthly representative and the heavenly original. When the gap between these manifests itself too palpably, this creates pressure toward a more differentiated conception. The Egyptian texts mentioned reflect this. The situation during the Egyptian First Intermediate Period, says Voegelin, was potentially fruitful: "From the depths of despair there might have arisen a soul purged of illusions about the world and willing to face its iniquity with the strength that flows from faith in a world-transcendent god. A new man, guided by the god who was manifest nowhere except in the loving movement of his soul, might have set himself the task of creating a government that would rely less on the cosmic divinity of institutions and more on the order in the souls of the men who live under them" (*OH*, 1:95). In actuality, however, the breakthrough did not occur there or at that time.

Why it did occur at the times and places it did is mysterious, as is the fact that it has occurred in different ways—in the manner both of noetic and of pneumatic differentiations. The mystery, of course, as should be clear from the theoretical exposition in part 1 of the present study, is inherent in the process: the movement of the soul into luminosity of existence is simultaneously a human seeking and a divine drawing. The social and human conditions for the quest may all be present, but the breakthrough is not simply a human endeavor; there is also a divine breakthrough or irruption into man, and there is no way that this can be predicted. It takes place where and in whom it will.

History has left us records of several occasions on which such breakthroughs have occurred. They are not confined exclusively to the Hellenic and Israelite-Christian historical streams, but these are the ones that have become most prominent in the background of Western readers, and it is on these that Voegelin focuses for purposes of discussion.[7] They differ in some important ways, but there is no radical discontinuity between them. In the Hellenic experience it is the noetic seeking that is emphasized, and in the Israelite and Christian it is the spiritual inrush of divine presence—but in neither case is the emphasis absolutely exclusive. The Hellenic differentiation develops in a process generated by an experience of crisis and of resistance to disorder, and through this it arrives at noetic understanding of the soul's order. The Israelite experience begins at the other end, with the pneumatic or spiritual experience of the divine calling and the manifestation of the One God as the source of order (for further discussion of this comparison, see *OH*, 2:51).

The earliest account of such a breakthrough in the pneumatic mode is that which describes the call to Abraham: "It is an order that originates in a man through the inrush of divine reality into his soul and from this point of origin expands into a social body in history. At the time of its inception it is no more than the life of a man who trusts in God; but this new existence, founded on the leap in being, is pregnant with future" (*OH*, 1:194, commenting on Genesis 14–15). At that time the new order did not yet extend beyond the soul of the individual in whom the divine irruption took place, but there were others subsequently in whom the call was heard again, among the patriarchs, Moses, and the prophets, and it succeeded, at least to some degree, in forming a community of people who became the bearers of the covenant not only on their own behalf but also on that of subsequent peoples in whom the call has been reenacted in part through their mediation.

It might seem strange, considering the speculative character of

7. The earlier volumes of *Order and History* tended to speak of these historical streams as if they were the only ones, or at least the only major ones; but, as was explained earlier, volume 4 represents a shift to increased awareness of the diversity of the spiritual centers that have been historically effective. See *OH*, 4: 1–6.

historiography dealing with the ancient world, especially when one goes back as far as the second millennium or so B.C., that Voegelin should so confidently identify Abraham as the fountainhead of this historical stream. He is aware of the problems involved and discusses them, but there is an important principle to which he believes he must be faithful. He formulated it in *The New Science of Politics* when he said that "the substance of history is to be found on the level of experiences, not on the level of ideas" (p. 125). It was in fidelity to the same principle that he also said, in "Reason: The Classic Experience": "The unfolding of noetic consciousness in the psyche of the classic philosophers is not an 'idea,' or a 'tradition,' but an event in the history of mankind" (*Anam.*, pp. 111–12). Similarly, he objected in "History and Gnosis" to Bultmann's dismissal of the importance of the historical existence of an actual Jesus and spoke, in "The Gospel and Culture," of the origin of the Gospel of Christ in "the experience of an extraordinary divine irruption in the existence of Jesus" (p. 80). His discussion of the question of a historical Abraham serves to illustrate the principle: it is not a question of the exact date of the story and the trustworthiness of its details but of "the authenticity of the experience that is communicated by means of the story" (*OH*, 1:195). Clearly, he says, those who wrote the story had themselves had the experience it describes, "for nobody can describe an experience unless he has had it, either originally or through imaginative re-enactment." Equally clearly, since the original experience, like its reenactments, was a real event, it has to have taken place sometime, and the Biblical record of it is what we have: "The spiritual sensitiveness of the man who opened his soul to the word of Yahweh, the trust and fortitude required to make this word the order of existence in opposition to the world, and the creative imagination used in transforming the symbol of civilizational bondage [the symbol of *berith*, or covenant] into the symbol of divine liberation—that combination is one of the great and rare events in the history of mankind. And this event bears the name of Abram" (p. 195).

When this new spiritual order did manage to extend itself beyond the souls of that one man and his immediate family, it was through the agency of another concrete historical person, Moses. Again the Biblical account is the only one available, but without the assumption of an historical reality approximating that described, the origin of the Israelites as a people would be unintelligible:

> If there was a clash between the orders of Israel and Egypt, it had its origin in an experience of Moses.
>
> The transformation of the indifferent and recalcitrant Hebrew clans into the Israel of Yahweh must have taken some time, as well as the efforts of a strong personality. It presupposes the existence of the man who could bring the people into the present under God because he had entered into it himself. Moreover, the formula of Israel as the Son of God could hardly have been intelligible and effective, unless the people had been penetrated with Egyptian civilization to a certain degree; and its creation, in particular, points to a man who lived so intensely as an Egyptian that he could conceive it in its full weight as the abrogation of Pharaonic order. [Pp. 392–93]

Somehow Moses persuaded the Israelites, still recalcitrant and divided, to make their departure with him from the only civilization they knew, but which had become for them a Sheol. They were not yet a people, but became one through further experiences that took place during the years of wandering. Sheol, Exodus, and Desert, says Voegelin, form a complex of symbols that have their meaning only in relation to one another. Exodus is only aimless flight until one pauses to seek a direction and finds one in the movement of transcendence:

> When the spirit bloweth, society in cosmological form becomes Sheol, the realm of death; but when we undertake the Exodus and wander into the world, in order to found a new society elsewhere, we discover the world as the Desert. The flight leads nowhere, until we stop in order to find our bearings beyond the world. When the world has become Desert, man is at last in the solitude in which he can hear thunderingly the voice of the spirit that with its urgent whispering has already driven and rescued him from Sheol. In the Desert God spoke to the leader and his tribes; in the Desert, by listening to the

voice, by accepting its offer, and by submitting to its command, they·at last reached life and became the people chosen by God . . . a people that moved on the historical scene while living toward a goal beyond history. [P. 113]

This is a mode of existence—the Exodus not *from* but *within* reality—that is fraught with dangers of derailment. It is existence in truth, but it is fragile, says Voegelin, because the goal beyond history can easily seem to merge with necessary and good goals to be attained within history. The two experiential forces governing Israel's self-interpretation were their transcendental Yahwism and the requirements of their pragmatic existence as a nation. The ambiguity of two central symbols can serve to exemplify the difficulty. The first to become historically problematic, according to Voegelin, was the symbol of the Promised Land. Spiritually they had reached their true home even in the desert of Sinai when they had passed from the cosmological Sheol and the Desert of aimlessness into the Kingdom of God through their acceptance of the Covenant: "Pragmatically, however, the Exodus from bondage was continued into the conquest of Canaan by rather worldly means; further, to a Solomonic kingdom with the very institutional forms of Egypt or Babylon; and, finally, to political disaster and destruction that befell Israel like any other people in history" (p. 114). Under the pressure of the pragmatic necessity of effective government and military defense, the symbol of Kingship, in turn, passed from the exclusive Kingship of Yahweh to that of his anointed earthly representative. The result was a Chosen King who became preeminent over the Chosen People and stood closer to God, who now made a special covenant with the royal house: "The King became the mediator of Yahwist order in the same sense in which a Pharaoh was the mediator of divine order for his people" (p. 272). The idea of theocratic order, which had prevailed during the period of the Judges, was a symbol which articulated and kept conscious "the experienced tension between divine and human constitution of society" (p. 247). Pragmatically it was inadequate to the situation that later developed, but when it was lost, says Voegelin, so also was some of the spiritual substance that had been gained through Exodus, Desert, and Covenant.

The problems connected with Canaan and Kingship, however, were only symptoms of a more difficult underlying problem: the residual compactness of the Israelite experience. As Voegelin analyzes it, the differentiation of consciousness that took place among the ancient Israelites never progressed as far as did the noetic differentiation among the Greeks. What was lacking in particular was individuation; the Israelites tended to have little sense of what the Greeks symbolized as the individual soul, but experienced the spiritual life only compactly, by way of the group: "In Israel the spirit of God, the *ruach* of Yahweh, is present with the community and with individuals in their capacity as representatives of the community, but it is not present as the ordering force in the soul of every man, as the Nous of the mystic-philosophers or the Logos of Christ is present in every member of the Mystical Body, creating by its presence the *homonoia*, the likemindedness of the community" (p. 240). This prevented the development of philosophy, which according to Voegelin requires the explicit experience of divine presence as an ordering force within the individual *psyche* of the philosopher, and it also made difficult the differentiation of the conflicting implications, mundane and transcendental, of the compact symbols of Chosen People, Promised Land, Anointed King, and so on.

The spiritual pressure of the divine calling continued, however, or at least repeatedly revived, and it expressed itself in the ways that it could under such conditions of compactness. In *Israel and Revelation* Voegelin traces the manner in which in the eighth century, with Amos, the line of prophets began who understood that the failure of Israelite order had its source not in external enemies but in the people itself. In the absence of philosophical reflectiveness by which the disorder of man and society could be diagnosed and the right order of the soul defined, the only alternative response to the experienced disorder of the later monarchies in north and south, Voegelin says, was the prophetic call to return to the Covenant and the traditional laws in which it expressed itself. Voegelin compares the prophet Hosea with Plato to show the dimensions of the problem:

> The prophet tried to describe a society in crisis, and he found the root of the evil in the "want of knowledge" concerning matters divine. Up to this point his analysis was literally the same as Plato's in the *Republic*. Plato, as Hosea, diagnosed the evil as an ignorance of the soul, an *agnoia* concerning the nature of God. But Plato could proceed from his insight to an analysis of the right order of the soul through its attunement to the unseen measure. And he even developed the concept of "theology," in order to speak in technical language of true and false conceptions of divinity. Under the condition of the more compact experiences and symbols in Israel, Hosea could not find the answer to his problems in the attunement of the soul to the divine measure, but had to seek it in a renewed conformity of human conduct to the measure as revealed in the "word" and the "law" of God. [P. 327]

Properly carried out, in fidelity to the spirit of the ancient tradition, this was not an inadequate response, but it suffered, says Voegelin, from the same ambiguous compactness it was trying to deal with. In particular there was the ambiguity of Law, as expression of the divine drawing toward the transcendental pole of perfect righteousness, and of laws as particular prescriptions requiring interpretation if they are to be applied appropriately to varying individual situations—in other words, requiring attunement to the transcendental measure. There was also the ambiguity of the position of the prophet as the one through whom the call is issued: the prophet could be interpreted as one who experiences the divine drawing, reports it, and invites the hearers to attend to its pull within their own consciences, or he could be interpreted as the spokesman through whom particular legal prescriptions are issued. The prophets themselves, says Voegelin, took the spiritual and existential line of interpretation: "We interpret Prophetism as the struggle against the Law [in the sense of a prescriptive code], as the attempt to disengage the existential from the normative issues" (p. 447). Their interpretation of the prophetic role as such, and particularly of Moses, the prototypical prophet, followed the same line:

> The Moses of the prophets is not a figure of the past through whose mediation Israel was established once for all as the people under Yahweh the King, but the first of a line of prophets who in the present, under the revelatory word of Yahweh, continued to bring Israel up from Egypt into existence under God. . . . The recall of the past blends, therefore, into the call in the present. They both belong to the same continuum of revelation, which creates historical form when it meets with the continuum of the people's response. [Pp. 428–29]

This contrasts with the compact interpretation of Moses, word of God, and Law set forth by the Deuteronomists, in whose understanding the immediacy of existence under God is broken by the myth of the authoritative author of the Pentateuch, represented as standing between people and God as the Egyptian Pharaoh stood between people and gods: "The word of God had become the Book of the Torah written by a Moses who had become a Pharaonic mummy" (p. 365).

Both styles of interpretation ran parallel to one another—as one would expect, since the ambiguity of a compact symbol can always be counted on to elicit different readings from interpreters who exist on differing levels of compactness and differentiation of consciousness. On the one side the pressure toward individuation and clearer differentiation led toward the breakthroughs of Jeremiah, the second Isaiah, and eventually of Jesus. On the other it led to the exclusivism and legalism attacked under the symbol of the "Pharisees" by the gospel writers. The tension between the two styles and levels of interpretation has never been resolved, nor, Voegelin would probably say, will it ever be as long as there remains the possibility of different levels of development among human beings. Israelite and Jewish compactness did not culminate once and for all in Christian differentiation; Christian history also has its legalists, dogmatists, and literalizers. And so did the Hellenic—before, during, and after the great noetic breakthroughs.

Hellenic culture was motivated from the beginning by concern with problems of order and disorder. In fact, it was to this concern that the term *paideia*, or "culture," referred: it did not refer, in the conventional modern sense, to the totality of the society's customs and literary and artistic artifacts but to the quest for true excellence in the formation of the well-ordered human being. According to Voegelin's tracing of the development of Greek thought in *The World of the Polis*, we may see this, for example, in the *Iliad*, in its focus on the course of the pathological syndrome in which Achilles, through lack of the good judgment that Aristotle was later to call *phronesis*, gave way to temptations to excesses of pride and anger—forces that when well regulated are the energies that are formed into the *arete* (true excellence) of the warrior. We may see it also in Hesiod's organization of his *Works and Days* as an exhortation to his unjust brother, Perses. He called Perses back from the disorder of his rapacity toward proper recognition of divine order symbolized by Zeus and his daughter Dike (Justice) and by Eris (Strife)—not the evil Eris but a second Eris, the good one, who incites men to peaceful competition in pursuit of the *arete* not of the warrior but of the industrious farmer (*OH*, 2:139).

Excellence and justice came to be conceived of in various ways during the course of the Hellenic reflection on the theme, but what is important is the continuous search for the most adequate way of understanding and enacting them. Gradually the shift from one conception of perfect excellence (*arete*) to another forced into consciousness the transcendental dimension both of the search and of man: "What they found was not the one true Arete but a whole series of Aretai. With each new discovery the claim for superior rank of the previous discovery was broken; and in the end the problem had to arise whether the latest discovery invalidated all previous ones, or whether each discovery differentiated a certain sector of human experience so that only a balanced practice of all the Aretai fully expressed the potentialities of man" (pp. 192–93). The solution, which Voegelin says was finally worked out with full explicitness by Plato, was that all of the particular forms of human excellence had to be differentiated from the Good as such, and that human perfection lay not in a particular form of strength, skill, or other excellence, but in the continuous, dynamic ordering of the entire personality through attentive responsiveness to the pull of the transcendental pole of the tension of existence: "The search for the true Arete ends in the discovery that the Aretai are habituations of the soul which attune the life of man with transcendent reality; with the full differentiation of the field of Aretai there emerges the 'true self' of man, the center at which he lives in openness toward the transcendental highest good, the Platonic Agathon. The transition to the ordering survey of Aretai means that the Agathon has been discovered as the principle of order in the soul" (p. 193).

It was mentioned earlier that one of the major differences Voegelin sees between the Israelite and Greek processes of differentiation is that the Greek form developed a clearer sense of the individual soul as the experiential center of the tension of existence—the center at which the divine drawing that motivates the search is sensed and at which the human response of decision is made. This, too, can be seen developing in the earliest period, as in Agamemnon's apology to Achilles (*Iliad* 19. 78–144):

> The king casts the responsibility for his unjust action on a whole assembly of gods (Zeus, Moira, Erinys, Ate) who blinded him. But when the blindness falls from him, and he becomes seeing again, he assumes responsibility for his action and offers amends. . . . The analysis by means of the symbolism of "blindness" and "seeing" is of considerable interest for the later development of a theory of action. For Homer is on the way toward discovering what the philosophers will call the "true self," that is, the area in a man's soul in which he is oriented toward noetic order. When the true self dominates, then the man "sees"; and through the retroactive recognition of "blindness," the misdeed is integrated (as it were by a "conscience") into the acting self. [P. 105]

The association of "self" with "seeing," that is, with experience, and with responsible decision is of the first importance for an understanding of the noetic differentiation as Voegelin conceives it. The Greek discovery of the "soul" must not be understood as the discovery of an entity, even if it came at times to be symbolized in that way, as in the Orphic conception or in the proofs of an "immortal soul" in Plato's *Phaedo*. As the first part of the present study suggested, from Voegelin's point of view the idea of a soul-entity is a hypostatizing conception carried over from the primary experience of the cosmos into the discussion of the differentiated experience of existence; it casts a mode of existential experience in the form of a thing, about the existence or survival of which there can be arguments. Voegelin recognizes the influence of the "Orphic knowledge of the soul" on Xenophanes and Heraclitus, and on the subsequent tradition, but what constitutes this as genuine knowledge in the existential sense (*episteme*) is the experience not a speculation about an entity (p. 165).[8]

The second and third volumes of *Order and History* trace the Hellenic process of noetic differentiation in detail, but a brief summary will serve here to indicate the main lines of the development and of Voegelin's analysis of it. The exploration in the medium of imaginative literature continued in poetry and drama, especially tragedy, which Voegelin defines, with reference to the practice of Aeschylus in particular, as a quest for existential order: "The truth of the tragedy is action itself, that is, action on the new, differentiated level of a movement in the soul that culminates in the decision (*proairesis*) of a mature, responsible man. The newly discovered humanity of the soul expands into the realm of action. Tragedy as a form is the study of the human soul in the process of making decisions, while the single tragedies construct conditions and experimental situations, in which a fully developed, self-conscious

8. It is also worth mentioning that the *Phaedo*, as the dialogue proceeds, moves from the hypostatizing style of discussion to the experiential, with emphasis on the life of the soul as a participation in the modes of existence of divinity.

soul is forced into action" (p. 247). The literary exploration tracing from Homer was joined around the seventh century by a stream of early philosophers and cosmological speculators, such as Thales, Anaximander, Xenophanes, Heraclitus, and Parmenides, which eventually culminated in the work of Plato and Aristotle.

Xenophanes's critique of the seemliness of the representation of divinity by Homer and Hesiod was mentioned in chapter 4. What is important about it is that for Xenophanes the inadequacy of myth was not simply a matter of inaccuracy; rather the myth was "an obstacle to the adequate understanding of the order of the soul" (p. 171). The motivating force behind his critique of anthropomorphism, as Voegelin analyzes it, was an experience of divine and human universality as an order in which all men participate and to which all owe a common loyalty and reverence. Xenophanes, says Voegelin, was "a religious genius who discovered participation in a nameless realissimum as the essence of his humanity" (p. 180). This supreme reality had to be represented as a "greatest god" for all men —rather than black-haired for the Ethiopians and red-haired for the Parthians—because it was "correlative to the experienced transcendence of existence common to all human beings." The problem with anthropomorphism, from this point of view, was not that it represented the divine by analogy with man but that it represented it in a way that correlated with idiosyncrasy and disorder in humanity: anthropomorphic symbolism "corresponds to a past phase in the self-understanding of man" (p. 176). Knowledge and existence depend on one another; just as the order of being becomes visible only to one whose soul is well ordered, so also right order in the soul will be impeded by an inadequate symbolization of ultimate reality.

Parmenides carried further the same line of reflection. The mystical transport represented in his poem by the journey to the goddess brought him to an experience of absolute "Being" and to the discovery of *nous* as the organ of the soul by which nonsensual, intelligible reality is experienced. The "Is!" of Parmenides was the first step in the process by which *nous* became the symbol for the power of apperceptive participation in reality and *psyche* came to symbolize the site of such conscious participation: "With the Parmenidean consciousness of the way that leads toward the border of transcendence, the soul itself moves into the field of philosophical speculation. We can speculate about transcendent Being because the soul is a sensorium of transcendence" (p. 221).[9] For Parmenides, *nous* is the power by which the soul can function as such a sensorium, while the content of Being is articulated by the further faculty of *logos*, which Voegelin says appears here for the first time in the sense of a capacity for logical argumentation (p. 209).

Heraclitus explored the soul in far greater depth than Parmenides did. He did not attempt to analyze Being through logical explication. Rather when he said that "the soul has a logos that augments itself," he was speaking of the power of inquiry that seeks the transcendental *sophon*, the divine wisdom, and that depends on the anticipating urges of hope (*elpis*) and faith (*pistis*) to orient it in the right direction (p. 228). It is in the thought of Heraclitus, says Voegelin, that there begins to form the idea of the "order of the soul" that will unfold fully in the Platonic dialogues: "Both Heraclitus and Plato . . . agree that no composition can lay claim to 'truth' unless it is authenticated by the movement of the psyche toward the *sophon*. The problem of truth now is differentiated so far that the loving movement of the soul toward the 'Alone Wise' is recognized as the source of such truth as the production of the thinker or poet may have" (p. 227).

The discovery of the soul and the struggle for right understanding of the order of the soul took centuries. It reached a climax, according to Voegelin, in the soul of Socrates and in his impact on Plato. The important achievement of Plato, and one that took him beyond Socrates, lay in the clarity with which he differentiated the ordering function in the soul from any form of wisdom that the soul could have. Socrates, if the dialogues represent him accurately, had

9. Compare with Parmenides's absolute "Is!" Augustine's reference to God as "the great Is" in *Enarrationes in Psalmos* 101. S. 2. 10. 47 (Dekkers and Fraipont, eds., 40: 1445): "Magnum ecce *Est*, magnum *Est!*" ("Behold, this is the great *Is*, the great *Is!*").

tended to equate virtue with knowledge, a position that was itself only one step removed from the Homeric notion of right action through "seeing." Plato himself, says Voegelin, seems to have thought along this line in his early dialogues, but in the *Republic* he presents an interpretation of the soul in which "we find a *sophia* [wisdom] that is nourished from the rational part of the soul, the *logistikon*, present in all men at all times, but still of no avail unless a virtue higher than wisdom sees to it that wisdom will indeed prevail in the soul over the passions" (*OH*, 3:111). Plato's term for this regulative virtue is *dikaiosune*, or "justice," the same term that is translated as "righteousness" in the New Testament. It is closely related conceptually both to the *pistis* (faith) of Heraclitus and to the *phronesis* (practical wisdom, prudence) of Aristotle. It is a power through which a transcendental good, the *agathon*, which is truly (in the phrase of Solon) an "unseen measure," is discerned through love and actively imitated in the decisions that concretely order the soul in fidelity to that love. It is this principle—that the transcendental is known through love rather than by means of a direct, intuitive "look"—that constitutes the essential difference, as was explained in chapter 3 of the present study, between *episteme* and *gnosis*, as Voegelin analyzes the basic concepts to which these terms refer. The insight that discerns the transcendental pole of the good as such has no more particular content than does the "Is!" of Parmenides, and there is no way it can be converted into information that could be taught to one who lacks the divine gift of sensitivity to its pull: "Concerning the content of the Agathon nothing can be said at all. That is the fundamental insight of Platonic ethics" (p. 112). Its transcendence places it beyond the reach of propositions, except insofar as they point toward it analogously. It is a living law, the tension of existence, and does not incarnate itself in prescriptive laws but in the concrete processes by which the soul, in its decisions, seeks attunement to it: "The vision of the Agathon does not render a material rule of conduct, but forms the soul through an experience of transcendence."

Aristotle's term for the person so formed, the person who can discern the true good because he is capable of the true wish, is *spoudaios*, the mature man—that is, the man who through noetic development and the practice of responsible decision and virtuous action has attained full human stature. The science of ethics, for Aristotle, is the self-explication of such a person, because the existential structure he embodies is the *kanon kai metron*, the norm and measure, of existential truth (p. 300).[10] Ethical truth has its locus in the process in which he exercises his characteristic virtue of *phronesis*, the art of right decision, in particular transactions from case to case; ethical truth is the truth of existence, and the *spoudaios* is the one who dwells in that. For this reason ethics could not be for Aristotle, any more than it was for Plato, a set of rules. The criterion of well-ordered existence for Aristotle, says Voegelin, is its openness to the divine ordering force, and this is not a precept but something that happens. "Die Ethik," says Voegelin, "ist darum nicht ein Korpus von Sätzen, sondern ein Seinsereignis, das sich das Wort zur Aussage über sich selbst gibt" ("ethics is therefore not a body of propositions, but an existential event, which articulates itself to itself").[11]

And yet there are differences of level of existential truth among human beings—of level of compactness and differentiation, of openness and closedness of existence, of fidelity or infidelity to the structure of being, of order, lack of order, and ill order. Plato discussed this problem in *Republic* 9. 572–73, under the figure of the tyrannical man, who is dominated by the "great winged drone" of insatiable appetite, the *eros tyrannos*—the equivalent symbol in Plato for the evil Eris of Hesiod. The person whose character becomes formed in this way has no sensitivity to the true directional tension, because the drone slays "any opinions or appetites accounted worthy and still capable of shame."[12] Such a person cannot

10. In *Nicomachean Ethics* 1113a29–35.
11. German *Anamnesis*, p. 128 (my translation); English *Anam.*, p. 65.
12. *Republic* 573b, trans. Paul Shorey, in Hamilton and Cairns.

be persuaded through an appeal to conscience, because a conscience, as Voegelin says, "can only be as good as the man who has it." [13] The *eros tyrannos* generates not mere lack of order but perverted order capable of stubborn resistance once it establishes a foothold in the soul. As Plato describes the path of development in that direction, the oligarchic and democratic types of human being—in the nomenclature he uses—are stages on the way to that condition.

Persons formed, to whatever degree, by appetite require guidance toward true order, and under such circumstances this can only take place through precepts coming from those wiser than they. Plato was much preoccupied with this problem in his later dialogues, especially the *Statesman* and the *Laws*. He seems to have gone through a slow process of gradual disillusionment about the possibility of creating a community of individuals, well ordered through existential attunement, who could act as true statesmen in society. The *Statesman* shows a recognition that even if there could be such people, they would still have to make their order effective in the community as a whole through legal prescriptions, which would always remain subject to unintelligent application by those on lower levels of existential development than the statesman himself. The *Laws* apparently reflects the final stage in his realization of the difficulties involved in the attempt to incarnate divine order among actual human beings. The *Republic* had hoped that there could be a substantial group of people ordered through the vision of the *agathon* in such a way that "the *nomos* [law] could enter their souls so that they would become a *nomos empsychos* [living law]"; however, in the *Laws* "men . . . are equal because the *nomos* is equally beyond them all" (*OH*, 3:233). Instead of the vision of the *agathon*, what they have here is only the pull of the golden cord in conflict with the stronger pulls of the other cords that draw them, and this pull is represented as taking the form of divinely given laws. Instead of *nomos* as the presence of the divine spirit, they have the laws that come from the Athenian Stranger, in whom alone the spiritual *nomos*

13. "The Oxford Political Philosophers," *Philosophical Quarterly*, 3 (1953): 114.

becomes luminous: "This spirit is not present in the souls of the equal men; it has solidified into a decree (*dogma*) of the polis; and this *dogma*, while it may be renewed and expanded by the citizens of the polis, is not created by them" (p. 233).

The problem with which Plato was wrestling in these dialogues is that the noesis that first developed among the major Hellenic philosophers, both by its nature and by its situation in the actual world, lies open in two directions: dogmatism and mysticism. This is why Voegelin so frequently speaks of Parmenides, Heraclitus, Plato, and Aristotle as "mystic-philosophers."[14] To the extent that men are actually philosophers in the original sense, they are engaged in an experiential, mystical ascent to luminous participation in existential truth; and the term *nous* was the language symbol through which these particular men expressed their experience of such apperceptive participation. What they came to know through *nous* was the *nomos* that is the tensional structure of reality and that when consciously accepted becomes *nomos empsychos*. If this is to be spoken of, however, it must be put into language, and language requires interpretation. And what requires interpretation may, unfortunately, be interpreted poorly. Symbolization, by its very nature, is always ambiguous. The interpreter may trace his way back through the symbol to the experience—in this case the existential truth—that engendered it; or, prevented from that, perhaps through compactness of consciousness or through existential closure, he may go astray and attach the symbol to some other real or imaginary experience. This is the process through which what Voegelin calls "secondary symbolisms" develop: symbols that originated in genuine noetic experience become literalized or immanentized and thereby not only take on new meanings but act to impede recovery of the original meaning.

The term Voegelin has come to use for this process is "doctrinization." The philosopher leaves a trail of symbols by which his hearer can follow him into luminosity of existence. The hearer, on the

14. As was mentioned earlier, Voegelin has also applied the same term to himself. See Sebba, "Prelude and Variations on the Theme of Eric Voegelin," p. 665.

other hand, may interpret the philosopher's truth not as existential but as propositional, so that what was experiential insight becomes only the memory of words. In the philosopher's experience in the divine-human Between, the symbols are not separate from the insight they express, nor is the experience separate from the reality of which it is the luminous presence, but when the hearer converts the symbols into a doctrine, then the reality of the Between becomes eclipsed, and *aletheia* is reduced to *doxa*:

> The language symbols belong, as to their meanings, to the Metaxy of the experiences from which they arise as their truth. As long as the process of experience and symbolization is not deformed by doctrinal reflection, there is no doubt about the metaleptic [participatory] status of the symbols. . . . If the metaleptic symbol which is the word of both god and man is hypostatized into a doctrinal Word of God, the device can protect the insight gained against disintegration in society, but it also can impair the sensitivity for the source of truth in the flux of divine presence in time which constitutes history. Unless precautions of meditative practice are taken, the doctrinization of symbols is liable to interrupt the process of experiential reactivation and linguistic renewal. When the symbol separates from its source in the experiential Metaxy, the Word of God can degenerate into a word of man that one can believe or not. [*OH*, 4:56]

Voegelin has said that "classical noesis and mysticism are the two predogmatic forms of real knowledge in which the *logos* of consciousness became optimally differentiated."[15] It should now be clear why: they are continuous with one another. Noesis is not simply a human mode of cognition; it is simultaneously the luminosity of being. From the beginning of the Hellenic philosophical reflection, with Parmenides, *nous* and Being were not entities but the subjective and objective poles of a single experience. This was still the case in the thought of Aristotle, in spite of his tendency to intellectualize and immanentize what he had learned

15. "Die klassische Noese und die Mystik sind die zwei prä-dogmatischen Wissensrealitäten, in denen der Logos des Bewußtseins optimal differenziert wurde." German *Anamnesis*, p. 333 (my translation); English *Anam.*, p. 192.

from Plato. For Aristotle, the *bios theoretikos*, the contemplative life, transcended the merely human level because in *nous* the human and divine meet and participate in one another: "the Aristotelian nous is more than the intellect that becomes active in the sciences of world-immanent objects. The nous as the *theiotaton* [the "divinest part" of man] is the region in the soul where man transcends his mere humanity into the divine ground" (*OH*, 3:306).

But from almost the beginning of the discovery of reality through experience and symbolization the process of deformation into secondary symbolisms was also under way. In the usage of Parmenides, *nous* and Being had their meaning as symbols in the explication of an experience of transcendence, but his younger contemporary, Anaxagoras, interpreted *nous* not as the apperceptive dimension of the experience but as a part of being, the "'finest' and 'purest' among things" (*OH*, 2:293). It is an excellent example of the generation of a secondary symbol:

> The procedure of Anaxagoras in solving his problem [the question of what it was that linked the Being discovered in mystical transport and the world of *doxa*] is characteristic of what may be called sophistic thinking in a technical sense. The problem of the mystic-philosopher, as well as his symbols (Nous and Being) are accepted, while the experience of transcendence, which lies at the root of the problem and motivates the creation of the symbols for its expression, is abandoned. As a consequence, the symbols of transcendence will now be used, or rather misused, in the speculation on immanent problems. [P. 294]

It is difficult, Voegelin says, to tell just how far Anaxagoras proceeded in the immanentizing direction, because his extant writings are so fragmentary, but his practice sketched out, at least, "the style of the sophistic intellectual," which "permits men who are no philosophers in the existential sense to express their opinions on problems involving the experience of transcendence with the usurped authority of the existential philosopher."

This is a description, as far as the particulars are concerned, of the pattern of derailment into secondary symbolism among the Greeks, but the derailment is not different in essence from that of the Deuteronomists in Israel or from the later Christian process of dogmatizing. Symbols can always be ill interpreted, and in any milieu, as long as history continues, there will always be interpretations reflecting diverse levels of existential formation among the interpreters.

Nor is there any essential difference in any of the three cases in the existential truth that becomes deformed. It has become a convention of the doxographic tradition built on the doctrinization of the noetic symbols that there is a radical difference between Philosophy or "natural reason," on the one hand, and Revelation on the other, but this is the expression of an attempt on the part of generations of theologians "to monopolize the symbol 'revelation' for Israelite, Jewish, and Christian theophanies" (*OH*, 4:236).[16] Voegelin's discussion of Parmenides and Aristotle on *nous* and of Plato on the experience of *metaxy* existence should already have made it clear that for them the discovery of reality is just as much a revelation as it is for those traditions that emphasize the irruption at the pneumatic center, and there is no reason why the historian should deny their interpretation of the experience: "Unless we want to indulge in extraordinary theological assumptions, the God who appeared to the philosophers, and who elicited from Parmenides the exclamation 'Is!', was the same God who revealed himself to Moses as the 'I am who (or: what) I am,' as the God who is what he is in the concrete theophany to which man responds." (p. 229).

The continuity of classical noesis with mysticism indicates, and is an aspect of, its continuity with the pneumatic differentiations in Israel and in Christianity. It was one of the features of the Ecumenic Age that the symbolisms produced in these different modes of theophanic experience were brought into contact and eventually forced to integrate with one another, at least to a degree. This was rendered possible, moreover, by the parallelism of structure in the

16. For a more extensive discussion of Voegelin's conception of the relation between reason and revelation, see Eugene Webb, "Eric Voegelin's Theory of Revelation," *The Thomist*, 42 (1978): 95–122.

essential experiences. Aristotle had developed the term *homonoia* to describe the manner in which the formation of the souls of men through *nous* could serve as the bond of society. Paul was able to adapt the same term for his own central concept of *homonoia* in the Christian community through common participation in the *nous* of Christ (*OH*, 3:364). Similarly, when Paul said that "the new covenant written by the spirit (pneuma) in the heart," which is the love of God, is as much God's knowledge of man as it is man's of God, he was striving to articulate the same mode of existential knowledge that Aristotle symbolized as the mutual participation of the divine and human in *nous*:

> That the resplendence of knowledge in the heart has its origin in divine action is explicitly stated in such passages as 1 Cor 8:1-3:
>
> > We know that "all of us possess knowledge (*gnosis*)."
> > Knowledge (*gnosis*) puffs up, love (*agape*) builds up.
> > If anyone imagines he knows something, he does not
> >   yet know as he ought to know.
> > But if one loves God, one is known by him.
>
> The words are addressed to members of the Corinthian community who "possess knowledge" as doctrine and unwisely apply it as a rule of conduct; such possessors of truth are reminded that the knowledge that forms existence without deforming it is God's knowledge of man. In a similar admonition to the Galatians Paul writes (Gal 4:8-9):
>
> > Formerly, when you did not know God, you were enslaved to beings who are not really gods at all; but now that you have come to know God—or rather to be known by God—how can you want to return to the weak and beggarly elemental spirits and be their slaves? ["The Gospel and Culture," p. 79]

Again, this is in essence the same structure of knowing through being known that Plato was pointing toward when he had his Socrates conclude the *Gorgias* with the myth of a Last Judgment. Voegelin comments: "to experience itself permanently in the presence of the judgment . . . is the criterion of the curable soul" (*OH*,

3:45). True knowledge in the existential or epistemic sense is not the holding of opinions but a participation, dependent on the creative divine presence, in the luminosity of being. It does not make the human knower the master of his existence, but requires his submission, in humility, to the divinely grounded structure. To exist consciously in the Between is to recognize that perfection of being lies in the Beyond and that man stands always below it and can turn toward it only through repentance. Judgment and repentance are inherent in the very structure of human existence as a tension toward the Beyond. To refuse them is to attempt to eclipse the tension through *scotosis*, and this is to reject existence itself on the only terms on which it is possible to one whose mode of existence is participation in, rather than identity with, being.

Although the Christian experience of revelation is marked, first in Jesus, then in Paul, John, and others, by a shift in the dynamics of theophany from the seeking at the noetic periphery to the divine drawing at the pneumatic center, "the noetic core . . . ," says Voegelin, "is the same in both Classic Philosophy and the Gospel movement. There is the same field of pull and counter-pull, the same sense of gaining life through following the pull of the golden [c]ord, the same consciousness of existence in an In-Between of human-divine participation, and the same experience of divine reality as the center of action in the movement from question to answer" ("The Gospel and Culture," p. 80). The pneumatic irruption in the Christian case, however, the divine breakthrough that becomes luminous at the center and casts its light over the field as a whole, unfolds fully the directional tendency in reality and the character of the goal that defines it (*OH*, 4:251).

In the Christian experience and its exegesis, moreover, the universality of the divine pole finally becomes clear as it becomes fully differentiated from the elements of the cosmic setting in which it was first embedded. Commenting on the parallel between the "I am" of the *ego eimi* sayings of Jesus in the Gospel according to John and the "I am" of the thornbush episode in Exodus, Voegelin points out the difference in level of differentiation they represent:

The revelation of the "I am" to Moses is still so deeply embedded in the primary experience of the cosmos that it must surround itself with such cosmological symbols as the voice of an intracosmic god of the fathers who speaks from a prodigial thornbush; and it constitutes, not everyman's humanity, but the qualities in Moses that enable him to lead Israel collectively from bondage in a cosmological empire to its freedom under God in history. The "I am" in Jesus, on the other hand, reveals itself as the living presence of the word in a man; it does not intend to establish a people in history but will, for every man who responds to its appeal, dissolve the darkness and absurdity of existence into the luminous consciousness of participating in the divine word. [P. 14][17]

As that luminous experiential reality disentangles itself from the various particular symbols in and through which it manifested its presence—thornbush, Chosen People, prophet, Tables of the Law, and so forth—it reveals its universality as "the true light that illumines every man who comes into this world" (John 1:9). The reality that is discovered and lost in history, and that continues to draw and to reward the faithful seeker, is one—not one truth of opinion to which all must assent but one *aletheia*, one luminosity of being, in which all are invited to dwell and in which all may become one through the *homonoia*, the shared life, luminosity, and love, that unites them.

17. The contrast Voegelin makes here and in other places between Christianity and the Israelite tradition is one to which Jewish thinkers especially might reasonably take exception. It is an important lacuna in Voegelin's coverage of the Western tradition that he has never discussed the Rabbinic Judaism developed after the Second Temple period. Of course, no one scholar can go into every aspect of such a large historical field, and Voegelin explores more of it and with greater analytic penetration than probably any other person, but this particular gap in his inquiry has the unfortunate effect of leaving the religion of Israel illuminated almost exclusively from the angle of Christian reflection. To look at the same historical and textual data from a Rabbinic point of view would open up quite different possibilities of interpretation. It is indicative of this problem that in *Israel and Revelation*, p. 372, Voegelin speaks of the Deuternomic defection into scripturalism and legalism as the major point of demarcation between the history of Israel and that of the Jews. Nowhere has he discussed the Rabbinic tradition expressed in the Talmud and in medieval and modern Jewish writings.

The spiritual revelation that took place in Jesus and in the early Christians was a conscious experiential fullness articulated in symbols that were drawn in part from myth and in part from theoretical philosophy. From the mythic tradition came such symbols as dying and rising, Son of God, divine Incarnation, and so on. From the language of theory came such symbols as *logos*, *aletheia*, and *homonoia*. For the most part, the main burden of articulation and communication in the early period of the Christian movement was borne by symbolism of the mythic type. From Voegelin's point of view this was natural, not only because theoretical conceptualization tends to be a late development but also because by the very nature of the matter a spiritual revelation is more effectively communicated through symbols that speak to the whole human being—to the heart and will as well as the mind. Such communication is not a simple matter of the encoding of information; rather it takes place through a complex process in which recognition of shared spiritual experience is elicited, new existential possibilities of order in the soul are elucidated, and a voluntary response of commitment to these possibilities is invited. The effective communication and the response of the person, on all the levels to which an appeal is made, are simultaneous. For there to be such response at all there must be understanding, but even a very compact understanding will suffice in the beginning.

To the extent, however, that the transcendent God known in the revelation is apprehended as a God of Truth, fidelity to the demands of the revelatory experience will require that faith seek understanding—not only compact understanding but the fullest and most lucid understanding possible. In Christian history, the theological tradition that stemmed from acceptance of this implication of its spiritual experience involved a long process of adapting philosophical symbolism and methods of inquiry. Over a period of time it resulted in a high degree of theoretical articulateness. It also produced a considerable amount of what Voegelin would consider speculation beyond experience—speculation that, as in the case of the numerous millenarian movements Christianity has spawned since its beginnings, could prove dangerous to the "balance of consciousness" and to a realistic appreciation of the fact that human existence, even spiritually regenerated human existence, is always lived in the Between. At its best, however, the theological tradition of Christianity made major contributions, Voegelin believes, to the process in which the content and structure of experiences of transcendence are rendered explicit.

Aquinas's discussion of *fides caritate formata*, faith animated and brought to mature form by love, is an example of such theoretical articulation of spiritual experience. This concept—as well as the experience of divine-human *amicitia*, or mutual love, that it expresses—is for Voegelin the culminating element of what he considers a fully adequate, intellectually and spiritually comprehensive philosophy of history.[18] In the unpublished manuscript on the history of political thought on which Voegelin was working in the 1940s, he said that Hellenic civilization had no parallel to the principle enunciated in 1 John 4:8: "He who does not love, does not know God; for God is love."[19] This is the experiential insight, according to Voegelin, that lies at the root of Christianity as such and at the root of Aquinas's teaching that fully formed, spiritually mature faith is animated from within by the love of God. The amplification of this doctrinal nucleus by Aquinas into a systematic philosophy of man and society, he says, was the medieval climax of the interpenetration of Christianity and Western civilization. This

18. For references to the *Summa Theologica* where Aquinas discusses the concept of *fides formata*, see chapter 8, note 21. A reader wishing to investigate Aquinas's thinking on this subject in detail can find valuable help in the explanatory notes and appendixes to St. Thomas Aquinas, *Summa Theologiae*, vol. 31: *Faith (2a 2ae, 1–7)*, trans. and ed. T. C. O'Brien (New York: McGraw, Hill, 1974).

19. This discussion appears in the manuscript in the section on "Luther and Calvin," which along with other sections on medieval sectarian movements and seventeenth-century Puritanism will soon be published under the editorship of William C. Havard. An even stronger statement of the Johannine conception of the Christian spiritual life as one of divine-human participation may be seen in 1 John 4:16: "God is love; he who dwells in love is dwelling in God, and God in him."

he considers to constitute the standard by which the further course of Western history has to be measured, and in his view that further course has involved the disintegration of the spiritual and doctrinal nucleus of the *amicitia* between God and man to which it gave expression. Luther's counterdoctrine of justification through faith alone (*sola fide*), which explicitly denied the possibility of *fides formata*, Voegelin describes as the first deliberate attack on the doctrine of *amicitia* and a major step in the spiritual disintegration of Christian culture.

To speak of such matters, however, brings us to the subject of the next chapter, which will treat some of the basic patterns of cultural breakdown, on individual and social levels, by which Voegelin believes the existential reality discovered through the openness of the soul has been lost. The present chapter has been concerned with Voegelin's tracing of the historical process in which experiences of transcendence have been reflected upon and symbolized, both in mythic and in theoretical language, and through those symbolisms have been offered as possibilities of existence to anyone able to hear the invitation. This is a process that can be studied historiographically, because sufficient records have been left to make a chronological tracing possible, at least for the Western world, which is the civilizational area with which Voegelin has been principally concerned. It would be seriously misleading, however, if this manner of discussion gave the impression that Voegelin considers Western history to fall into two neat packages—one involving the discovery of reality and the other its loss—as though the business of the ancient world had been exclusively truth and the formation of the soul and that of the modern world exclusively error and deformation. The discovery of existential truth has not been the exclusive accomplishment of Greek philosophers, Israelite prophets, and Christian saints. It is a process that takes place again and again, and ultimately each person must make the discovery for himself. This may be facilitated by the examples of those who went before and by their legacy of symbols, but the reappropriation of those symbols must always be an active process. Spiritual formation is not a gift that can be passively received through cultural transmission, even if each seeker does begin from an existential starting point that has already been shaped, on its human side, by the cultural tradition of his community.[20] Without the divine drawing, there would be no seeking; and without the cultivation of virtuous habits by which the pull of the iron cords of passion and appetite are resisted, there would be no effective sensitivity to the divine drawing. But even where good habit and the pull of the golden cord intersect, the free response of the individual to the possibility of a larger life would still be required, as well as his willingness to pay whatever price of suffering, sacrifice, and self-surrender his own situation might demand of him.

Where enough individuals begin again the search for reality in this way, they can reinforce each other's efforts so that a movement of cultural renewal can take place. This has happened over and over in the course of history. Israel had its moments of heightened spiritual sensitivity scattered among various periods, separated sometimes by centuries. The same was true of Greece, as well as Christian civilization and the modern West.[21] Once following a lecture in which Voegelin had talked extensively about the modern loss of the sense of transcendence and its symbolism, he was asked if there were no positive developments in our own century.[22] He

20. Cf. Gadamer's discussion in *Truth and Method*, pp. 267–74, of "effective-historical consciousness" and the idea of tradition as a sort of moving horizon which carries forward from the past to the present the fundamental questions regarding possible projects of living.

21. In "What Is Political Reality?" Voegelin gives a poignant account of the process by which Albert Camus, for example, worked his way painfully past the alternatives of absurdism and ideological dogmatism to the affirmation that there is no other accomplishment than that of self-transcending love: "there is no fulfillment other than that of love, meaning the renunciation of self and dying to the world. Going on to the end. Disappear. To dissolve oneself in love. It will be the power of love which then creates, rather than myself. To lose oneself. To dismember oneself. To deny oneself in the fulfillment and the passion of truth." Camus, *Carnets* (Paris, 1964), 2: 309–10, quoted in *Anam.*, trans. Niemeyer, p. 171.

22. The conversation took place March 3, 1976, after a lecture at the University of Washington. The questioner was Professor Rodney W. Kilcup.

answered with a long list of philosophical thinkers who he said had made important contributions to the recovery of what had been lost. The list included Husserl, Heidegger, Jaspers, and Bergson. He especially emphasized at that time that with Husserl had come an important turnaround in modern thought, away from dogmatism and the opacity of secondary symbolisms and toward renewed attention to concrete experience. Voegelin's indebtedness to the stream of thought these thinkers represent, as well as his differences from them, were discussed early in the present study. His own rediscovery of existential reality in its experiential fullness has been part of a process of rediscovery that has been under way for some time, but which is still only beginning.

One must hope that it will continue. Whatever cultural benefits this brings, however, the burden of individual search and discovery will always remain. The discovery of reality does not take place once and for all so that it may be looked back upon as an event in the past; it is a continuous process to which all human beings are called. From Voegelin's point of view this is what history in the most proper sense of the word is: a movement into existential truth by way of right order in the soul, the *dikaiosune* (justice or righteousness) of Plato and of the New Testament, and by way of reflective intelligence—an appropriation of reality that is simultaneously moral and theoretical.

CHAPTER 6

The Loss of Reality

JUST as existential reality must constantly be discovered and rediscovered, so also, in the actual course of events, is it constantly being lost. One reason is that the expression of truth takes place in symbols, and symbols require interpretation. The interpreters, however, are not always prepared, morally, intellectually, or spiritually, for the task. As a result, they may attribute new, distorted meanings to the symbols of the philosopher. As Voegelin said regarding the Sophistic misuse of the symbols of pre-Socratic and Platonic philosophy, "In Plato's immediate environment the sophist is the enemy and the philosopher rises in opposition to him; in the wider range of Hellenic history, the philosopher comes first and the sophist follows him as the destroyer of his work through immanentization of the symbols of transcendence" (*OH*, 3:63).[1]

This process can result in what is much more destructive than a simple misunderstanding. It can produce new derivative symbols, secondary and even tertiary, which appear the same as the original, primary symbols and usurp their place. The word "God," for example, may be used to refer to Ockham's supreme entity instead of to Aquinas's *Ipsum Esse*, or the word "transcendence" may be imagined as referring to a movement in space. The secondary symbol can be extremely difficult to expose as such. Even to explain that there are different possibilities of interpretation can be a challenge. For one thing, the philosopher can never be sure what his words will mean in the ears of his "sophisticated" audience. Many in his audience, even if he catches them on the alert so that they understand for a moment, can be counted on to slip back quickly into more familiar

1. See also the chapter on the Sophists, *OH*, 2:267–331.

and more easily imageable meanings. And it is possible that many will never understand at all. The primary symbols express genuine philosophical experience, and their correct interpretation requires parallel experience on the part of the hearer. Experience, however, only becomes philosophical when it is both transcendentally oriented and reflectively conscious, and this is not a universal condition. In the absence of this it is inevitable that the symbol will become disengaged from its original engendering experience and attached to nonphilosophical experiences, such as the perception or imagination of mundane objects and speculation regarding their existence or nonexistence or their possible forms.

To those committed to them, the secondary symbols will come to seem the authentic articulation of truth, which will itself be immanentistically conceived as correctness of opinion regarding a reality known "from without." Philosophy in turn will cease to be a way, or an existential process, as it was for Plato, for example, and will become a subject matter.[2] Voegelin has described the basic pattern of derailment in his chapter on the Sophists in *The World of the Polis*:

> The problem of the mystic-philosopher, as well as his symbols . . . , [is] accepted, while the experience of transcendence, which lies at the root of the problem and motivates the creation of the symbols for its expression, is abandoned. As a consequence, the symbols of transcendence will now be used, or rather misused, in the speculation on immanent problems. A peculiar style of thinking develops that permits men who are no philosophers in the existential sense to express their opinions on problems involving the experience of transcendence with the usurped authority of the existential philosopher. This is the style of the sophistic intellectual. [P. 294]

There are several ways in which immanentizing patterns of interpretation may be said to distort philosophy. One is that, as was

2. Cf. Lewis, *Surprised by Joy*, p. 225: "Once, when he [Dom Bede Griffiths] and [Owen] Barfield were lunching in my room, I happened to refer to philosophy as 'a subject.' 'It wasn't a *subject* to Plato,' said Barfield, 'it was a way.' The quiet but fervent agreement of Griffiths, and the quick glance of understanding between those two, revealed to me my own frivolity."

explained in the third chapter, genuine philosophical knowing is a process in which the experience of human existence and its proper order are explicated from within, whereas philodoxic speculation treats existence as though it were an external object. Another is that such speculation tends to be motivated by a desire for certainty—to know whether the thing speculated about really exists and to know it exactly as it is, in a comprehensive view.

Voegelin's principle that the direction-defining poles of an experience of transcendence must not be hypostatized has been referred to already. Its purpose is to protect philosophical inquiry against both forms of distortion mentioned above. To imagine the transcendent pole, for example, as though it were an entity independent of the experience in which it is known would be to conceive of it as something to be known from without—not in the experience of love, trust, and hope in which it discloses its actual loveliness and worth. If hypostatized it would become simply one more entity among others about whose possible worth and character one might argue even if its existence were granted. If one believed it could really be known with certainty in this externalizing manner, moreover, this would imply a mode of knowledge that does not rely on the mediation of reflective consciousness and its analogical symbols. Ultimately this would imply a conception of man that denies his real situation in the Between and imagines him as situated already in the Beyond, at least in his cognitive capacity.

The claim to absolute knowledge of ultimate reality is the destruction of philosophy as *zetema*, or existential quest—that is, the reflective process in which one enters into the truth of existence as known from within.[3] As a designation for this sort of absolutist claim that attempts to overleap the human condition Voegelin has drawn on Plato's term "eristics," which contrasts with "dialectics," or the manner of inquiry represented in dialogue (see *Philebus* 17a).

---

3. Cf. Jaspers, *Philosophy*, 1:45: "Awakening to myself, in my situation, I raised the question of being. Finding myself in the situation as an indeterminate possibility, I must *search for being* if I want to find my real self. But it is not till I fail in this search for intrinsic being that I begin to philosophize."

Dialectic, says Voegelin, is the activity by which the human being explores his real situation in the Between as viewed from various perspectives and as represented in the interpretive models that express them (*Anam.*, p. 107). Eristic thought, in contrast (the name of which is formed from the Greek word for strife, *eris*), contends that there is only one point of view, its own, and that what it sees from this angle is not in any way a matter of interpretation but the reality itself, known with certainty and stated with finality. Another term Voegelin frequently uses for this sort of claim is "dogmatism."[4] The essence of dogmatism, as he conceives it, is the attempt to arrive at a final answer that will close off the possibility of further questioning. The fundamental stance of eristic thought is defensive, not exploratory. Nothing is more threatening to a dogmatist than openness to further questioning. Eristic, therefore, is the characteristic expression of what Voegelin calls closed existence; dialectic is the expression of open existence.

It should be clear that what is claimed in the eristic or dogmatistic manner is not existential knowledge, or *episteme*, as Voegelin, following Plato in particular, uses the term, but *gnosis*. Even in the classical period there was a tendency for the distinction between *episteme* and *gnosis* to blur, especially when *episteme* was associated with certainty. The association is understandable. Where one's knowledge is grounded in immediate experience, even if this is reflectively mediated in consciousness, one feels a confidence and perhaps even certitude that one cannot feel about objects of speculative opinion. The lover of God is convinced of the divine loveliness, for example, because it is apprehended in the experience of love. Similarly, the experience of actual existence grounds the principle of contradiction. It is only a small step from this to the idea, expressed for example by Aristotle, that *episteme* is knowledge of that which is necessarily so and why (see *Posterior Analytics* 71b8–34). Another

---

4. For Voegelin's discussion of dogmatism, see, for example, *OH*, 3:368–69; "On Readiness to Rational Discussion," p. 280 (translation of "Diskussionsbereitschaft" [1959]); "The Gospel and Culture," pp. 61–66; *Anam.*, pp. 186–88.

symptom of the disintegration of the classical *episteme* and its conversion into *gnosis* may be seen in the dissociation Werner Jaeger notes between Aristotle's conceptions of *phronesis* (practical reasoning) and *sophia* (theoretical understanding). According to Jaeger, Plato had so intimately linked moral insight (*phronesis*) with theoretical knowledge of the Idea of the Good, that it had become virtually synonymous with such terms as *sophia*, *nous*, and *episteme*; and in his earlier writings, such as the *Protrepticus* and the *Eudemian Ethics*, Aristotle had used the term in the same way.[5] By the time he wrote the *Nicomachean Ethics*, however, he was separating theoretical knowledge from the moral insight of the lover of the Good, and treating theory as the knowledge of what is most general as compared with *phronesis*, which inquires into the particular practical case. This is a step toward the interpretation of *episteme* as a neutral knowledge from without, accessible to anyone with the proper intellectual capacity, regardless of his moral condition. The confusion, Voegelin believes, was only incipient in Aristotle, but the claimants to philosophy and knowledge who followed him had aims of their own and were willing to make use of their predecessors in whatever ways would further their pursuit of cognitive and even pragmatic mastery of ultimate reality.

To summarize the underlying issue briefly, *episteme*, in what Voegelin considers the best use of the term, is knowledge of existence from within as ordered by the love of the transcendental *summum bonum*. *Doxa*, on the other hand, is speculation about that which is known from an external perspective. Because *episteme* is grounded in involvement in the existence that is known, it may claim a sort of certainty as compared with *doxa*, which always has the character of a speculative opinion. Its certainty, however, is that of actual experience not certainty about what lies outside experience, and even the certainty it has is limited by the fact of mediation in reflective consciousness. A claim to certainty regarding that which is known from without is a claim to *gnosis*, as is also a claim to be able to

5. *Aristotle: Fundamentals of the History of His Development*, 2d ed., trans. Richard Robinson London: Oxford University Press, 1962), pp. 436–37.

bypass interpretive mediation in the knowledge even of what is known from within. Whether it claims to know from within or from without, *gnosis* claims to be an immediate perception of the real as it is in itself. It also tends to claim to be dependent neither on reasoning ability nor on moral rectitude on the part of the knower, though the gnostic may consider himself the recipient of inspirations from a higher, spiritual source. The possibilities of variation are broad, and gnosticism has manifested itself historically in many forms.

The claim to *gnosis* and to the freedom it would grant from the conditions of *metaxy* existence constitutes, as Voegelin sees it, the basic pattern of philosophical and existential derailment leading to the loss of reality. His study of the history of this loss extends in his various writings from classical to modern times and covers such figures, besides those already mentioned, as Joachim of Fiore, Siger de Brabant, Genghis Khan, Machiavelli, Tamerlane, Thomas More, Voltaire, Helvétius, d'Alembert, Turgot, Condorcet, Hegel, Auguste Comte, John Stuart Mill, de Maistre, Nietzsche, Bakunin, Kropotkin, and Marx. This is far too large a body of material to be studied here in any detail. The basic pattern of Voegelin's analysis, however, can be made clear.

Voegelin is well known for his use of the concept of "gnosticism" in the analysis of modern intellectual, spiritual, and political disorder. His concept is based on the use of the term in the ancient world, but it is broader both in conception and in coverage. This, of course, makes for problems, both philosophical and historical, which are further complicated by the enormous recent expansion of documentary material from the Gnostics of approximately the second to fourth centuries A.D., owing to the discovery of the Coptic Gnostic library at Nag Hammadi in Egypt.[6] In April 1978 a con-

6. The entire collection of Gnostic texts from Nag Hammadi, totaling fifty-two tractates, primarily Christian but including some Hellenic, Jewish, Zoroastrian, and Hermetic material as well, has been published in translation in *The Nag Hammadi Library in English*, ed. James M. Robinson (San Francisco: Harper and Row, 1977). The texts discovered were Coptic translations from Greek originals.

ference was held at Vanderbilt University on "Gnosticism and Modernity," primarily to discuss the application of the term to modern phenomena and Voegelin's use of the term in particular. Voegelin himself participated in the conference and described how he began his inquiry into ancient Gnosticism after writing *Die politischen Religionen* (1938). He realized subsequently that this book's treatment of modern quasi-religious mass movements, such as Nazism and Fascism, as revivals of paganism was inadequate. The reason, he explained, was that paganism was an expression of the "truth of the soul," of open existence in relation to transcendence, while the modern movements were expressions of an attempt to distort reality in a fundamental way. He decided that there must be a more appropriate heuristic concept for their analysis than "paganism." Gnosticism seemed a likely candidate, and he subsequently went to discuss it with such specialists as Hans Jonas and Gilles Quispel.

Ancient Gnosticism, however, strongly tended toward apoliticism, since it denigrated life in this world in favor of escape from it through some sort of secret teaching or *gnosis*. Voegelin's own interest was in the forms that a claim to *gnosis* could take when there was an interest in drawing on the power of such knowledge for the transformation of the present world. He found considerable evidence of the development of immanentistic interpretations of *gnosis* in, for example, the hermetic and magical traditions and speculative constructions of history such as Joachim of Fiore's. The hermeticists, magicians, and alchemists sought a *gnosis* of the secrets of man and nature that would confer power over them. Joachim and those inspired by him looked for the coming of a Third Kingdom of the Spirit in which all Christians would be inspired by the Holy Spirit to the extent that institutional authorities, either secular or churchly, would no longer be required.[7] This kind of speculation

7. For the linkage between Gnosticism and Hermeticism, see the articles by Jean Doresse, "La Gnose" and "L'Hermétisme égyptianisant," *Histoire des religions*, vol. 2, ed. H.-C. Puech (Paris: Gallimard, 1972), pp. 364–497. Two excellent papers on this subject and its relevance for an interpretation of the concept of Gnosticism were presented at the conference on "Gnosticism and Modernity":

has served as historical background for such diverse later developments as Renaissance Humanism and the Enlightenment, Hegel's
theory of the absolute epoch, Auguste Comte's theory of a new age
of Positive Science, Marx's theory of a transformed humanity in a
communist society, and Hitler's dream of a New Order and
Thousand-Year Reich.[8]

The fact that the ancient, classical form of Gnosticism tended
toward rejection of the world rather than its transformation has
made Voegelin's use of the term controversial, and at the conference
just mentioned he said himself that he would probably not use that
term now if he were starting over again, because besides what is
known currently as Gnosticism the pattern of derailment he is
interested in has included many other strands, such as apocalypticism, alchemy, magic, and theurgy, as well as such modern deriva-
tives as scientism and the various developments listed above.[9] The

Stephen A. McKnight, "Gnosticism and Modernity: A Reappraisal," and James
L. Wiser, "From Cultural Analysis to Philosophical Anthropology: An Examination of the Concept of Gnosticism." These and other papers from the conference
are to be published in a volume edited by Richard J. Bishirjian. McKnight
emphasizes the element of discontinuity between Gnosticism and Hermeticism,
however; he points out that Gnosticism was characteristically a transcendentalizing enterprise in which the world is rejected; Hemeticism, in contrast, is primarily oriented toward the production of improved conditions in the world. See his
essay, based in part on his conference paper, "The Renaissance Magus and the
Modern Messiah," *Religious Studies Review*, 5(1979): 86–88. Voegelin has discussed Joachim in many of his writings, but most extensively in *The New Science of
Politics*, pp. 110–13, 119, 126–27, 139, 184.

8. For Voegelin's discussion of these topics, see particularly *The New Science of
Politics*, "More's Utopia," *Österreichische Zeitschrift für öffentliches Recht*, n.s., 3
(1951): 451–68, "On Hegel: A Study in Sorcery," and *From Enlightenment to
Revolution*. Writing on the basis of Voegelin's pattern of analysis, Klaus Vondung, *Magie und Manipulation: Ideologischer Kult und politische Religion des Nationalsozialismus* (Göttingen: Vandenhoeck und Ruprecht, 1971), offers a more detailed
study than Voegelin has himself of the role of magic in the National Socialist
imagination.

9. Cf. an interview with Voegelin, "Philosophies of History," *New Orleans
Review*, 2 (1973): 136. For the view of a historian of religions on the derivation of
the ethos of modern science from ancient magical and alchemical traditions, see
Mircea Eliade, *The Forge and the Crucible: The Origins and Structures of Alchemy* (New
York: Harper and Row, 1962), pp. 172–78.

term is not at all inappropriate, however, as long as one distin-
guishes between it and the ancient movement that bears its name,
since both that transcendentalizing movement and the other immanentizing ones share the common feature of a claim to absolute
knowledge in the form of *gnosis* and to power deriving from that
knowledge. To keep the distinction clear, the name of the ancient
Gnostic movement will be capitalized; the term "gnosticism," uncapitalized, will be used for all movements based on claims to *gnosis*
of any sort.

The fundamental dynamic of gnosticism in any of its forms is
rooted, as Voegelin said at the conference, in the fact that if one
wishes to escape from the tension of existence in the Between, there
are only two ways to do so. One is to seek escape from the world into
the Beyond—as was the case with the ancient Gnostic
movement—and the other is to draw the Beyond in some manner
into the world. The latter can be attempted in various ways. One
may claim cognitive and pragmatic mastery of mundane existence
(in the case of magic and alchemy) or of divine reality (in the case of
theurgy). Or one may claim to have special knowledge of a new age
about to dawn in which oneself and one's followers will play a
leading role. One may also believe oneself chosen by destiny, by
God, or by the "dialectics of history" to be the agent through which
the new age will be brought about. The possible variants, both
theologizing and secularist, are numerous.

Voegelin's analysis of gnostic developments in history may also
seem to be characterized by abrupt leaps between, for example, the
ancient Gnostics and a medieval thinker such as Joachim or between
Joachim and a modern figure such as Marx. There are two reasons
why transitions of this sort seem so abrupt. One is that the scholarly
literature on this subject is already massive, and Voegelin assumes
his readers have some familiarity with it. He does not feel it necessary to spell out all of the links between the thinkers he discusses. In
placing Marx in the tradition of Joachim, for example, he has not
felt obliged to prove that Marx knew of Joachim's thought, because
anyone who has studied Marx can be expected to know that he was

an admirer of Thomas Münzer, the leader of the left wing of the German Reformation, and that Münzer in turn considered himself a follower of Joachim. The pattern of the three ages of history, moreover, has had many manifestations from the time of Joachim to the time that Lessing introduced the idea of a Third Kingdom of enlightened humanity into modern German thought in his *Education of the Human Race* (1780).[10] The recurrence of the pattern would be significant even if Lessing had not known, as in fact he did, that Joachim was the source of this kind of speculation.

Another reason for the seeming abruptness with which Voegelin moves from the gnosticism of one period to that of another is that the writings he has published so far do not represent all the details of his research. When he abandoned the nearly finished history of political thought in the 1940s and went on to write *The New Science of Politics* and *Order and History*, he left tacit many of the steps of transition that he had discussed in the earlier work. That he would not feel like writing all over again such a lengthy historical treatment is understandable, but it is also understandable that many readers would wonder how one gets, as Voegelin does in chapters 4 and 5 of *The New Science of Politics*, from ancient Gnosticism to Joachim of Fiore in the twelfth century and from him to the English Puritans of the seventeenth century. The intermediate steps were covered in the section entitled "The People of God" in the unpublished work. There he showed, step by step, how the ideas of the Puritan sectarians and their claim to be a spiritual elite inspired directly from on high could be seen to derive from gnostic or quasi-gnostic patterns of thought that entered the West by way of the writings of Pseudo-Dionysius, found echoes in the religious thought of the West itself, and were developed further and circulated more widely through the writings of Scotus Erigena. This gnostic stream subsequently inspired various medieval sects, such as

10. For a brief discussion of this document and its influence on some modern literary figures, see Eugene Webb, *The Dark Dove: The Sacred and Secular in Modern Literature* (Seattle and London: University of Washington Press, 1975), pp. 34–36. For the influence of Joachim himself, see pp. 22–24, 34–35, 132–33.

the Albigensians, as well as ecclesiastical reformers such as Joachim, and through him passed into the thought of Boniface VIII in *Unam sanctam* and Dante in the *Convivio* and into the Franciscan Spirituals and various later sects, such as the Ortliebians, Paracletes, and Adamites, and finally into the Puritan enthusiasts of the seventeenth century. The projected publication of this material under the editorship of William Havard will fill in the historical picture considerably.

The gnostic claim may be made in diverse ways. Gnostic thinkers may claim special knowledge through intuitions of an intellectual sort, but their claims may take emotional or volitional forms as well. An emotional gnostic may claim, for example, to grasp truth immediately through feelings in the heart, or a volitional gnostic may claim that his own will is so perfectly attuned to the will of God that whatever he wishes is a revelation of God's will (or history's, etc.). As Voegelin put it in *The New Science of Politics*:

> The attempt at immanentizing the meaning of existence is fundamentally an attempt at bringing our knowledge of transcendence into a firmer grip than the *cognitio fidei*, the cognition of faith, will afford; and Gnostic experiences offer this firmer grip in so far as they are an expansion of the soul to the point where God is drawn into the existence of man. This expansion will engage the various human faculties; and, hence, it is possible to distinguish a range of Gnostic varieties according to the faculty which predominates in the operation of getting this grip on God. Gnosis may be primarily intellectual and assume the form of speculative penetration of the mystery of creation and existence, as, for instance, in the contemplative gnosis of Hegel or Schelling. Or it may be primarily emotional and assume the form of an indwelling of divine substance in the human soul, as, for instance, in paracletic sectarian leaders. Or it may be primarily volitional and assume the form of activist redemption of man and society, as in the instance of revolutionary activists like Comte, Marx, or Hitler [P. 124].

The gnostic may be consciously antireligious, but there is a sense in which the claim to *gnosis* is always a claim to revelation or revelatory experience. Voegelin's own theory of revelation was touched on in the third chapter in connection with the distinction between what he calls the noetic and pneumatic differentiations.[11] Both noetic experience and spiritual experience, as Voegelin understands them, involve revelation—since the seeking is always also a being drawn—but there is a fundamental difference between Voegelin's concept of revelation and the gnostic approach. For Voegelin there is only one form of revelation, and this is an awakening of love for the true and the good, or for the "divine ground." This sort of revelation contains no informational content; rather it stimulates a search for truth that may result in particular judgments, but this is a search that always must take the form of reasonable inquiry. It is discursive not intuitive. Revelation for the gnostic, in contrast, provides particular information about what is the case, what is right, and so on, and does so without the need for critical inquiry. Its judgments are considered above criticism, and the gnostic thinker characteristically refuses to allow further questioning on the subject.

The intellectual gnostic, in essence a philodoxic dogmatist, characteristically attempts to inculcate his ideas in others—by force if necessary. In doing so he gains psychological support for his own beliefs—the illusion that what is uncertain becomes certain if everyone believes it—and the pleasant feeling that he is a benefactor of mankind. The latter, of course, applies whether the members of mankind are willing or unwilling recipients of his benefactions. Resistance on the part of his hearers can even give him the sense of exaltation that accompanies martyrdom for the sake of an "ideal." The reason for the passion that attaches to "ideals" in this way is that the dogmatist, despite his effort to flee from the question to a final, exhaustive, and tension-free answer, does not cease to be human. He does not cease, that is, to be involved in the tension of existence, which, whether it is recognized or not, always has a transcendental dimension. When he turns his attention away from

11. For a further discussion of this topic, see Webb, "Eric Voegelin's Theory of Revelation."

the pole of the beyond toward the immanent *doxa* in his attempt to eclipse mystery, the "tension toward the beyond" nevertheless remains and confers a quasi-transcendental "ideal" status on the object of his belief, "an absolutism of conviction that stems from the transcendental implications of the animating experiences" (*OH*, 3:368).[12] Much of Voegelin's analysis of modern political and intellectual history is a tracing of the dynamics of such misdirected absolutism of the ideal, which a figure as early as Solon (sixth century B.C.) had already recognized as a major source of disorder in human existence.[13]

Gnostic tendencies, in their particular historical embodiments, may manifest themselves in many forms, but there are characteristic features that may be noticed in all of them, and a discussion of the gnostic configuration as such can serve here in place of the detailed discussion of particular forms that Voegelin offers in his historical studies of the modern period from Siger through Marx.

One widely recognized feature of gnosticism is its tendency toward dualism. The ancient Gnosticism is famous for its abhorrence of the world and the flesh, but dualism in a somewhat modified form is characteristic of immanentizing gnosticisms as well. In the latter case, the dualism is not one between this world and a transcendental Beyond but rather between the present world and a new one that is hoped for. Either way the gnostic feels a sense of alienation from his present world and hopes for deliverance from it. The deliverance is to come through the transformation of the aspirant or of his world.

The transformation itself may be imagined as happening in a variety of ways, but frequently it is expected to take place through

12. Cf. 3:82: "An 'ideal' in this sense, however, is precisely what Plato calls a doxa." For the early modern development of the symbolism of "ideals" as a substitute for the realm of transcendental mystery, see "More's Utopia" (1951), pp. 458–60, 463–64, and 467.

13. *OH*, 2:197: "The Doxa is the source of disorder; renunciation of Doxa is the condition of right order, Eunomia. When man overcomes the obsession of his Doxa and fits his action into the unseen measure of the gods, then life in community will become possible. This is the Solonic discovery."

some form of technical manipulation (it is worth remembering that for a gnostic even prayer can be manipulative) based on the special knowledge given in the *gnosis*. From this point of view there is little or no need for moral preparation for the transformation. As is well known, the Manichean Gnostics with whom Augustine was involved in his youth believed it made no difference what immoralities one practiced with the body, since the flesh was evil under any circumstances and was to be left behind entirely when one finally gained salvation. At the other extreme of the chronological scale there is Bakunin's or Kropotkin's insistence that the present generation is so corrupted by the old world that if it tried to prepare for change by any means other than sheer destruction, it would contaminate the new world; the transformation of man is to take place not by gradual moral reformation but by the magical effect of the experience of total revolution and the orgy of destruction it will involve (see *From Enlightenment to Revolution*, pp. 218–19, 228–32).

Because the *gnosis* of the gnostic visionary is special information possessed only by the few, not the universal tension of existence or love of God in which all are involved whether they realize it consciously or not, gnostic movements tend to divide mankind into an elite (the knowers and masters of technique) and the masses, the nonknowers, who at best can be followers of those who know.

Depending on whether the particular gnostic configuration is contemplative or activist in form, the elite leaders may have as their role withdrawal into contemplation and ascetic practices (as in the case of the medieval Cathari) or the active inauguration of the New Age (as in the case of more recent mass movements such as Communism and National Socialism). The activist effort frequently takes the form of what in "The People of God" Voegelin has called "eschatological violence," an attempt to force the wheel of history to turn by deeds that violate ordinary morality but which are considered to be beyond good and evil because they will secure the transition from a world of iniquity to a world of light. Even sheer destructiveness and terrorism are interpreted from this point of view as the manifestation of divine or at least superhuman energies working through man—the breaking in of the New Age.

These, at any rate, are the basic features of the gnostic pattern of thought. They may vary in particular manifestation, and some features will be emphasized in some places and times and deemphasized in others, but the basic pattern remains the same. All of the features tend to be present at least to some degree, because they are linked logically by their connection to the conception of knowledge as *gnosis* and the conception of man that goes with this.[14] The opposite of *gnosis* is the *episteme* of the philosopher, as Voegelin understands this term, or the *cognitio fidei* of the religious faithful. The former has been studied at length already. The latter has been discussed more briefly, but it will be one of the principal subjects of the following chapter.

14. Although Voegelin's discussion of *gnosis* and gnosticism concentrates on Western manifestations, there are also Eastern versions of gnosticism as well. An example of a controversy in Asian thought regarding the basic issue whether human wisdom could aspire to *gnosis* may be seen in the incident known as the Council of Lhasa, which took place in the eighth century A.D. The controversy was between Chinese Ch'an monks, represented by Hsüan-tsang, and Indian monks represented by Kamalaśila, over whether the *jnana* (the Sanskrit cognate of *gnosis*) gained through Ch'an meditation took place through pure intuition and conferred infallibility or whether reason played a necessary role in the Buddhist approach to liberating understanding. The Chinese denied that there could be a structured, rational approach to *jnana* and claimed that it came in a sudden illumination not caused in any way by the mental processes preceding it. It amounted to a leap to intuitive ultimate knowledge, and the one who possessed that knowledge was supposed to be beyond criticism—with regard either to his cognitive claims or his moral conduct. The Indian counterclaim was that one could approach the ultimate insight possible to man, which they called *prajna* (a combination of intellectual insight and the insight that can be gained through meditation), by gradual stages involving the study of philosophical texts such as those of Nagarjuna. Hsüan-tsang and Kamalaśila are supposed to have debated these issues formally. The resolution of the controversy at the council was of considerable political as well as religious and philosophical importance for the subsequent history of Buddhism in Tibet. See Paul Demiéville, *Le Concile de Lhasa* (Paris: Imprimerie nationale de France, 1952). I am indebted for information regarding this controversy to Dr. William Stablein and Mr. Christopher Wilkinson.

PART 3

EXODUS

History and Transcendence

CHAPTER 7

The Philosophy of Religion

"Sir," the woman said, "you have no bucket and this well is deep.
How can you give me 'living water'? Are you a greater man than
Jacob our ancestor, who gave us the well, and drank from it himself,
he and his sons, and his cattle too?"   John 4:11–12

THE only cure for a radically gnostic interpretation of the universe,
Voegelin has said, is "to drop gnosis and return to the original
sources of order in the soul, that is to the experiences of faith" (*From
Enlightenment to Revolution*, p. 275, n. 7). It is appropriate to consider Voegelin's philosophy of religion after the discussion of gnosticism and the loss of reality, because on the level of society as a
whole—not just the small section of society constituted by
philosophers—religion is the positive counterpart of the gnostic
movements. It is in the religious dimension of society that the
ordering experience of the love of God is effectively communicated
and the invitation to the truth of existence is issued. It is also
appropriate to consider Voegelin's philosophy of religion near the
end of this study of his thought in general, because, as he said in his
essay on Toynbee (1961), at a certain point in the process of his own
existential *zetema*, the philosopher of history comes to realize that
there is a sense in which history proper is the history of religion
("Toynbee's History as a Search for Truth," p. 191). History in the
full sense, that is, is a movement toward a transcendent goal that is
known with the greatest adequacy possible to man in the ordering
experiences of trust, hope, and love and in the life these constitute
and the symbols they engender.

The concept of faith, it is true, may be corrupted into that of a

211

nonrational intellectual certainty—that is to say, into a claim to *gnosis*—but according to Voegelin this is not what it has been for the authentic mainstream of religious tradition, and his analysis is borne out both by the evidence of a sense of the analogical character of religious symbols on the part of ancient peoples, as discussed in the second chapter, and by the explicit theological teaching of so widely respected a spokesman for Christian religious thought as Aquinas. When Voegelin says in *The New Science of Politics* (p. 122), "Uncertainty is the very essence of Christianity," he is consciously echoing Aquinas, who said that "imperfect knowledge belongs to the very notion of faith, for it is included in its definition, faith being defined as *the substance of things to be hoped for, the evidence of things that appear not* (Heb. 11:1)." [1] One of the finest formulations of the problem of faith, says Voegelin, is that of Aristotle discussing the mystery religions in his work *On Prayer*: "Those who are being initiated are not required to grasp anything with the understanding [*mathein*], but to have a certain inner experience [or passion, *pathein*], and so to be put into a particular frame of mind, presuming that they are capable of the frame of mind in the first place." [2] Voegelin goes on to comment on this that "the *cognitio Dei* through faith is not a cognitive act in which an object is given, but a cognitive, spiritual passion of the soul," in which the ground of

1. Aquinas, *ST*, Ia–IIae, q. 67, a. 3. Voegelin refers in his footnote to q. 4, a. 1. See also *Science, Politics, and Gnosticism*, p. 108. On Aquinas's conception of the relation between thought and belief, see T. C. O'Brien, "'Sacra Doctrina' Revisited: The Context of Medieval Education," *The Thomist*, 41 (1977):498: "The affirmation here of a *doctrina*—a logic in that sense—comes out of an understanding of belief. That act is not a logic, not a discursive discipline, even though St. Thomas does like to compare a believer's attitude towards God with that of pupil to master. But belief in itself is simple assent, a cleaving to God Himself as He attests the truths of salvation. The assent is accompanied, however, by thought, by pondering: *cum assensione cogitatio*; it is a movement of mind not yet fulfilled by vision. The personal cleaving to God, belief in its essence, prompts many human responses: the Cathedral of Chartres, the paintings of Fra Angelico, the music of Bach, the poetry of the liturgy. And, in St. Thomas's view, thinking."

2. Aristotle, *On Prayer*, quoted in *OH*, 3:275, from a translation by Werner Jaeger, *Aristotle*, p. 160.

being is experienced (*OH*, 3:275). It is experienced, that is, as the goal of the soul's love and as the force that draws it in its striving. When faith is conceived of in such ways as these, it is the precise opposite of *gnosis*, and a steadfast commitment to it can preserve the balance of consciousness by counteracting the all too human desire for perfect knowledge.

Unfortunately this balance is difficult to maintain, and so religion, for many, slips almost inevitably into dogmatism. The danger of such derailment is compounded, according to Voegelin, by the fact that none of the spiritual irruptions which in the ancient world gave rise to the great religions and to philosophy ever managed to work out "a fully balanced symbolization of order that would cover the whole area of man's existence in society and history" (*OH*, 4:301). "The human responses to the divine irruptions," he says, "rather tend to accentuate different aspects of the one truth of man's existence under God." Then there is the fact that to be communicated the experience of existential truth must be formulated in propositions, which may be misinterpreted as representing *doxai* about objects beyond experience. In technical theological expression this problem is further aggravated by the tendency of abstract language to become dissociated from its experiential roots: "For the more abstract the language of the tension becomes, the more liable is its user to forget that the language is part of the divine-human encounter in which man's tension toward the ground becomes luminous to itself" (p. 39). At its most authentic, religious language is not simply description of religious experience, but is that experience itself in articulate form in consciousness. This is "the idea-word . . . , living and with a soul, of which the written word justly is called no more than an image," spoken of by Plato's Phaedrus (*Phaedrus* 276a, quoted in *OH*, 3:19). Religious language, however, cannot always be used and understood at its most authentic, because it has the responsibility of bearing the living truth from generation to generation and from higher existential levels to lower. "The emergence of a language of truth," says Voegelin, "is part of the mystery of a truth that constitutes history by revealing itself. However, the hierophantic event that engenders the language passes with the man who has been graced by it, while the language remains in the world. When it enters history, truth has to carry the burden of death and time; and in the hands of lesser thinkers, who are sensitive to the truth in a measure but are not able to reactivate the engendering experience fully, the surviving truth of the language can acquire a status independent of the originating reality. The truth of reality living in the symbols can be deformed into a doctrinal truth about reality" (*OH*, 4:39).

In a world in which people are at different stages in the ascent to existence in truth—whether because the divine drawing works on them with different degrees of force or because they differ in maturity of experience—it is inevitable that religious language will be taken by some to express doxic speculations. Some followers of a religious tradition, moreover, may be expected to cling deliberately to that level of interpretation, perhaps because they are apprehensive about the possibly elitist claims of those with more spiritual insight or perhaps because it seems to them that the "subjectivity" of religious experience might threaten the objectivity of the God whose honor they uphold.

These are not entirely reprehensible motivations from Voegelin's point of view. Dogmatism, he has said, may have "the civilizational purpose and effect of protecting an historically achieved state of insight against the disintegrative pressures to which the differentiated truth of existence is exposed in the spiritual and intellectual turmoil of the ecumenic situation" (pp. 43–44).[3] It was to deal

3. For some other references by Voegelin to the positive value of doctrinal formulations, see *OH*, 1:359; "Liberalism and Its History," *Review of Politics*, 37(1974): 515; and "Toynbee's History as a Search for Truth," pp. 196–97. Cf. Gadamer, *Philosophical Hermeneutics*, p. 17: "Genuine speaking, which has something to say and hence does not give prearranged signals, but rather seeks words through which one reaches the other person, is the universal human task—but it is a special task for the theologian, to whom is commissioned the saying-further (*Weitersagen*) of a message that stands written." In an unpublished lecture delivered at the University of Washington, March 3, 1976, Voegelin suggested that dogmatism originates as a resistance to the corruption of genuine religious insights.

with the needs of just such a situation, he points out, that Cicero developed the older Latin term *religio* "into the symbol that comprehends protectively both the truth of existence and its expression through cultic observance and doctrine" (p. 44).

Dogma is a dangerous remedy, however, and it is for this reason that Voegelin often seems to have so ambiguous an attitude toward religion.[4] Religion is not just any process of spiritual movement into increased participation in existential truth, but an organized, socially mediated process involving individuals on many levels of moral, intellectual, and spiritual preparedness. It necessarily involves symbolizations, including doctrinal formulations, appropriate for those on the lowest as well as the highest levels. If it did not, it would not fulfill its function as the carrier of truth to all who need it. But this means also that it necessarily carries implicit within it not merely a possibility but an active tendency toward deformation into doxic speculation. Voegelin recognizes the need for religion and for doctrine, but he writes as much against their dangers as in defense of their importance.

The danger of dogma is that once the need for it is accepted, one may seek to find a perfect doctrinal formulation that will express truth in its fullness with final validity. If this temptation is succumbed to, the necessary and beneficial dogmatics of religion will degenerate into dogmatism, which was defined in the preceding chapter as the attempt to arrive at a final answer that will close off the possibility of further questioning. The worst harm that can follow from this is the distortion of authentic human existence that can take place through the loss of the fundamental movement of questioning, in which, as Voegelin has said, "man's experience of his tension . . . toward the divine ground breaks forth in the word of enquiry as a prayer for the Word of the answer" ("The Gospel and Culture," p. 62). The answer to the existential question, the tension of existence, is not an item of information about an

4. Cf. *OH*, 1:376: "it looks as if in Deuteronomy we were touching the genesis of 'religion,' defined as the transformation of existence in historical form into the secondary possession of a 'creed' concerning the relation between God and man."

external object, according to Voegelin's way of thinking, but a symbol articulating the experienced transcendental pole of the tension itself, and it has no proper meaning apart from the experience it expresses.

This existential deformation is the worst of the dangers of dogmatism, but there are others as well. The attempt to fix the expression of truth at one point of formulation can cause the loss of the meaning even of that formula, since later generations will approach it from the point of view of their own conceptual language, and where perfect and eternal validity is claimed the changes in language are likely not to be noticed. The result will be that each generation will read its own meanings into the formula while believing it is perfectly faithful to "the truth once delivered to the saints." And of course there will be no idea that that truth was ever anything but doxic.

Thoughtful theologians have become aware of this problem. A medieval thinker like Aquinas had little sense of history and the importance of historical context for interpretation, but those who think in his tradition in the twentieth century now take account of it. Bernard Lonergan, for example, makes a distinction for precisely this reason between what he calls "dogmatic theology" and "doctrinal theology." "Dogmatic theology," he says, "is classicist. It tends to take it for granted that on each issue there is one and only one true proposition. . . . In contrast, doctrinal theology is historically-minded. It knows that the meaning of a proposition becomes determinate only within a context" and that contexts vary with time, the differentiations of human consciousness, and so on (*Method in Theology*, p. 333).

What is more serious still, the hermeneutic problem is not simply a matter of language and concept. It also has to do with the substantive existence articulated in the symbols. The most dangerous social effect of dogmatism, warns Voegelin, may be the loss of both existential truth and cultural substance: "If it be forgotten that the answer of the construct depends for its truth on the understanding of existence that has motivated it; if it be erected into an idol valid for all time; its effect will be the very opposite of protection. For the sensed, if not clearly known, invalidity of the symbol at a later point in history will be extended by the critics of the symbol to the truth nevertheless contained in it. An obsolete symbol may have the effect of destroying the order of existence it was created to protect" ("On Debate and Existence," p. 147).

In connection with this, there is the problem, of course, of distinguishing between those symbols that are genuinely obsolete and those that only appear so because their original meanings have been lost through the process Voegelin refers to as "deculturation."[5] Much of Voegelin's study of historical symbols has been an effort to make such distinctions and to establish the basis for them. The central criterion is that of the symbols' ability to function adequately in existential elucidation. Deculturation involves the loss of personal ability for this, and where this takes place the symbol will inevitably be misused if it continues to be used at all. Its recovery will in turn restore vitality to the symbols. It may happen, however, that an advance in the differentiation of consciousness may render the continuing use of a symbol problematic. A symbol such as the Promised Land, for example, or that of the promise of progeny to Abraham, which originally served well in the articulation of an experience of transcendence, may later become an impediment to such experience unless it is transformed into what amounts to a new symbol through radical reinterpretation. This is precisely what happened, according to Voegelin, when the Promised Land symbol and that of the Kingdom later became interpreted

5. It should be explained that Voegelin uses the term "culture" not, as many now do, to refer to the artifacts, customs, and literary remnants of a society but to refer to the process of spiritual formation through which the members of a society are oriented toward the true and the good. In this, Voegelin follows the Greek use of the term *paideia*, of which *cultura* became the Latin translation. Deculturation, according to Voegelin, takes place both on the level of society and that of the individual as the ordering experiences are lost and the symbols that expressed them become corrupted accordingly. For Voegelin's discussion of deculturation, see, for example, *From Enlightenment to Revolution*, p. 233; "The Gospel and Culture," pp. 74–75; "Immortality," p. 238; "More's Utopia," p. 468; and "On Paradise and Revolution," *Southern Review*, n.s., 7 (1971):27–29.

in eschatological terms and when the symbol of the People of God came to be interpreted as referring not to a particular ethnic group but to the universal spiritual calling of humanity (see *OH*, 1:343). Some symbols, such as these, are capable of such transformation, so that it is only the earlier compact meaning that becomes obsolete. Others are not, and to attempt to return to them, at least for those who have really advanced beyond them, would be a degeneration. The cosmological symbols of ancient Near Eastern religion, for example, became displaced as a result of the spiritual advances made by Judaism, Christianity, and Islam. As Voegelin says in the introduction to *The Ecumenic Age*, "Only when man has become conscious of divine reality as moving his humanity, not through its presence in the cosmos, but through a presence reaching into his soul from the Beyond, can his response become luminous as the immortalizing countermovement toward the Beyond" (*OH*, 4:16–17). This last can be gained only by the differentiation between divine ground and cosmos, and a retrogression to compact cosmological symbolism would involve its loss.

These, then, are the dimensions of the problem of doctrine as seen from the point of view of one who, like Voegelin, recognizes not only the importance of dogma and of religion in Cicero's sense but also their perils. Perhaps the best way to outline a solution to this problem congruent with Voegelin's general approach to the philosophy of religion would be to draw once again on Polanyi's useful distinction between focal and subsidiary awareness. As was discussed in the second chapter, Polanyi considers language to function well when focal attention is not on the linguistic expressions themselves but on what they intend. The same principle would apply to doctrinal formulations of religious meaning. Doctrine, from this point of view, belongs in subsidiary awareness; in proportion as it becomes an object of focal awareness it becomes opaque and ceases to perform its mediating role between the faithful and the divine reality they intend. Or to put it another way, faith may be directed toward or focused on different points. One may focus one's trust on God as He is in Himself, on His mysterious and ultimately ineffable reality, or one may focus it on the dogmatic formulation. Ideally, faith is an act of self-transcendence, which is the case when the focus is God Himself. But to direct one's faith toward the divine reality—focusing in the direction of what can be no object at all for human consciousness—is arduous and requires considerable spiritual maturity.

When the focus is a doctrinal statement, there are two possibilities—one destructive of the spiritual life and one essential to it. It is this that makes the issue so complicated. In placing one's trust in a doctrine, one may, for example, be making the object of faith one's own knowledge as formulated in the doctrine. The result in such a case will be not self-transcendence but self-inflation—faith not in the mysterious reality of God but in one's own *gnosis* of God. Or, in the case of what we have seen Aquinas speak of as *fides informis*, faith as doctrinal assent, one may trust a spiritual tradition based on and leading toward genuine self-transcendence. Any beginner in the religious life must in fact go through a stage in which *fides informis* is his principal mode of knowledge of things divine—simply because he is a beginner. And even when he gains maturity of spiritual experience and begins to understand the traditional doctrines from within, as it were, so that they become subsidiary to the experienced truth that shines through them, he will continue to live at least in part on the level of one who does not understand all the potential meaning of the symbol. The doctrine will become, one might say, not perfectly transparent but only translucent. As long as one continues to live in the Between, and from Voegelin's point of view there is no escaping it, there will always be symbols mediating existential truth for the human knower. In the experience of mature religious faith, moreover, in *fides formata*, the highest knowledge that is possible is not a *gnosis* but self-transcending love. Even the greatest saint lives not simply on the highest level of *faith vitalized by love* but between unformed and perfected faith, so that dogmatic symbols are always needed to direct one's attention beyond the level of existential penetration of truth that one has already spiritually reached.

For this reason, despite his reservations about the present state of the churches and his distrust of dogma as used in them, Voegelin is not an anti-institutional thinker. As he said at the end of his discussion of Heraclitus in *The World of the Polis*, there will always be differences of existential level among human beings: "And in order to make this hierarchical structure effective in social practice, institutions will be required for continuing and transmitting spiritual insights, as well as the intellectual culture that is necessary for their exposition and communication, through the generations, and for mediating them to the many [through] processes of education appropriate to their receptiveness" (*OH*, 2:240). Despite their dangers, the authority of religious institutions and the dogmas they use in the mediation of their truth will remain the indispensable means by which those who lack maturity of spiritual experience and understanding may be led to higher levels.

In this process the dogma should function in the manner of a lens—to focus the attention of the faithful not on the dogma itself but beyond. In traditional theological discussion the distinction between apophatic and cataphatic theology is a strategy for insuring this. Cataphatic theology proceeds by affirmations of positive qualities attributed to God, as when one says God is just, loving, and so on. Apophatic theology goes on from the initial affirmations to deny that these qualities attributed to God may involve any of the kinds of limitation they must take on in human understanding.[6] Again it is a matter, as was discussed in the second chapter, of analogy. A dogmatic formulation functions properly as long as its analogical character remains clear so that it can focus one's attention through the analogy toward the mystery it shadows forth. In the ordering experience of *fides caritate formata*, Voegelin would say, the love itself, the *caritas*, becomes a focusing device directing one's atten-

6. For a discussion of the history of the development of the distinction between negative or apophatic theology and affirmative or cataphatic theology, see Jaroslav Pelikan, *The Christian Tradition: A History of the Development of Doctrine*, 3 vols. to date (Chicago: University of Chicago Press, 1971–), 1:347–48, and 2:30–32, 54–55, 258–59, 264–70. For Aquinas's discussion of this issue, see his treatise on "The Names of God," *ST*, I, q. 13.

tion toward the deepest, or highest, level of reality—the divine love in which the humanly experienced tension of existence is an analogical participation. The theologian's dogma, for Voegelin, becomes, like the philosopher's myth, an invitation to participate in a truth that is not propositional but existential—not a formula but a life.

Unfortunately, believes Voegelin, at the present time "the deforming doctrinalization has become socially stronger than the experiential insights it was originally meant to protect" (*OH*, 4:58). This is why his own attitude toward religion in general and toward Christianity in particular is a divided one, a matter which often perplexes his Christian critics.[7]

Although his works touch at least briefly on a fairly wide range of religious traditions, including Judaism, Islam, and Hinduism, the religion on which his discussion has tended to center is Christianity, which he considers to have articulated more fully than any other the differentiation of consciousness toward which both the noetic and pneumatic theophanies of the ancient world were ultimately directed.[8] He ended his *Israel and Revelation* with an indication that the fulfillment of the mysteries the Israelite prophets were exploring

7. The question whether Voegelin's thought is or is not compatible with orthodox Christianity has been one of the principal preoccupations of Voegelin's critics. For a sampling of comparatively recent articles dealing with this theme, see Thomas J. J. Altizer, "A New History and a New but Ancient God?" *Journal of the American Academy of Religion*, 43 (1975):757–64; Bruce Douglass, "A Diminished Gospel: A Critique of Voegelin's Interpretation of Christianity," in Stephen A. McKnight, ed., *Eric Voegelin's Search for Order in History* (Baton Rouge: Louisiana State University Press, 1978), pp. 139–54; John A. Gueguen, "Voegelin's *From Enlightenment to Revolution:* A Review Article," *The Thomist*, 42 (1978): 123–34; John Hallowell, "Existence in Tension: Man in Search of His Humanity," *Political Science Reviewer*, 2 (1972): 181–84 (reprinted in the McKnight book); Gerhart Niemeyer, "Eric Voegelin's Philosophy and the Drama of Mankind," *Modern Age*, 20 (1976): 28–39; and Frederick D. Wilhelmsen, "The New Voegelin," review of *The Ecumenic Age, Triumph*, January 1975, pp. 32–35.

8. Voegelin discusses Muslim thought briefly in *OH*, 4:142–45, and *Science, Politics, and Gnosticism*, pp. 113–14; and Hinduism in *OH*, 4:319–22. He does not discuss Rabbinic Judaism at all, but limits his treatment of Judaism to what he considers the Deuteronomic defection into legalism, *OH*, 1:372, 376; see above, chapter 5, note 17.

would be unfolded in the "good news about Jesus" (*OH*, 1:515). And in *The New Science of Politics* he described "the appearance of Christ . . . the revelation of the Logos in history" as the acme of a giant cycle overarching the cycles of the single civilizations, ancient and modern (p. 164).

That Voegelin associates himself personally with the Christian tradition, moreover, is indicated by the way he speaks of the contrast between his own way of thinking and that of such thinkers as Condorcet and Turgot as one between the "Christian humanist" on the one hand and positivist intellectuals on the other (*From Enlightenment to Revolution*, p. 133). And when he said of Toynbee's recognition of the importance of religion in history that "sooner or later, when engaged in a study of this kind, he would have to confess himself either an existentialist of the nihilistic variety, or a philosopher and Christian," it must have been clear to him that this observation would apply to himself as well ("Toynbee's History as a Search for Truth," p. 190). In fact his critique of Toynbee is implicitly as much a description of Voegelin's own positive conception of the philosopher of history as it is a set of criticisms of Toynbee himself. The last of those particular criticisms seems especially significant for Voegelin's understanding of his own relation to the Christian religion. Speaking of Toynbee's belief that "his knowledge as an historian had not only shown that all attempts to formulate spiritual truth in intellectual terms had ended in failure, but convinced him that the feat could not be accomplished at all," Voegelin describes this as the symptom of "a dilettantism with regard to questions of reason and revelation, philosophy and religion, metaphysics and theology, intuition and science, as well as communication, that could easily be overcome by anybody who wanted to overcome it" (pp. 196–97).

That Voegelin himself finds such questions problematic may make him seem to some readers virtually an agnostic, but this statement makes it clear, as much of the present study should also have, that this suspicion is unfounded. Awareness of problems does not make a philosopher a skeptic; rather it is a sign of the serious-ness of his interest in truth. Nor is Voegelin's attitude toward Christianity one of intellectual detachment. That he does not be-lieve philosophy is a detached activity devoid of spiritual commit-ment should also be clear by now, but his further observation on Toynbee's "unwillingness to complete the *zetema* in spite of a clear knowledge of what its end would have to be" can serve to underscore this point: "The situation on the level of overt argument points to the more deeply seated difficulty that Toynbee is sensitive to the word of God insofar as it has become historically tangible in dogma-tic symbols and ecclesiastic institutions, but that he does not hear the word as spoken to him personally" (pp. 197–98).

By itself this way of speaking would appear to make the question of Voegelin's Christianity a simple one, and it would probably not be inferring too much to say that Voegelin acknowledges himself "a philosopher and Christian," specifically a "Christian humanist," and that he considers himself to hear the word of God and to respond to it personally. The question is not nearly so simple, however. Many of Voegelin's critics, including Gerhart Niemeyer, who translated and edited the English *Anamnesis*, have expressed serious reservations about Voegelin's understanding of Christianity. In his review of *The Ecumenic Age* Niemeyer criticized Voegelin particularly for the way he sets aside the question of the uniqueness of the Christian revelation and of the Incarnation in Jesus. He even went so far as to say, "It seems that this once Voegelin has ap-proached a great spiritual reality from a standpoint extraneous to it."[9] Also there is the fact that Voegelin is not a regular participant in the liturgical life of any Christian communion.

For this last there are biographical reasons. Voegelin was born of a Lutheran father and a Roman Catholic mother and was raised in the Lutheran church. His own experiences with the church, both

9. Niemeyer, "Eric Voegelin's Philosophy and the Drama of Mankind," p. 35.

Protestant and Catholic, however, have been traumatic.[10] To understand Voegelin and his concerns as a philosopher, political scientist, and historian, and also as a religious man it is always necessary to remember his historical circumstances. Just as his steadfast opposition to gnostic thinking in all of its manifestations derives from his own experience of the threat of death and the reality of exile at the hands of the Hitlerian corruption of the gnostic, apocalyptic, and magical streams that have flowed into our own century out of antiquity and the Middle Ages, so also his coolness toward the institutional expressions of Christianity derives from disappointing experiences with its representatives. In his case this was not a matter of a few dogmatistic or manipulative pastors, but was massive in scale. He speaks in conversation of how in Vienna in the 1930s all of the clergy he knew except one were Nazis, and his contacts with clergy in Eastern and Western Europe since the war seem to him to indicate a similarly opportunistic attitude on their part toward the communist powers.

Voegelin has not written his criticisms of the churches, and this is not the place to speak in detail of what those criticisms might be if he wrote them, but even a devoted Christian, if he is honest and responsible in his loyalty to Christianity's essence, must acknowledge that Christian institutions and their official representatives have hardly presented an inspiring spectacle in the twentieth century. The modern tendency to interpret Christianity as a system of doctrines, moreover, has led to the near eclipse of the spiritual, mystical side of Christianity, which is what Voegelin considers its essential core. This is a problem, moreover, that is not just recent,

10. One may gain a sense of the type of Christian teaching to which Voegelin was probably exposed in his youth by considering Karl Jaspers's description of his Lutheran confirmation class in "Philosophical Autobiography," p. 76: "The instruction given to those to be confirmed was a joke to us and ridiculous (the pastor gave the geography of hell, told with grotesque phantasy that the Pope goes daily into the Castle of Angels in order to touch the heaped-up gold, asserted that the fact that the stars did not collide proved God's guidance, that we would be saved by the fact that Christ was nailed to the cross, etc.)"

but one which Voegelin sees running through at least the last five centuries or so:

> The crack in the precarious balance of a Christian order becomes unmistakable in the high Middle Ages, with the ominous bifurcation of faith and fideism in the parallel movements of Mysticism and Nominalism. In the sixteenth century, a Christianity that has become doctrinaire explodes in the wars of religion; and their devastations, both physical and moral, arouse wave after wave of disgust with dogmatism, be it theological or metaphysical. . . . And with the seventeenth century begins the incredible spectaculum of modernity—both fascinating and nauseating, grandiose and vulgar, exhilarating and depressing, tragic and grotesque— . . . with its ideological dogmas piled on top of the ecclesiastic and sectarian ones and its resistant scepticism that throws them all equally on the garbage heap of opinion. ["Immortality," p. 238][11]

Much of the history of Christianity, in other words, seems to Voegelin the history of its derailment from what it might have been and from what it perhaps still could be, but is unlikely to be. As Voegelin said in *The Ecumenic Age*, "a history constituted by the noetic and pneumatic theophanies of a Plato and Paul can advance to the further differentiations of mysticism and, correspondingly, tolerance in dogmatic matters" (*OH*, 4:261). But in the actual course of events it has not done so. Voegelin's assessment of Christianity in its historical embodiment might well be summed up as follows: the spiritual substance of Christianity is the very bread of life, but those who bear it are unworthy of it and tend all too often to lose sight of it, offering stones in place of bread. And this is not just a matter of the clergy and clerical vested interests; all of the faithful who corrupt the spiritual truth of existence into opinion share in the failure of the Christian religion.

11. Cf. *Science, Politics, and Gnosticism*, p. 109, on the idea that the social success of Christianity by the time of the High Middle Ages made faith vulnerable because great masses could not endure the thin thread of certitude offered through *cognitio fidei* and began to look for greater certainty from arguments and doctrines.

Even if one accepts Voegelin's criticisms of the historical Christian religion as it has taken shape—and an honest Christian must acknowledge that there is truth to them—Voegelin's response is not the only one possible to a reasonable and responsible person who faces the question whether to practice his religious fidelity inside or outside the institutional church. But one who chooses to remain within the church should also recognize that Voegelin's own decision is not an impossible one either. Various forms of responsible religious practice are possible, and the choice of one is a decision that each must make for himself.

From all of this it would seem that an interpreter who wished to put together an argument to the effect that Voegelin is not a Christian would be able to find as much evidence for his position as one who argued the opposite. The resolution of this apparent dilemma, however, cannot best be found by settling for one side or the other, but by refining the question. The most penetrating question is not whether Voegelin is a Christian or not but what is the shape of his particular variety of Christian thought—for that his thought is Christian in at least some sense seems incontestable. Those of his critics who have attacked his treatment of Christianity have in effect been arguing not that Voegelin is not a Christian at all but that he is not a Christian by their standards. And he would agree. Their argument is really that he is not an orthodox Christian, but there have been unorthodox Christians from the beginning, and there must be all the more when orthodoxy progressively narrows itself through doctrinization.

Another pertinent question about Voegelin's Christianity is: in what ways is he more or less traditional or orthodox in his interpretation of Christianity than are many of the prominent figures in modern theology? That question is too large, of course, to be taken up in any detail here, since it would involve a survey of many other thinkers and an attempt to define the limits of their orthodoxy as much as his. A few observations, however, might at least be interesting, even if they must remain rather fragmentary. First, though, it will be necessary to consider briefly the question of the nature of orthodoxy as such.

The matter of what "orthodoxy" refers to in Christian usage is complicated by the fact that the term is used rather differently, or at least with different emphases, in the Eastern and Western sections of Christendom. The word *doxa* in Greek not only means "opinion" or "particular judgment," as has been discussed already, but it also means "glory," "splendor," and "praise." The Western Church has tended to emphasize the idea of opinion or doctrine in connection with the term, so that it is interpreted primarily as meaning "right opinion" on doctrinal matters. The Eastern Church, on the other hand, has emphasized the idea of divine glory and praise of that glory, so that for the Eastern Orthodox the term has tended to mean not only right opinion but even more "right praising."[12] Voegelin has not discussed Eastern Orthodox theology, but in many ways he would probably find it more congenial than the Western tradition with which he has been in tension, especially since the Eastern Church has preserved more of the tradition of Plato than has the Western on the whole and has always put more emphasis on the mystical side of Christianity. The present discussion, however, can be simplified by focusing only on the Western use, since it is the form of Christianity that has mainly concerned Voegelin.

Even when orthodoxy is interpreted as a matter of right doctrine, it is still necessary to determine what this means. One possible interpretation would be that orthodoxy is made up of a set of exhaustive formulations of religious truth and of faithful adherence to these. The reasons orthodoxy, when interpreted in this manner, would be antithetical to Voegelin's way of thinking should be

12. For discussion of this issue from an Eastern Orthodox point of view, see Nicolas Zernov in *The Concise Encyclopedia of Living Faiths*, ed. R. C. Zaehner (London: Hutchinson, 1977), pp. 83–84. Zernov says: "It is significant that 'Orthodoxy' is translated in all Slavonic languages by the word *Pravoslavie* which means 'right praise,' the purely doctrinal element being thereby eliminated. 'Orthodoxy' is translated in a similar fashion into Arabic and other oriental languages."

sufficiently clear already; this would reduce truth from existence to proposition, and the claim that the propositions are exhaustive would be gnostic in character. It is possible, however, to interpret orthodoxy not as a set of exhaustive formulations but as a framework of constant symbolizations within which theology, as the effort to understand reflectively the content of the faith they express, can take place. Interpreted in such a way, orthodoxy would not be incompatible with Voegelin's philosophical principles, but could be seen as the practice of fidelity to existential truth mediated by historical symbols. In fact, in this sense Voegelin's entire enterprise as a philosopher of history might be described as an orthodoxy, just as it is also orthodox in the sense of the practice of right praising both of the divine reality and of its adequate symbolic expressions.

To solve the problem of Voegelin's orthodoxy as simply as this, however, would be too easy; it would bypass the question of the extent to which Voegelin's own thinking on basic Christian notions corresponds to or differs from the credal definitions that for many Christians serve as the standard of orthodoxy in the doctrinal sense. To do so, moreover, would also be to lose the potentially important challenge offered to the theologian by Voegelin's interpretations of basic Christian concepts. Something the professed adherent of credal orthodoxy can sometimes forget is that dogmas do not have simple and obvious meanings: they have to be interpreted. They are the analogical expressions of inexhaustible mysteries. The difficulty with a purely doxic conception of dogma is that it overlooks the analogical use of language in doctrinal formulas and presupposes that it is possible to know precisely what the doctrines mean. Voegelin's own approach to Christian doctrine is epistemic, in the sense of this term as it was discussed in the third chapter. This means that in approaching Christian doctrine Voegelin seeks to understand it as an explication of existential experience and to do so systematically, in a manner consistent with what he believes to be sound philosophical principles. To the orthodox Christian, Voegelin offers a challenge that can serve as a stimulus to greater intellectual penetration of the mysteries of faith and to more adequate articulation of the meanings of the doctrines to which he is loyal.

To readers not familiar with twentieth-century theological discussion it might seem that divergencies between Voegelin's and more standard Christian thinking would lie in questions of the miraculous and of the historical accuracy of the Biblical accounts of the life, death, and resurrection of Jesus. Voegelin does, after all, speak of the "Pauline myth" of the risen Christ, and he says that modern debates regarding demythization and the "'historicity' of Christ" derive from the destruction of "consciousness of analogical truth" through the "'historization' of the myth" (*OH*, 4:250, 113; see also pp. 265–66). It is necessary to remember, however, that Voegelin's use of the term "myth" is not that of a positivist; by "myth" he does not mean a false account of purported matters of fact. What he means is a true account of existential reality as known epistemically, or from within. He makes this issue quite explicit in his discussion of the controversy between Bossuet and Voltaire:

> The mythical language was, at the time of its original employment, the precise instrument for expressing the irruption of transcendent reality, its incarnation and its operation in man. In the age of Christ and the centuries of early Christianity, this language was not a "myth" but the exact terminology for the designation of religious phenomena. It has become a "myth" as a consequence of the penetration of our world by a rationalism which destroys the transcendental meanings of symbols taken from the world of the senses. In the course of this "de-divinization" (*Entgötterung*) of the world, sensual symbols have lost their transparency for transcendental reality; they have become opaque and are no longer revelatory of the immersion of the finite world in the transcendent. Christianity has become historized in the sense that a universe of symbols that belongs to the age of the myth is seen in the perspective of categories which belong to an age of rationalism. In this perspective only, when symbols and dogmas are seen in a "literal," disenchanted opaqueness from the outside, do they acquire the "irrationality" which brings them into conflict with logic, with biology, history, etc. [*From Enlightenment to Revolution*, p. 21]

From Voegelin's point of view, the controversy—which was really an eighteenth- and nineteenth-century one—between those who attacked the historicity of miracles and those who defended them was merely a symptom of the fact that both opponents and defendants had come to accept an externalizing, doxic framework of discussion.

The territory of dispute has since shifted considerably. By far the greater number of the prominent figures in twentieth-century theology—including, for example, Rudolf Bultmann, Paul Tillich, Karl Barth, Emil Brunner, and Reinhold Niebuhr—have in their various ways accepted the positivist critique of miracles, and many have gone some distance toward separating the symbolism of the Christian story from history altogether.[13] Voegelin, in comparison, takes the historicity of Jesus and the divine Incarnation very seriously, as the earlier quotation from *The New Science of Politics* indicated. If one wishes to find a modern reduction of Jesus to a disincarnate symbol, one can find much better evidence of it in such thinkers as Tillich or Bultmann. According to Voegelin, "tearing the drama of participation asunder into the biography of a Jesus in the spatio-temporal world and eternal verities showered from beyond would make nonsense of the existential reality that was experienced and symbolized as the drama of the Son of God" ("The Gospel and Culture," p. 90).[14] A Gospel, he says, "is neither a poet's work of dramatic art, nor an historian's biography of Jesus, but the symbolization of a divine movement that went through the person of Jesus into society and history" (p. 92). It is neither a humanly created symbol, that is, nor a positivistic description of external events; rather it is the expression of a concrete experience of tran-

13. See the chapter, "Disengagement from History," in Alan Richardson, *History: Sacred and Profane* (Philadelphia: Westminster Press, 1964), pp. 125–53, for a discussion of each of these figures in this respect. Richardson excepts Niebuhr, however, from the general pattern (p. 127, n. 1).

14. It is precisely this sort of separation between factual history of the sort investigated by historians and a suprahistorical realm of meaning that Richardson finds in Tillich, Brunner, Barth, and Bultmann. See *History: Sacred and Profane*, pp. 133–39.

scendence that originated in Jesus and that he enabled his disciples
to share in.

To speak in this manner is clearly to speak of divine presence as
incarnate in the fullest possible sense in the historical person, Jesus
of Nazareth. The doctrine of Incarnation is the center of orthodox
Christian theology, and the question of Voegelin's relation to that
tradition can be addressed most economically by discussing his
conception of this doctrine. It should come as no surprise that
Voegelin is critical of the doctrinal formulations of the principle of
Incarnation. In *Israel and Revelation* he says, "With the appearance of
Jesus, God himself entered into the eternal present of history," and
adds that "the mystery of the Incarnation itself, of the consubstantiality of God and man, is impenetrable"; but he says further, in criticism
of traditional dogmas, that its meaning for history "is as far from
satisfactory positive expression today as it was at the time of Jesus and
his generation" (*OH*, 1:345, text and n. 19).[15] Still, he has also
spoken more favorably of orthodox formulations in other places and
has discussed their interpretation in the light of his understanding
of man and man's relation to the divine.

At the heart of his interpretation of Christian doctrine is Voegelin's fundamental belief that man must not be hypostatized into a
purely intramundane, immanent entity. An interpretation of the
doctrine of Incarnation that began from such assumptions would be
entirely inadequate from his point of view. Since he considers the
tradition of metaphysics that has played so prominent a role in
theology to be just such an immanentizing, if Voegelin were to
address himself to theological debate, he would probably say that

15. One may compare Voegelin's way of speaking in criticism of Christian
dogmatic formulations with that of such an eminent theologian as Reinhold
Niebuhr, *The Nature and Destiny of Man: A Christian Interpretation*, 2 vols. (London: Nisbet, 1941–43), 2:62: "When Greek thought seeks to express the idea
that 'God was in Christ' and made Himself known in history in the Incarnation,
it tries to state this truth in metaphysical terms. This means in effect that an
ultimate truth, transcending all human wisdom and apprehended by faith, is
transmuted into a truth of human wisdom and incorporated into a metaphysical
system."

much interpretation of the doctrine of Incarnation has been distorted by a tendency of that sort. In particular he would be critical of the common tendency to interpret divine presence as something unique in Jesus and absent from other human beings.[16] His own way of thinking, as has been shown, is quite the opposite. The interpretation of man through Plato's symbol of the *metaxy* is central to Voegelin's thought, and when he does discuss specific Christian doctrines, he draws on that symbol for their explication.

Also fundamental to his approach, of course, is the assumption that the Christian doctrines, insofar as they are genuinely meaningful, express actual experience—both that of Jesus presumably and that of those who formulated the doctrines. They are not mere ideas or doxic speculations for Voegelin, even if they may have been that for some Christian interpreters. Nor are they expressions of the experience of Jesus alone, because if they were they could not communicate effectively to others. They would be uninterpretable in principle. Paul's discussion of the revelation of the Son of God in him (Gal. 1:16), according to Voegelin, articulated "his experience of the God who enters him through the vision and by this act of entering transfigures him"—even if the formulators of dogma in the fourth and fifth centuries inverted the Platonic procedure of using a likely myth and reinterpreted the Pauline myth of the Son of God in pseudophilosophical terms using "the philosophically secondary, semihypostatic language of 'natures'" (*OH*, 4:256, 267). When Voegelin discusses the classic dogmas of the later period, therefore, he assumes that they refer back to the experience of someone, such as Paul, even if they give it a rather indirect expression. It is also possible, although Voegelin does not discuss this, that despite their hypostatizing language the Fathers of Nicaea and Chalcedon may have known in their own lives the experiences in question.

16. For a more detailed discussion of this point with special reference to Aquinas's speculations that in addition to the graces of sanctification he shares with other human beings, Jesus must be supposed to have a special *gratia unionis* (grace of union) to explain his uniqueness, see Webb, "Eric Voegelin's Theory of Revelation," pp. 118–21.

Voegelin's most direct discussion of a Christian dogma is in "Immortality: Experience and Symbol" regarding the Chalcedonian Definition of the Faith. The Council of Chalcedon, which culminated the process of formulation of doctrine that began in Nicaea in 325, met in 451 to settle the questions raised by Apollinaris and Eutyches. The earlier councils had decided that God and Man were united in Jesus, but they had left the manner of the union sufficiently open that further disputes arose. Apollinaris suggested that in Jesus the divine Logos replaced what in other human beings was the rational soul or mind. This made the Incarnation merely the presence of a divine mind in a human body, a condition unique to him. This was not considered adequate to the principle that the divine Son "had to be made like these brothers of his in every way" (Heb. 2:17). Nor was the suggestion of Eutyches "that our Lord was of two natures before the union, but after the union one nature" (divine only).[17] The Definition of Chalcedon itself was that there were two natures, divine and human, united in the one person of Jesus. Voegelin says of this formulation: "This valiant attempt of the Patres to express the two-in-one reality of God's participation in man, without either compromising the separateness of the two or splitting the one, concerns the same structure of intermediate reality, of the *metaxy*, the philosopher encounters when he analyses man's consciousness of participation in the divine ground of his existence. The reality of the Mediator and the intermediate reality of consciousness have the same structure" ("Immortality," p. 263; cf. *OH*, 1:474). This is to say that Incarnation and *metaxy* are, in Voegelin's terms, "equivalent symbols," as he immediately goes on to say.

This means, of course, that from Voegelin's point of view the Incarnation is not something that takes place exclusively in Jesus, but is the same mystery of divine-human participation in which all human beings are involved—to the extent that they actually rise to their potential humanity. "Transfiguring incarnation . . . ,"

17. "The Admissions of Eutyches," in Henry Bettenson, ed., *Documents of the Christian Church*, 2d ed. (London: Oxford University Press, 1963), p. 69.

Voegelin says, "does not begin with Christ, as Paul assumed, but becomes conscious through Christ and Paul's vision as the eschatological *telos* of the transfiguring process that goes on in history before and after Christ and constitutes its meaning" (*OH*, 4:270). In fact it is the universality of divine-human participation or Incarnation, although it may vary in degree, that makes the symbolism of Incarnation in Jesus intelligible for those to whom it speaks. As he said in "The Gospel and Culture" (speaking of Peter's recognition of Jesus as Son of God in Matthew 16:16 and the statement by Jesus in John 6:44 that "no man can come to me unless he is drawn by the Father who sent me"), "nobody can recognize the movement of divine presence in the Son, unless he is prepared for such recognition by the presence of the divine Father in himself. The divine Sonship is not revealed through an [*sic*] information tendered by Jesus, but through a man's response to the full presence in Jesus of the same Unknown God by whose presence he is inchoatively moved in his own existence" (p. 91).

The term "inchoatively" here is essential to Voegelin's meaning, as is also the reference to Incarnation as the "eschatological *telos*" of history. To an uncareful reader it might sound as if Voegelin's theory of the Incarnation puts all human beings on a single level with Jesus, which would indeed be a considerable departure from Christian orthodoxy. Voegelin, however, has no such intention. The mystery of divine-human participation is realized in different degrees by different people depending on the divine drawing and on the willingness of the individual to dwell in the truth of existence rather than in an illusory Second Reality.[18] It is a matter, in other

18. It is perhaps worth reminding the reader that fundamental to Voegelin's thought is the principle that the divine drawing (in theological terms "grace") and the human seeking are one and the same movement of the soul. From this point of view, it is not that the divine drawing is given first, then accepted or rejected by a detached receiver. Rather the two movements are simultaneous, but with the human seeking dependent on the attractive power of the good that is sought. Voegelin respects the integrity as well as the mysteriousness of human freedom, but there is neither Pelagianism nor Molinism in his conception of man's dependence on divine grace.

words, of openness of existence as compared with existential closure, of willingness to surrender to the love of God, the tension of existence, or of pulling back from it. Perfect openness of existence, however, lies beyond the ordinary human being, who is as much between existential openness and closure as between the other poles of the *metaxy*. This is why Voegelin speaks of it as eschatological. It is the supposition of the Christian, and Voegelin shares this supposition, that in Jesus there was perfect existential openness and a fullness of divine-human participation that was unique among men. The symbolism of Incarnation, he says, expresses "the experience, with a date in history, of God reaching into Man and revealing Him as the Presence that is the flow of presence from the beginning of the world to its end" ("Immortality," p. 263).

This means, Voegelin goes on to say, that "history is Christ written large," and because Incarnation and *metaxy* are equivalent symbols, "this last formulation is not in conflict with the Platonic 'Man written large.'" To be truly human, in other words, is not something given as the presence of a static "nature"; rather individuals participate to varying degrees in the perfect humanity that is realized fully in Jesus, and they do so to the extent that through the drawing of divine grace they become like him.[19] It is precisely this movement toward fullness of divine-human participation, toward Christ, that constitutes what Voegelin considers to be history in the true sense of the word.

This philosophy of man and of history is not at all incompatible with Christian orthodoxy. Voegelin's interpretation of man as in movement toward Christ, in whom his potential humanity is fully actualized even as it is raised to transfiguration in the divine glory, is in fact in fundamental harmony with that of Aquinas in his article, "Whether Christ Is the Head of All Men?" to which Voegelin refers:

19. Cf. *OH*, 4:305: "Universal mankind is an eschatological index." On Aristotle's conception of the problem of potential versus actual humanity, see *OH*, 3:363–64, 367. On the relation between this theme and Voegelin's conception of the Incarnation, see Webb, "Eric Voegelin's Theory of Revelation," pp. 118–20.

We must therefore consider the members of the mystical body not only as they are in act, but as they are in potency. Nevertheless, some are in potency who will never be reduced to act, and some are reduced at some time to act; and this according to three degrees, of which the first is by faith, the second by the charity of this life, the third by the fruition of the life to come.

Hence we must say that if we take the whole time of the world in general, Christ is the Head of all men, but according to different degrees. For, first and principally, He is the Head of such as are actually united to Him by glory; secondly, of those who are actually united to Him by charity; thirdly, of those who are actually united to Him by faith; fourthly, of those who are united to Him merely in potency, which is not yet reduced to act . . . fifthly, of those who are united to Him in potency, which will never be reduced to act.[20]

The movement into fullness of divine-human participation involves, as was said, a choice of openness of existence. Its threshold, for Voegelin as for Aquinas, is faith, because the openness that must be chosen is openness to the pain of love. Without a basic trust in the power and graciousness of transcendent Being—the trust that the deepest longings of the soul will find their fulfillment as man's life is perfected through grace in death—no one could have the courage to surrender the protective shield of cultivated illusions with which fallen man in closed existence insulates his heart. This basic trust opens up the heart so that the depths of longing in it can be consciously suffered. This is man's exodus both into the reality of the soul's life and into the divine reality beyond it. Faith is the means of entry into love, which is a life lived in fidelity to the ordering tension of existence that leads beyond the world. It is this life, of surrender to the love of God conferred on man by divine grace, that for Voegelin constitutes existentially the truth of history and its order.

20. *ST*, III, q. 8, a. 3. The text of "Immortality," p. 262, incorrectly refers to this article as *ST*, III, q. 8, a. 2.

CHAPTER 8

The Philosophy of History

> . . . the flux of existence does not have the structure of order or, for
> that matter, of disorder, but the structure of a tension between truth
> and deformation of reality.
>
> Voegelin, "Equivalences of Experience and
> Symbolization in History" (p. 220)

THE central challenge for a philosophy of history, in Voegelin's
view, and the point where most founder, is that of maintaining the
balance that is required for open existence in the field of existential
tensions.[1] This involves a balance between the claims that the immanent and transcendent dimensions of human experience make on
the human being who lives "between" them. What the term
"philosophy of history" is commonly taken to mean—from a
philodoxic point of view—is an immanentist speculation on the
structure of history that claims to be able to define its dynamics and
their necessary workings and thereby to predict the pattern in which
it will inevitably unfold and disclose its final meaning. Hegel and
Marx are probably the most prominent exemplars of this approach,
and Voegelin has commented on their thought at length.[2] It should

1. Voegelin calls this the "postulate of balance"; See *OH*, 4:228.
2. On Hegel, see "On Hegel: A Study in Sorcery." For a dissenting interpretation of Hegel by a political philosopher generally very sympathetic to Voegelin's
way of thinking, see Germino, "Two Conceptions of Political Philosophy," in
The Post-Behavioral Era, pp. 243–57. On Marx, see *From Enlightenment to Revolution*, pp. 240–302. Both also figure prominently in *Science, Politics, and Gnosticism*. Other philosophers of history whom Voegelin discusses in various places—
and who represent from his point of view a wide range of degrees of adequacy and
distortion—include Herodotus, Thucydides, Polybius, Ssu-ma Ch'ien, Augustine, Joachim of Fiore, Voltaire, Condorcet, Turgot, Schelling, Comte,
Burckhardt, Nietzsche, Collingwood, Spengler, Bergson, Jaspers, Rudolf
Bultmann, Ernst Cassirer, Hannah Arendt, and Arnold Toynbee.

not be necessary here, however, to go into the details of his criticism of this kind of philosophy of history; an understanding of the basic principles of his thought makes clear from the start that any attempt to interpret human existence in time as an immanent enterprise with an inevitable and fully knowable meaning is the expression of a failure to recognize its character as a movement in the *metaxy*, the field of tensions "between" Man and God, time and eternity, opacity and luminosity, imperfection and perfection of being. For man to have an immanent structure of the sort that could ground such a philosophy of history he would have to be already a completed being, at least in the sense of having a determinate, knowable essence or nature.

It is the nature of man, however, to have no nature of this sort. This is not a paradox; it is simply a matter of clarity in the use of the term "nature" as applied to man. Man's nature, as Voegelin, along with the classical philosophers, has analyzed it, is existence in the Between. It is a process, a quest, a struggle for truth and for order. It cannot be definitively grasped as an object of *doxa*, but can be known only existentially—through experiential involvement in its mystery. *Metaxy* existence is not a phenomenal datum: "Life is not given . . . ," says Voegelin, "life to be gained requires the cooperation of man" (*Anam.*, p. 105).[3] It is the nature of man to be in the position of having to make this cooperative response to the attraction of the experiential pole that represents perfection of being; it is the very essence of humanity to be always "on the way" to completeness.

Just as the history of philosophy, according to Voegelin, is largely the history of its derailment, so also is that of the philosophy of history. The study of particular derailments in the thought of individual thinkers is less interesting than an analysis of the various

3. Cf. Mircea Eliade, writing on the experience of human existence as represented in widely recurrent patterns of religious symbolism, in *The Sacred and the Profane: The Nature of Religion*, trans. Willard R. Trask (New York: Harcourt, Brace, 1959), p. 100: "Religious man is not *given*; he *makes* himself, by approaching the divine models."

kinds of derailment that are possible. These fall into two general patterns: the immanentizing and the transcendentalizing. Both involve either the eclipse of the experience of *metaxy* existence or a deliberate refusal to accept its conditions.

The basic form of the transcendentalizing mode of derailment is represented particularly clearly by the Gnostic movement of the early centuries of the Christian era, though it is a pattern of experience and symbolization that is perennial. Voegelin traces it back at least as far as the First Intermediate Period of Egyptian history.[4] Its motivating experience is a mood of alienation. This mood may develop at any time, because it is rooted in the very structure of existence itself as an especially acute sense of one's distance from perfect being: "The symbol 'alienation' is meant to express a feeling of estrangement from existence in time because it estranges us from the timeless: we are alienated from the world in which we live when we sense it to be the cause of our alienation from the world to which we truly belong; we become strangers in the world when it compels conformity to a deficient mode of existence that would estrange us from existence in truth" ("Immortality," p. 268). As it first develops—for example, in the Egyptian case studied in "Immortality"—the alienation from disordered mundane existence may be the beginning of a quest for true order, and it can aim ultimately not at flight from the world but at the attunement of the world's order to the order of divinely grounded being. When the hope for such attunement is sufficiently thwarted, however, by the resistance of disordered existence, then the world can seem permanently cut off from the possibility of true life. In such circumstances the tension of existence takes on a negative character, because it comes to seem not a movement toward the Beyond but a static condition in which the longing for transcendental perfection will

4. For a discussion of this pattern as represented in the anonymous text, "Dispute of a Man, Who Contemplates Suicide, with His Soul," dating from ca. 2000 B.C., see "Immortality: Experience and Symbol," passim. There is a discussion of the development of Hellenistic Gnosticism as an analogous pattern on p. 270.

always remain frustrated. This is a common enough situation, and it need not always lead to the transcendentalizing form of derailment; any way out of the tension will do. In Gnostic-transcendentalizing, however, the escape sought is a leap out of the *metaxy* into the Beyond, which is imagined as man's "true home," his own original mode of being, from which he has "fallen"—for one elaborately mythicized reason or another—into the "world."

It is clear that the Gnostic sense of alienation grows out of the same structure in experience that, in the case of properly differentiated consciousness, gives rise to the distinction between world and being. The difference, according to Voegelin, is that in the Gnostic case the differentiation of consciousness is not fully carried through, to the point that the tension itself and its inherent directional tendency would become visible; rather the level of imagination that has to think in terms of "things" seizes on the experience and casts it in a hypostatizing mold: "the symbols of alienation are recognizable as hypostases of the poles of existential tension. The 'world' we discern in the perspective of our existence to partake of both time and the timeless is dissociated, under the pressure of the mood, into 'this world' of existence in time and the 'other world' of the timeless; and as we 'exist' in neither the one nor the other of these worlds but in the tension between time and the timeless, the dissociation of the 'world' transforms us into 'strangers' to either one of the hypostatized worlds" (p. 269).

Ironically, what begins in this way as a flight from the experience of frustrated existential tension tends to exacerbate the frustration by legitimizing and thereby reinforcing the mood of alienation and by establishing a framework in which there can be no real homeward movement, because the poles of the tension have become isolated from one another. "When the luminosity of noetic consciousness is deformed," says Voegelin, "into an 'anthropology' of intramundane man and a 'theology' of a transmundane God," or, for that matter, into the *gnosis* of a transmundane original Manhood, "the theophanic event will be destroyed, and with it . . . the experience of participation" (*OH*, 4:313).

Any refusal to acknowledge the tension of existence and its

character as a condition in which the immanent and transcendent poles of the tension meet in the humanity that is constituted by its participation in them will preclude the experiential knowledge of divine presence in which alone the deepest longings of the human soul can find their fulfillment. This is true whether the denial operates in a transcendentalizing or an immanentizing manner. The result is that the tension which could be experienced as a joyful movement of theophany becomes either a state of anxiety, in which one fears inevitable frustration, or of ennui, in which the tension is buried in unconsciousness and reduced to a dull ache and a sense of directionlessness. Various writings of Voegelin's have traced these developments from classical to modern times.[5] It is a matter, as he describes it, of existential health or disease—the soul's openness to its own experience or its perverse attempt to close itself off in voluntary ignorance—and of the tonality, joyful or anxious, that this gives to the tension:

> The health or disease of existence makes itself felt in the very tonality of the unrest. The classic, especially the Aristotelian [referring to *Metaphysics* 1072b–1073b], unrest is distinctly joyful because the questioning has direction; the unrest is experienced as the beginning of the theophanic event in which the *nous* reveals itself as the divine ordering force in the *psyche* of the questioner and the cosmos at large; it is an invitation to pursue its meaning into the actualization of noetic consciousness. There is no term for "anxiety"; the tonality of being scared or frightened by a question to which no answer can be found is characteristically absent from the classic experience; the "scare" had to be introduced by the Stoics [Voegelin cites Chrysippus (third century B.C.) and Cicero], as a pathological phenomenon, through the adjective *ptoiodes* [fearful]. In the modern Western history of unrest, on the contrary, from the Hobbesian "fear of death" to Heidegger's *Angst*, the tonality has shifted from joyful participation in a theophany to the *Agnoia ptoiodes* [fearful ignorance], to the hostile alienation from a reality that rather hides than reveals itself. [*Anam.*, p. 10]

5. See particularly "Reason," "On Hegel," and *From Enlightenment to Revolution*, esp. pp. 53–73.

Voegelin goes on in the same passage to speak of Hegel, Marx, Freud, Sartre, Claude Lévi-Strauss, and Samuel Beckett.

Perhaps because of the prestige of the sciences of physical nature and the widespread modern skepticism about metaphysical reality, the transcendentalizing versions of flight from historical existence in the *metaxy* have generally been less popular in the modern age than the immanentizing. Of the persons mentioned above, probably only Samuel Beckett would closely fit the pattern of Gnosticism represented by the Valentinians, Sethians, Manichaeans, and other groups in late antiquity, and he would qualify not because of his hypostatizing affirmation of a transcendental realm of true being but because of the negativity of his depiction of man's life in the world. For obvious reasons a transcendentalizing version of the flight from the tension of existence is currently more easily found among theologians—on varying levels of sophistication.

One case—a sophisticated one—that Voegelin has discussed in detail is that of Rudolf Bultmann.[6] According to Voegelin's analysis, the heart of Bultmann's thinking on history is to be found in the pronouncedly Gnostic character he gave to the existentialism he adapted from Heidegger. This, says Voegelin, shows up particularly in his denial of the relevance of the Old Testament and the

6. Voegelin has devoted one entire essay to Bultmann: "History and Gnosis," in *The Old Testament and Christian Faith*, ed. Bernhard W. Anderson (New York: Herder and Herder, 1969), pp. 64–89. He also discusses him more briefly in *OH*, 4:311–12 (in connection with Bultmann's debate with Karl Jaspers in *The Question of Demythologizing*), and p. 326. There is a large body of scholarship on Bultmann; for a sympathetic, but not uncritical basic exposition of Bultmann, with emphasis on his links to Heidegger, see John Macquarrie, *An Existentialist Theology: A Comparison of Heidegger and Bultmann* (London: SCM Press, 1955). For treatments of Bultmann specifically as a philosopher of history, see Richardson, *History: Sacred and Profane*, pp. 139–47; and Langdon Gilkey, *Reaping the Whirlwind: A Christian Interpretation of History* (New York: Seabury Press, 1976), pp. 220–26. Since Bultmann is highly regarded as a New Testament scholar, it is perhaps worth mentioning that Voegelin considers his writings to be indispensable for the study of the New Testament, even though he is very critical of Bultmann for the way he considers him to uproot the Israelite and Christian symbols from historical experience—both the experience of ancient Israel and that of the historical individual, Jesus of Nazareth.

history of Israel generally for Christian thought, except insofar as it represents the "Law" from which Christian existence is supposed to be free—with "Law" interpreted not as the expression in Israelite experience of the divine drawing (what Plato called *helkein*), and the appeal that this makes for human cooperative response, but as an immanentist "natural" mode of existence, what Bultmann refers to as "unbelieving existence in freedom." The reason for Bultmann's rejection of Israelite historical experience is that for him the Christian faith is essentially a movement out of history that takes place in the believer's personal encounter with Christ in the present: "the Now receives eschatological character through the encounter with Christ, because in this encounter the world and history come to their end and the believer as a new creature is *entweltlicht* [unworlded]."[7]

The fundamental issue in the controversy between Voegelin and Bultmann has to do with the principle that *helkein* and *zetesis*, the divine drawing from the transcendental pole and the human seeking from the immanent pole, are not different movements but one and the same movement of the soul. Bultmann, according to Voegelin's reading, is tempted to deny the irreducibly paradoxical structure of the tension of existence and to dissolve the tension by disvaluing the human seeking. Voegelin's argument is, in essence, that in what Bultmann calls eschatological encounter the world and history do not come to an end, but in fact manifest their true nature as dimensions of a concrete movement of transcendence, which always takes place under conditions of finitude.

Bultmann's interpretation of the New Testament, says Voegelin, is not adequate to the text, because it is based on an existentialist conception of man much narrower than the Biblical one. Ironically, says Voegelin, this existentialism takes its name from the denial of validity to everything but the moment of a man's flight from actual existence in the Between toward an eschatological future in which man will escape from temporal incarnation. "Historicity," in

7. Bultmann, "Geschichte und Eschatologie im Neuen Testament," *Glauben und Verstehen*, vol. 3 (1960), quoted by Voegelin, in his own trans., "History and Gnosis," p. 79. English trans., E. Kraft, *New Testament Studies*, 1 (1954):5–16.

Bultmann's usage, becomes revised into a term designating the mode of existence of one who becomes *entweltlicht* of both world and history, and "history" is termed "profane" to indicate its lack of reality and value.

This is not to say, however, that Bultmann's reading of early Christian thought is entirely fallacious. In fact the New Testament reflects a sense of estrangement in the world that to some extent parallels the modern experience of alienation from which the existentialist trend has originated. The hermeneutical failure, according to Voegelin, lies in concentrating on that one aspect of the concern to which the historical texts give expression and ignoring others. A distortion is founded on a partial truth, and that is an important source of its appeal. "A good deal of the fascination Heidegger's work holds for the unwary," says Voegelin, "is due to the subtle blending of truth presented with conviction and untruth through omission" ("History and Gnosis," p. 65). A gnostic thinker, he says, has special appeal in troubled times like our own, because under conditions of chronic disorder it becomes so easy to feel that not only the world as we know it but the world as such is alien. The core of Bultmann's thinking is not an "objective" appraisal either of historical documents or of the human situation, says Voegelin, but "a gnostic existentialism that wills the annihilation of nature and history" (p. 88). What is in question is not, ultimately, the accuracy of an interpretation of existence, but a choice, a project of existence, and "against the existentialist will no argument is possible" (p. 89). This, by the way, is an excellent example of what Voegelin considers to be overlooked by the doxographic "history of ideas"; ideas may function not as representations of reality or even as imitations of earlier ideas but as symbols of existential projects.

From Voegelin's point of view, Bultmann is actually one of the more insightful philosophers of history among those he selects for detailed criticism, because his thought was founded on sensitivity to the experiential tension of existence. Most who begin to reflect on the meaning of history show comparatively little direct awareness of the tension, but tend to objectify its dynamism in an immanentist manner as a force moving mankind toward some form of mundane fulfillment. The central problem of the philosophy of history is to maintain a sense of the balance between the transcendental and immanent dimensions of man and his life in time. When this balance is lost sight of, then one may fail, as Voegelin considers Bultmann to do, to take seriously the fact that man is essentially incarnate, treating him as though he were really a spirit waiting for delivery from his fleshly prison so that he may return to his true home in a hypostatized Beyond. Or one may treat man as though he were an entirely natural entity devoid of spirit and essential freedom and governed by laws that need only to be discovered and mastered for an enlightened planner to be able to manipulate him effectively for his own good and for that of society— as defined, of course, by the manipulator.

The latter version of derailment—the immanentizing kind—is, as was said, the more popular in the modern period, but it also has had a long history. Because an immanentist philosophy of history at least takes the world and society seriously as problems, its representatives tend to be interested especially in organization. Broadly speaking, this organizing effort takes two forms. One appeals to an internal principle of order within the individual and attempts to evoke this through institutional arrangements. The other attempts to impose a pattern of organization by physical coercion. To speak of these, however, is to speak of ideal types. Certain historical movements have corresponded to them approximately, but in specific instances there is always the possibility of mixing the types or of veering at some point from one to the other. Voegelin has discussed extensively two historical movements that exemplify these ideal types, even if not always consistently: liberalism and ecumenic imperialism. Each has, at times, passed over into the other form. The liberal planner tends to begin with optimistic expectations about the innate goodness of man. But when men disappoint him, he can be tempted to coerce them. The world conqueror, on the other hand, may wish not only to be feared by his subjects but also to be loved, and when his efforts at coercion no longer seem fully effective, he can even be found making appeals to their loyalty and sense of responsibility. Both, however, share the initial assumption that man is an intramundane entity, governed by natural laws, from whom desirable behavior can be elicited or coerced by systems of social control.

Although the political and intellectual current known as liberalism has taken on various forms in the course of its history, most persons would probably agree that one of its characteristics is the expectation that substantial change can be effected in men through institutional arrangements with the result that man and society can be progressively perfected.[8] It is rare, however, that a liberal thinker asks serious questions about either human nature or the nature of institutions as such. Voegelin took up the theory of institutions in 1964 in "Der Mensch in Gesellschaft und Geschichte," an essay that addresses itself both to the substantial reality of institutions and to the common forms of misconception regarding them. The principal source of misconception is again the objectifying imagination that treats institutions as though they were static entities with an immanent nature that could be defined in a doxic manner. In actual use, the term "institution" is only a topical concept or category covering a wide range of more or less constant forms of relationship that seem prominent in a society. When the society itself is comparatively stable, the impression is reinforced

8. Voegelin discusses liberalism in detail in "Liberalism and Its History" (1960, trans. 1974) and "On Readiness to Rational Discussion." He discusses its early manifestations among the Enlightenment *philosophes* in *From Enlightenment to Revolution*. On the subject of institutions, see *OH*, 3:87, where Voegelin says that in the *Republic* Socrates restrains himself from practical political proposals so as not to give the impression that good order in a *polis* can be created through institutional arrangements: "He considers it, on the contrary, a symptom of disease in a polis when the citizens are feverishly active with patching up this or that gap in the law, but do not dare to touch the well-known source of the multitude of minor evils. They act like patients, permanently in search of a panacea, but unwilling to mend the way of life that causes the disease. . . . The goodness of a polis has its source not in the paradigm of institutions, but in the psyche of the founder or ruler who will stamp the pattern of his soul on the institutions."

that its institutions are more like "things" than processes. To develop an adequate theory of institutions, however, it is necessary to penetrate beneath this imaginative level to their character as dynamic processes and then to consider the nature of the dynamics that move them: "Theoretically these complexes must be analyzed into types of procedure or transaction {*Typen des Handelns*} for the actualization of order in society; the analysis must proceed further to the question of the order which is supposed to be actualized; and this again must be pursued to the question of human nature and its proper order."[9] What questions of this sort would ultimately lead to, says Voegelin, if they were pursued philosophically, as they were, for example, by Aristotle in the *Nicomachean Ethics* and *Politics*, is the realization that well-ordered human existence must be oriented through the love of divine perfection and is consequently as dependent on the pull (*helkein*) toward the pole of the *summum bonum* as it is on human effort (*zetesis*). The specific achievements of order that take place through the processes that we call institutions must therefore be understood not as the simple products of human action, as though they were human "creations," but as the results of divine-human encounter and cooperation.[10]

When the analysis is carried this far, what becomes clear is the central point that liberal thought, in all its forms, characteristically misses: the irresolvable mystery of human freedom and the concommitant limitations of institutions. As long as the mystery of divine-human participation in the Between persists—and there can be no escaping it, because it is what constitutes the substantial reality of "human nature"—there is no way that human adjustments of immanently conceived "institutions" can convert history from freedom into an inevitable course of progress, either toward the true

9. "Theoretish müβten diese Komplexe in Typen des Handelns zur Verwirklichung von Ordnung in Gesellschaft aufgelöst Werden; die Auflösung würde uns weiterführen zu den Fragen der Ordnung, die verwirklicht werden soll; und diese wieder zu den Fragen der menschlichen Natur und ihrer richtigen Ordnung."· "Der Mensch in Gesellschaft und Geschichte," *Österreichische Zeitschrift für öffentliches Recht*, n.s., 14 (1964): 1.

10. Ibid., pp. 9–10.

perfection of man or toward merely intramundane satisfactions. Man and his history will always remain mysterious, free, and dependent on the free graciousness of the divine drawing.

Again, however, one must recognize the element of truth in the liberal position. It is founded on a genuine insight, and an adequate philosophy of history must do justice to the truth that this involves. Liberal conceptions of order in history are not mere folly; what they are is one-sided. They overlook the transcendent dimension of the human project, but they notice the immanent one. They overlook the *helkein*, but they notice the reality and importance of *zetesis*. Institutions may not be able, as the liberal thinker characteristically hopes, to guarantee openness of existence, but they can facilitate it, and as long as man lives not only in the realm of spirit but also of the flesh, he requires socially established procedures in which his life may be ordered on that level as well. To the extent, however, that these are based on an immanentizing conception of man, their purpose will be vitiated, and to the extent that they are believed to be capable of acting as the sufficient cause of the perfecting of man, they will become enticements by which the "liberal" planner may be tempted down the path to totalitarianism. As Voegelin has shown in detail in *From Enlightenment to Revolution*, the transition from liberal advocacy of freedom from traditional constraints to the imposition of new ones in the name of "improvement," and ultimately to a totalitarian terror directed against those reluctant to be improved, is so gradual that the planner can remain quite unconscious of it—and untroubled in conscience.[11] In fact, the "idealism"

11. See, for example, the discussion (pp. 59–60) of the shortness of the step that separates Helvetius's plan for social control through the behavioristic reinforcement of socially desirable appetites from Jeremy Bentham's plan for a perfect prison in which the "inspector" would be able to observe every movement of the criminal and administer immediate correction (in Bentham's *Panopticon: Or, The Inspection House*) and ultimately from Lenin's plan for a perfect state in which all those suspected of capitalist inclinations would be kept under constant observation, which would be, in Lenin's phrase, "universal, general, national." See also *The New Science of Politics*, pp. 173–75, and Voegelin's debate with Hannah Arendt, "The Origins of Totalitarianism," *Review of Politics*, 15 (1953): 68–85.

of the liberal conscience may make it a source of moral support for imperial ambitions by legitimizing those ambitions as the efforts of a more advanced and "enlightened" people to "improve" those whom the march of progress has left behind.[12]

Liberalism is a modern current of thought, however, and imperial ambition has had a long history. It is the predominant feature of what Voegelin has termed the Ecumenic Age, which began at least as far back as the time of Alexander the Great.[13] To understand clearly the nature of the philosophical questions to which ecumenic imperialism gives rise, it is necessary to distinguish it from the imperial form of the earlier cosmologically ordered societies—such as those of Egypt and Mesopotamia—that preceded the ecumenic empires. These were "concrete" societies in the sense that there was an organic relation between the symbolism of order and its substance in the life of actual communities of persons sharing common experiences, memories, and loyalties. The ecumenic empires, for

12. See "Readiness to Rational Discussion," p. 272, for a discussion of "improvement" as the basic concept of J. S. Mill's anthropology and of his idea that, in Voegelin's summation, "the primary blessing is 'the permanent interest of a man as a progressive being,' " that "everything that furthers that interest constitutes a legitimate political demand," and that therefore "in the case of peoples with a low standard of civilization, despotism is a legitimate form of regime, provided that, and in so far as, it serves toward 'improving' the barbarians." See "More's Utopia" for a discussion of that work as the first evocation of a people that sets itself up as the standard of mankind: "The actual atrocities of Western colonial imperialism, of National Socialism, and Communism mark the end of a curve, of which the beginning is marked by the playful atrocity of the humanistic intellectual" (p. 468).

13. Voegelin has at different times offered varying indications of how he intends the temporal span of this "Ecumenic Age" to be marked. On the one hand he says, in "Configurations of History," p. 26, that it extends "from approximately the eighth century before Christ to the eighth century after Christ, at which time it had run its course," because, "it was realized that ecumenic empires were not the solution to organizing mankind as a unity." In "World Empire and the Unity of Mankind," *International Affairs*, 38 (1962): 170–88, on the other hand, he treats "the age of empire" as continuing until the present and speculates that perhaps the intramundane apocalyptics of imperialism may currently be performing a *reductio ad absurdum* on themselves so that this age will come to an end before too much longer.

their subject peoples, were virtually abstractions that attempted to impose themselves from above, with no recognizable roots in the history and culture of communities. In the earlier cases the imperial symbolism—the Egyptian pharaoh or Mesopotamian emperor, for example, mediating between human society and the society of the gods—served to express men's sense of the hierarchy of being and the preeminence of the transcendental order. It also, says Voegelin, suggested an incipient sense of spiritual universality:

> For the enlargements of the social horizon from tribal society to city-state, and further on to an empire which comprises the whole area of a civilization, are not mere quantitative increases in the number of population, but qualitative jumps in social organization which affect the understanding of human nature. They were experienced as creative efforts by which man achieved a differentiated consciousness both of himself and of the divine origin of an order that is the same for all men. Through the hard reality of empire, there begins to shine forth, as the subject of history, a universal mankind under God. [OH, 4:95]

A major difference between what Voegelin calls the cosmological and the ecumenic empires is that the latter lack the spiritual substance found in the experience of concrete societies. In the Alexandrian and Roman empires, as well as the Iranian empire that preceded them, the imperial order overarched societies but did not itself become the form of any society: "In none of these cases did the conquerors belong to the societies organized by them; in none of them did the resultant empire organize a Persian, Macedonian, or Roman society" (pp. 116–17). The new empires, says Voegelin, are "not organized societies at all, but organizational shells that will expand indefinitely to engulf the former concrete societies" (p. 117). An ecumenic empire, even when it becomes for all practical purposes an ecumene, is not an actual world, but is in search of a world.

The great mistake of ecumenic imperialism is that it fails to notice that the "world" it seeks to dominate is not an existent "thing," lying there waiting to be conquered, but a substantive order with a spiritual as well as a physical dimension.[14] Failing to notice this, it also fails to notice that in its crushing of concrete societies, it destroys the only spiritual basis for a genuine world:

> This new symbol [the "ecumene"] . . . was plagued with ontological difficulties. For the ecumene was not a society in concretely organized existence, but the *telos* [goal] of a conquest to be perpetrated. In the pursuit of the *telos*, then, the ecumene in the cultural sense turned out to be much larger than expected, and the conquest never reached its goal. Moreover, one could not conquer the nonexistent ecumene without destroying the existent societies. . . . When finally enough contemporarily living human beings were corralled into an empire to support the fiction of an ecumene, the collected humanity turned out to be not much of a mankind, unless their universal status as human beings under God [the spiritual dimension of their existence in the divine-human Between] was recognized. And when universal humanity was understood as deriving from man's existence in presence under God, the symbolism of an ecumenic mankind under an imperial government suffered a serious diminution of status. Philosophically, the ecumene was a miserable symbol. [*OH*, 4:171–72]

What ecumenic imperialism fails above all to notice is that what it is really engaged in is not mere conquest but, as Voegelin puts it, "an essay in world creation, reaching through all the levels of the hierarchy of being" and requiring attunement—both active (through *zetesis*) and passive (through *helkein*)—to the tensional pole indicated by such symbols as the "unseen measure," "transcendent Being," the divine Beyond, and so on ("World Empire," p. 179).

As with the other forms of derailment discussed, however, there is also a kernel of truth underlying the ecumenic imperialist conception of historical order. For one thing, it grows out of what amounts to an incipient, not yet clearly differentiated, version of the same sense of spiritual universality to which Plato gave expression in his

14. For a discussion of the etymology of the terms "world," *kosmos*, and *mundus*, see "World Empire and the Unity of Mankind," pp. 177–78.

symbol of the *metaxy* and which was also emerging into consciousness around the same time in Confucius and Lao-tse, the Buddha,
Zoroaster, the Israelite prophets, and others. The two are in fact
parallel phenomena linked by the fact that both, the conquerors on
the one hand and the prophets and philosophers on the other, are in
quest in their different ways of "universal mankind" (p. 171).[15]
That both recognize this feature of their enterprises and make it
central to their self-interpretation is what makes the "ecumenic age"
a configuration in history. The conqueror, however, never notices,
as the prophet or philosopher sometimes does, that "universal mankind is not a society existing in the world, but a symbol which
indicates man's consciousness of participating, in his earthly existence, in the mystery of a reality that moves toward its transfiguration. Universal mankind is an eschatological index" (*OH*, 4:305).

This very realization that "the fulfillment of mankind is an escha-
ton" and that "the end of all human action does not lie within this
world but beyond it" produces its own temptations ("World Empire," p. 184).[16] Another important truth that imperialism recognizes, as more differentiated and otherwise more adequate
philosophies of history sometimes have not, is that however
spiritual mankind may be, it always retains its physical dimension
and its situation in the cosmos made up of world and society as well
as of man and the gods, and it requires ordering on its lower as well
as its higher levels. An example of failure to appreciate this may be

15. Moreover, although one does not cause the other, but rather both arise
from an initial, not necessarily very clear experience of universal humanity (i.e.,
of human existence in the Between), the pressure of empire has historically had an
important influence on the development of philosophical consciousness, because
it has forced to heightened reflectiveness those who suffer its effects; in fact, some
of the earliest examples of historiographic writing—Herodotus, Ssu-ma Ch'ien,
and 2 Kings—have had as their principal subject matter the clash between an
imperial order and that of a traditional society with a cultural substance the
historian perceives as threatened and worth preserving; see "Configurations of
History," p. 27.

16. Voegelin speaks of Polybius and Saint Matthew as having gained the
quoted insights between them.

seen, believes Voegelin, in Augustine's argument in book 6 of *The City of God* against Varro's claims for the importance of a civil theology: "What St. Augustine could not understand was the compactness of Roman experience, the inseparable community of gods and men in the historically concrete *civitas*, the simultaneousness of human and divine institution of a social order. For him the order of human existence had already separated into the *civitas terrena* of profane history and the *civitas coelestis* of divine institution" (*The New Science of Politics*, p. 88). Augustine noticed the immensely important fact that "the structure of history is the same as the structure of personal existence," a movement in the Between following the tension toward transcendent perfection: "His conception of history as a tale of two Cities, intermingling from the beginning of mankind to its end, conceives it as a tale of man's personal Exodus written large" ("Immortality," p. 262). The transcendental emphasis, however, caused him to treat the earthly city as a place of disorder or false order and to overlook the truth that had been noticed by Varro, as by Plato before him, "that a society must exist as an ordered cosmion, as a representative of cosmic order, before it can indulge in the luxury of also representing a truth of the soul" (*The New Science of Politics*, p. 162). Augustine is in this respect only the most articulate of a wide range of Christian thinkers he typifies. Christianity, says Voegelin, for all its depth of insight into the eschatologically oriented structure of history, has "left in its wake the vacuum of a de-divinized natural sphere of political existence" (p. 162). The problem, says Voegelin, is that "the Church never quite disengaged itself from its apocalyptic origin—its apocalyptic unconcern about mankind in history narrowed its intellectual horizon so badly that it never developed an adequate philosophy of history" ("World Empire," p. 186).

It is no accident that Christianity and Gnosticism became so intermingled in the early Christian era that the effort to disentangle their strands or locate their continuities has become a rapidly growing academic specialty. The Christian experience of the homeward movement of the soul can easily lead to a loss of what Voegelin calls the "balance of consciousness," which requires one to remember that "the exodus from reality is a movement within reality"—that there is no stepping out of the Between and that even the "spiritual man" continues to dwell in the cosmos (*OH*, 4:227). Fidelity to "the postulate of balance" is one of the first requirements for the philosopher of history.

So far the various forms of derailment considered have all involved ways of misconstruing the field to be interpreted. They have in common a tendency to emphasize formulable patterns or *doxai*, and in this respect they share the fundamental error of assuming that the meaning of history can take the form of an opinion. Another requirement of the philosopher of history, besides that of maintaining his balance in the field of tensions, is that he retain a clear awareness of the distinction between mystery and puzzle. The two basic questions raised by Leibniz in his *Principles of Nature and of Grace* (Why is there something and not just nothing? Why is that something as it is and not different?) are not puzzles to be solved by an indefatigable researcher or a clever calculator ("On Debate and Existence," p. 147). They are indicators pointing to irreducible mystery. The attempt to reduce the mystery of existence to something for which an answer could be found is a fundamental misconstruction both of the field to be inquired into and of the nature of the inquiry itself. It is another instance of the tendency of what is called philosophy to turn itself into philodoxy. Philosophy is not in essence any construing of a field but a *zetema*. It develops interpretive models as it proceeds, but it does so with an awareness of their mythic or analogical character, and its primary concern is with the process itself by which the philosopher moves not mainly into a right view of things but into "existence in truth" or "openness." It is because Augustine realized this that, despite his partial lack of balance, his "tale" of the two Cities offers so much more adequate a theory of history than most.

One modern philosopher of history in whose work the dimensions of this problem become clearly visible is Arnold Toynbee, about

whom Voegelin has written at some length.[17] Voegelin considers
Toynbee's enterprise not merely a doxic speculation but a genuine
zetema, and this is why his *Study of History* exhibits significant
changes of basic conception as one reads through it. Voegelin once
asked Toynbee, who was having to respond to various critics during
a conference, what he thought of their attacks on him. His answer
was, "Well, you see I wrote these things twenty-five years ago, and
I have almost forgotten what they are, and now I must defend
them" ("Configurations of History," pp. 23–24). "Definitions in
the course of a *zetema*," says Voegelin in a comment on the shifts of
perspective in Toynbee's *Study*, "are cognitive resting points, which
articulate the view of reality that has been gained at the respective
stage in the existential advance toward truth. . . . Hence, the
definitions which articulate the view of reality achieved in earlier
stages of the *zetema* are liable to be superseded by definitions reached
at higher existential levels. In an existentially authentic *zetema* we
are faced, therefore, with a series of definitions, the later ones quali-
fying and superseding the earlier ones. . . . As a matter of fact,
the search for truth about the order of history has steadily advanced
through the volumes of the *Study* to higher existential levels"
("Toynbee's History as a Search for Truth," p. 184). The problem,
however, was that, in terms of the construing of the field, the basic
plan developed on the earliest existential level was retained to cover
studies on the last, and that, in terms of the existential movement
on the part of the philosopher, the *zetema* was truncated at a certain
point.

Toynbee's initial principle is well known: the smallest intelligible units for historical study are not individual states or societies,
linguistic communities, and so on, but civilizations. The plan was
to study the life cycles of these units, from genesis and growth to
breakdown and disintegration. During the course of the first six
volumes of the *Study*, however, difficulties with this approach became clear; the "social atoms" called civilizations were not self-

17. "Toynbee's History as a Search for Truth." See also *OH* 1:124–27, 133;
4:3–6, 173–74; and *From Enlightenment to Revolution*, p. 117.

enclosed but flowed into one another, particularly through the role of the type of configuration that Toynbee called a "universal church" in preparing, and giving form and life to, the successor civilization. The result was that Toynbee began to realize at least implicitly that his "smallest intelligible unit" was not intelligible simply in itself. His existential advance was the development of a sensitivity to spiritual movement in history. The subsequent four volumes of the work reflected these insights in their reclassification of the societies under study as "primitive societies," "primary civilizations," "secondary civilizations," and "higher religions"—arranged chronologically and genealogically on an ascending scale of value. These classifications continued, however, says Voegelin, to function within the framework of the initial assumptions about the intelligibility, organic character, and "philosophical equivalence" of the civilizational units.

This is a limitation of conception. More important still is the internal limit imposed on the *zetema* by Toynbee's "unwillingness to pursue his search to the end" ("Toynbee's History," p. 196), which would have led him, says Voegelin, to a position somewhat like that of Augustine if he had allowed the *zetema* to complete its natural course: "A search for truth is supposed to reach its goal, that is, a view of reality existentially informed by the *philia* of the *sophon* in the Platonic sense, or by the *intentio animi* toward God in the Augustinian sense. Toynbee does not reach this goal of the love of God, but stops short at a sensitive spiritualist's and historical connoisseur's sympathy with religions" (p. 184).

Voegelin's own inquiry into the nature of historical development has also had to go through some major reconceptions. His shift from the doxographic history of ideas to that of experiences and their symbolic expressions has already been discussed. That was a costly revision of his basic conception of historical studies, because he had nearly completed a several-volume work using the doxographic approach and had to abandon it and spend years exploring the implications of the new insight. More recently he has rethought a major aspect of the project of *Order and History*, because he believes he has noticed in it a fallacy that exemplifies what is probably the most pervasive source of misconstructions for all interpretations of history. This is the tendency of advances in insight to give rise to Before and After symbols that distort one's view of the field by masking the underlying continuity of human experience and the equivalence of the symbols that develop on different levels of compactness and differentiation of consciousness (see "The Gospel and Culture," p. 83).

The particular fallacy, as he describes it in the introduction to *The Ecumenic Age*, was "the conventional belief that the conception of history as a meaningful course of events on a straight line of time was the great achievement of Israelites and Christians who were favored in its creation by the revelatory events, while the pagans, deprived as they were of revelation, could never rise above the conception of a cyclical time" (*OH*, 4:7).[18] His investigations after the publication of the first three volumes of *Order and History* soon led him to the realization that this unilinear construction of history was a symbolic form that could be traced back as far as the third millennium B.C. to the pre-Israelite empires of the Ancient Near East. To this symbolic form, which traces a straight line of history from a divine-cosmic origin of order to the author's present, he gave the name "historiogenesis" as a parallel to the other already well recognized symbolisms of theogony, anthropogony, and cosmogony.[19] It was, in other words, a symbolic tale of the origins of a given society and served to round out the sequence of such forms relating to the gods, man, and the cosmos, the other three partners

18. This conception of the origins of the idea of history as a meaningful course directed toward a goal is still current among many historians. For a parallel expression of this idea at the time Voegelin was writing the first three volumes of *Order and History*, see Mircea Eliade, *The Myth of the Eternal Return: Or, Cosmos and History* (New York: Pantheon Books, 1954), pp. 102–8. For a more recent expression of it, see Thorkild Jacobsen, *The Treasures of Darkness: A History of Mesopotamian Religion* (New Haven: Yale University Press, 1976), p. 164.

19. Voegelin's first discussion of this was in "Historiogenesis," an essay of 1960 reprinted in the German *Anamnesis* and subsequently incorporated into *OH*, vol. 4.

in the compact quaternarian symbolism of the primary level of experience.

If this had been the whole of the matter, however, it would not have required any major reconception of Voegelin's project. What he also realized was that "the very unilinear history which I had supposed to be engendered, together with the punctuations of meaning on it, by the differentiating events, turned out to be a cosmological symbolism" (*OH*, 4:7). This meant that in his conception of the shape of Western history he had slipped into a compact pattern of interpretation that had been continuously recurrent from the time of the Sumerians and Egyptians, through the Israelites and Christians, right into the modern philosophies of history he had been trying to extricate himself from. It was a pattern of symbolization inappropriate to the level of differentiation of consciousness on which he was attempting to work and was therefore in unrecognized conflict with his thinking as a whole. It was even, he realized, an expression of a sort of spiritual imperialism by which one's own cultural group attempts to interpret history as centering on it alone and thereby virtually denies humanity—the experience of responsive movement in the Between—to other peoples. This was a chastening realization. It led him to the special preoccupations of *The Ecumenic Age*: "if the symbolism of a unilinear history with its climax in the present could be engendered by the experience of a cosmological empire being threatened and preserved, was there perhaps something of a 'leap in being' in the foundation of empire? and inversely, was there perhaps something imperial about spiritual outbursts?" (p. 7). It also led him to the realization that history, in its aspect as a configuration in time, was not nearly so susceptible to interpretation in terms of pattern as he had hoped. It was "not a story of meaningful events to be arranged on a time line" (p. 57). Rather it was "a disturbingly diversified field of spiritual centers," and the work of a philosopher of history would have to be "a movement through a web of meaning with a plurality of nodal points" (pp. 3, 57). "The process of history, and such order as can be discerned in it," he concluded, "is not a story to be told from the beginning to its happy, or unhappy, end; it is a mystery in process of revelation" (p. 6). The main need in the philosophy of history now, says Voegelin, is not for another construing of the field but rather a "return from symbols which have lost their meaning to the experiences which constitute meaning. . . . The great obstacle to this return is the massive block of accumulated symbols, secondary and tertiary, which eclipses the reality of man's existence in the Metaxy. To raise this obstacle and its structure into consciousness, and by its removal to help in the return to the truth of reality as it reveals itself in history, has become the purpose of *Order and History*" (p. 58).

These conclusions, of course, are not at all in conflict with the basic thrust of the initial three volumes of *Order and History* and of Voegelin's other work to this point. Rather they only express a more explicit realization of his fundamental approach. Nor do they invalidate the interpretation that there were genuine advances from compact to differentiated experience of reality and corresponding advances in the symbolization of the order of being. The differentiating events were historically real, in a variety of times and places, and were genuinely epochal in that they marked real advances and gave rise to the symbolism of Before and After.

The difficulty with the symbolism of epoch is not that there is no real and important change separating the period before from that coming after. Rather such symbolism produces, or else feeds into, the all too human tendency to interpret the change as a point of final transition from a past of darkness and folly to a present—the interpreter's own—of perfect, exhaustive wisdom:

Before Philosophy there was Myth; before Christianity there were pagan idols and the Jewish Law; before monotheism there was polytheism; and before modern Science, of course, there were such primitive superstitions as Philosophy and the Gospel, Metaphysics and Theology, which no self-respecting person should touch nowadays. Not everybody is as tolerant and intelligent as the Jesus who could say: "Think not I have come to dissolve the law and the prophets; I have come not to dissolve (*katalysai*) but to fulfil (*plerosai*)" (Mat 5:17). ["The Gospel and Culture," pp. 83–84]

Not only is this a fall into the philodoxic fallacy of interpreting the mystery of existence as a puzzle to which the solution has finally been found. It also betrays a virtually and sometimes literally murderous impulse to condemn one's predecessors as well as those contemporaries who have not yet advanced to the properly "modern" way of thinking.

The antidote to the hubris this involves is to remember that "the truth of reality is always fully present in man's experience [as the Between of the tension of existence] and that what changes are the degrees of differentiation" and to remember also the principle of the equivalence of the symbolisms that, on any level of compactness or differentiation, give expression to that constant core of experience (p. 84). There is a real advance, and a real Before and After, but it is not a change in the structure of reality, nor is it even the knowledge of a new truth. It is only an advance in clarity regarding the abiding reality of the encounter and interplay of poles in the divine-human Between. When history is understood in this light, it comes to be seen as a "trail of equivalent symbols," the epochal structure of which originates "when a truth of reality emerging from the depth recognizes itself as equivalent but superior [in differentiation] to a truth previously experienced" ("Equivalences," p. 233).

There have been three major groups, according to Voegelin, of such equivalent symbolisms expressing three experiences of truth—cosmological, anthropological, and soteriological (see *The New Science of Politics*, pp. 76–78). These articulate in varying degrees of compactness and differentiation three different, but constant and simultaneous, levels of the experience of human existence. The level of cosmological experience and symbolization corresponds to that of the primary experience of the cosmos. It involves a minimum of reflective self-awareness, but does articulate the field of experience in terms of the quaternarian structure already discussed—

man, the divine, the world, society—and in doing so takes adequate account, on its own compact level, of the polar structure of the tension of existence. Anthropological and soteriological truth correspond to the noetic and pneumatic differentiations respectively: the first is characterized by a greater emphasis on the role of noetic inquiry (the human *zetesis*), the second by a more emphatic sense of the spiritual inrush of divine ordering presence (the divine *helkein*) (see chapter 3).

Anthropological truth is the experience of a human being who asks questions regarding the true and the good, and in his search also feels himself pulled off course by distractions and forces of disorder, but who resists these for the sake of the good that he loves. Soteriological truth is the experience of one who finds himself falling in love in an overpowering way with the same ultimate ground of truth and goodness that the other senses in the distance. For this person the transcendental goal is not distant, nor does it seem abstract; rather it is experienced as an intensely personal presence, before Whom one must repent, and Who offers a possibility of existence toward which one feels drawn, but from which one also shrinks, because to enter into it would cost nothing less than a death and rebirth.

To be precise, however, it is only in a certain sense that one may say the anthropological and soteriological complexes of experience and symbolization represent different levels of differentiation. The fact that the structure of the differentiating event "reaches from a pneumatic center to a noetic periphery" means that there is also a sense in which the differentiated consciousness of existence is a single level, but one which may involve an emphasis on one or the other of its structural poles. An exclusive or predominant emphasis on either could lead to a failure to notice the wholeness and continuity of the theophanic experience. In this respect it is only together and balanced by one another that the noetic and pneumatic experiences constitute properly differentiated consciousness.

Still, it is *pneuma* that is preeminent. The human seeking and the divine drawing are aspects of a single movement of the soul, the directional tendency of the tension of existence; but an adequate explication of that movement or tension must recognize the priority of the divine pole as the structuring principle. The seeking is structurally dependent on the drawing, since it would not take place without an experienced attraction to a good felt to be worth seeking. Soteriological truth, therefore, represents a higher level of differentiated experience, because it articulates a clearer realization of this structural relationship and of the character of the divine pole as known not from the periphery but at the pneumatic center.

Voegelin has discussed these differences of level in some detail on two occasions, early and late in the course of his work since the turning point of the 1940s. In *The New Science of Politics* (pp. 77–78) he discussed it in connection with Artistotle's thesis that friendship between God and man was impossible because of their radical inequality: "The impossibility of *philia* between God and man may be considered typical for the whole range of anthropological truth. The experiences that were explicated into a theory of man by the mystic philosophers had in common the accent on the human side of the orientation of the soul toward divinity. The soul orients itself toward a God who rests in his immovable transcendence; it reaches out toward divine reality, but it does not meet an answering movement from beyond." He contrasts this with the Christian soteriological experience "of mutuality in the relation with God, of the *amicitia* in the Thomistic sense" (p. 78; cf. *OH*, 3:364). His reference here is to the *Summa Contra Gentiles* (III, 19) and the idea that the choices and movements of the human will are immediately ordained by God in his providential care for man.[20] When this providential ordering is responsively accepted in the soul that yields itself to it, it can culminate in the *fides caritate formata* (faith formed by love) that is the substance of divine-human *amicitia*, the friend-

20. "*Nam electiones et voluntatum motus immediate a Deo disponuntur. . . .*" Aquinas means that whatever the particular good sought, and whatever the deficiencies of the seeking, the will is always moved most fundamentally by the love of the good as such; cf. *ST*, Ia–IIae, q. 1, a. 6.

ship or mutual love in which the divine and human poles are apprehended as participating in one another (*The New Science of Politics*, p. 79).[21]

In *The Ecumenic Age* Voegelin discusses the same issue in the framework of a comparison of Plato and Paul. We have seen how highly he regards the *Timaeus*'s philosophical myth of the continuity of soul and cosmos, and of the two thinkers he considers Plato to have had superior critical consciousness and balance. In spite of this, however, he says that "the Pauline myth [of the death and resurrection of Jesus and of the soul's renewal through participation in the risen Christ] is distinguished by its superior degree of differentiation":

> In the first place, his vision carried Paul irresistibly beyond the structure of creation to its source in the freedom and love of divine creativity. Paul differentiated the truth of existence, *i.e.*, the experience of its ordering process through man's orientation toward the divine ground so far that the transcosmic God and his Agape were revealed as the mover in the theophanic events which constitute meaning in history. . . . Paul, furthermore, differentiated fully the experience of the directional movement by articulating its goal, its *teleion*, as the state of *aphtharsia* [imperishability] beyond man's involvement in the Anaximandrian mystery of Apeiron [the Boundless] and Time. . . . And finally, Paul has fully differentiated the experience of man as the site where the movement of reality becomes

---

21. Aquinas's discussion of love (*caritas*) as the vital principle (*forma*) of faith may be found in *ST*, IIa–IIae, q. 4, a. 3–5, and q. 23, a. 6. Aquinas's distinction between *fides informis* ("formless" or dead faith) and *fides formata* (animated or living faith) is related to the distinction discussed earlier between *doxa* and *episteme* (see chapter 3). *Fides informis* is a matter of correct opinions about God, and as such it remains a purely extrinsic relationship. It prepares the ground for *fides formata*, by orienting one doxically in the direction of truth, but it does not attain God as He is in Himself; that is, it does not constitute spiritual union with Him. *Fides formata* does constitute such union. See also ibid., IIa–IIae, q. 4, a. 1, on faith as the substance of things hoped for (Heb. 11:1). To understand Aquinas's thinking on this subject it is important to remember that for him knowledge was not a confrontational "look" at an object, as it came to be for Ockham and Descartes and much of modern thought, but a formal union of knower and known.

luminous in its actual occurrence. In Paul's myth, God emerges victorious, because his protagonist is man. He is the creature in whom God can incarnate himself with the fullness (*pleroma*) of his divinity, transfiguring man into the God-man (Col. 2:9). [*OH*, 4:250–51]

The meaning of the Pauline myth, in other words, is substantially identical with that of the Platonic *metaxy*, because the basis of each in experience is the same, but in the Pauline version it unfolds its full implications. They are equivalent symbolisms, but the Pauline is superior in its experiential penetration and its articulateness.[22]

The advance from cosmological truth through anthropological and soteriological truth is not, according to Voegelin, a movement from false to true, nor even from an old truth to a new and different one. It is a movement only toward fuller experience and clearer expression of one and the same truth of existence. As one emerges existentially into the *fides caritate formata* of providentially ordered divine union, one does not move out of the cosmos or beyond humanity. It is the same Between as ever that one lives in, only with more luminous presence and a clearer intention of fidelity to the divine drawing and to one's role in what Plato called the "serious play" (*Laws* 6. 769a):

> The field of the play is the soul of man, in which feelings, apprehensions, and *logismos* [reasoning] pull in different directions. The play is played by the gods in whose hands man is the *paignion* [plaything]. Man, however, is not an automaton; he himself, in so far as he "is one" [i.e., a man], has a part in the play; he has to play the rôle which is assigned to him of supporting the pull of the golden cord and resisting the drawings of lesser cords. . . . This play, then, is serious because it is ultimately directed by God, "the most serious." Man's part in it is equally serious because in this serious play he attunes himself to the divine direction. . . . The serious play is enacted by every man in his personal life by supporting the pull of

22. It is perhaps worth mentioning that Voegelin speculates that Plato may well have penetrated as far as Paul experientially but refrained from giving full expression to his insight lest it lead to apocalyptic expectations and loss of the "balance of consciousness"; see *OH*, 4:237–40.

the golden cord; it is enacted by man in community by celebrating the rites of the polis in conformity with the *nomoi* ["laws" expressing the divine drawing]. [*OH*, 3:235][23]

When man lives up to the role to which he is called, his entire existence becomes a kind of dialogue with Being in which he himself is articulated as reality through his participation in this divine-human *amicitia*. As Voegelin has said, in a comment on the Mosaic experience and symbolization of divine reality as the "I am" of the

23. For the myth of man as puppet of the gods, drawn by golden and iron cords, see Plato *Laws* 1. 644d–645c. For another version of the idea of "serious play" in Plato, see *Laws* 7. 817b–c, where the life of the well-ordered city is described as the truest and best of dramas: "we are ourselves authors of a tragedy, and that the finest and best we know how to make. In fact, our whole polity has been constructed as a dramatization of a noble and perfect life; that is what *we* hold to be in truth the most real of tragedies. Thus you are poets, and we also are poets in the same style, rival artists and rival actors, and that in the finest of all dramas, one which indeed can be produced only by a code of true law—or at least that is our faith" (trans. A. E. Taylor, in Hamilton and Cairns, eds., *Collected Dialogues*). It must be remembered, of course, that in classical Greece the term "tragedy" meant only a serious play in verse not a story of downfall, as it came to mean in medieval and renaissance literary theory. Aeschylus's *Eumenides*, for example, is a tragedy in which things work out well for everyone—protagonists, antagonists, and chorus. A classical Greek might likely have called Dante's *Commedia* his *Tragoedia*. It is here, by the way, that one of the significant points of difference between Voegelin and Toynbee becomes clearly visible. Toynbee is well known for his interpretation of history as tragic in the sense that its pattern is one of inexorable cycles of rise and fall. This involves a conception of tragedy more medieval than Greek. Voegelin does not think history susceptible of explanation in terms of any necessary pattern. Rather he considers history to be a function of man, which is to say that historical existence in its essential reality is a movement of transcendence involving a free response to an invitation to openness of existence—an invitation that comes from the Beyond of history. Voegelin also considers history a tragedy, but in the genuinely Greek sense exemplified in the quotation above from Plato and in such a play as *The Suppliants* of Aeschylus. Voegelin's own definition of tragedy appears in *OH*, 2:247: "The truth of the tragedy is action itself, that is, action on the new, differentiated level of a movement in the soul that culminates in the decision . . . of a mature, responsible man. . . . Tragedy as a form is the study of the human soul in the process of making decisions, while the single tragedies construct conditions and experimental situations, in which a fully developed, self-conscious soul is forced into action."

Thornbush Episode (Ex. 3:14), "the substance of the creative action is the 'word.' From the Beginning, reality is the divine word speaking in succession the evolution of being from matter through plant to animal life, until it speaks man who, in the persons of patriarchs and prophets, responds by his word to the word spoken by god in history. The reality of the cosmos, thus, becomes a story to be told by the man who participates responsively in the story told by the god." (*OH*, 4:13).[24]

This does not require that the human player know the script of the drama in which he is caught up: "Ultimately the cosmic play is in the hands of God, and only He knows its full meaning" (*OH*, 3:235, commenting on *Laws* 6. 769a). On the contrary, precisely what is required is that man recognize and acknowledge that he does not know. Only through this confession can he play his role well, avoiding the fratricidal war of opinions of those who mistake their *doxai* for existential truth. What man has, instead of the full and clear vision that would give him cognitive mastery of his existence and make him a rival to the creator, is something he would find very precious if only he would approach his role with appropriate reverence and humility: the sets and layers of equivalent symbols engendered by his experience of participation. These various levels of analogical expression of mystery, when they articulate genuinely open existence on the part of the human partner in the drama, simultaneously reveal and conceal a truth that is never directly perceived, but in which man is nevertheless immediately and luminously involved, through trust, love, and hope:

> The search for truth makes sense only under the assumption that the truth brought up from the depth of his psyche by man, though it is not the ultimate truth of reality, is representative of the truth in the divine depth of the Cosmos. Behind every equivalent symbol in the historical field stands the man who has engendered it in the course of his search as representative of a truth that is more than equivalent. The search that renders no more than equivalent truth rests ulti-

24. For a more extensive discussion of the Thornbush Episode, see *OH*, 1:405–14.

mately on the faith that, by engaging in it, man participates in the divine drama of truth becoming luminous. ["Equivalences," p. 234]

At the end of Mann's *Joseph*, Jacob has died and been buried in the family tomb at Hebron. Deprived of their father's protection, the brothers suddenly find themselves in fear of the outcast who might take vengeance on them. They fall down before Joseph and ask for mercy, but he tells them that in doing so they show that they have missed the meaning of their story. For which he does not blame them. "One can easily be in a story and not understand it," he says (p. 1207). Passionate and unreflective, they had never noticed the drama they were in. He, on the other hand, in his pride and youthful folly, had thought he knew the drama and his own role "far too well." Now, however, they are all in a position to realize with humility this divine calling and, in a spirit of mutual forgiveness and encouragement, to take up once again their part in the play. And so Joseph invites them to join him in returning to what is yet to unfold in "that quaint and comic land of Egypt":

> Thus he spoke to them and they laughed and wept together and stretched out their hands as he stood among them and touched him, and he too caressed them with his hands. And so endeth the beautiful story and God-invention of JOSEPH AND HIS BROTHERS.

Conclusion

THIS study of the thought of Eric Voegelin has been an attempt to set forth and explain Voegelin's theoretical principles and to show, at least briefly, how he applies them to the study of historical phenomena. It is the exposition of theory that has required the greater space, both because this is the most challenging aspect of Voegelin's work and because it is central to all of his writing. Once a reader has a clear understanding of Voegelin's philosophical foundations, it should be easy to take up any of the particular historical studies and see exactly what Voegelin intends there. The great value of Voegelin's historical work is that he approaches the study of history from a coherent philosophical point of view, placing the particulars in a theoretical framework that elucidates their potential meaning for the concerned participants of history.

What Voegelin works out and illustrates with a wealth of historical references is a theory of man as related essentially to transcendence, that is, as constituted in his humanity by his love of and loyalty to transcendental values. Every philosophy of history is founded on a theory of man. A major challenge for a philosopher working in this area is to develop an account of man that will be truly comprehensive, not reducing him to some one of his functions or aspects and not isolating him from the surrounding reality in which his existence as a whole is embedded. Voegelin's fundamental concept of existential tension, of which human existence is itself a particular expression, offers an economical yet richly suggestive basis for a nonreductionist theory of man and his history. His studies in the history of experience and its symbolization, moreover, make clear that such a theory of man has been implicit in the thought of the central thinkers of the Western philosophical and religious traditions. Voegelin does not present himself as the discoverer of radically new ideas—we would have reason to be suspicious of them if he did—but as a spokesman for principles that have been tested by the experience of generations.

The point of view from which Voegelin speaks, however, although it has deep historical roots, involves features that tend to seem unfamiliar to many contemporary readers, who are often unconsciously the heirs of theoretical choices tracing back to the divergence of nominalist from more traditional philosophical thinking in the late Middle Ages. The difficulty a reader may have with Voegelin is less one of agreement or disagreement—at least until the issues become clear—than of grasping his intention. It is hoped that the present study has elucidated the essentials of Voegelin's philosophy and made clear the elegant simplicity of its underlying pattern. It should now be possible to state concisely the basic principles of his thought:

1. To begin with, there is the principle that existence may be known from within and that it is properly known, from a human perspective, only in that manner; the attempt to confine knowledge to an externalizing perspective—to step outside of existence and contemplate it with neutrality—falsifies both knowledge and the reality known. For knowledge is itself involved in existence, and the reality known is one in which consciousness and concern are most intimately involved.

2. Man is inevitably a limited knower. This is both because his knowledge of existence is from within, not from without, and because it must be mediated through symbolic analogies. The only escape from symbolic mediation and analogy would be to know reality intuitively—not through reflection, and not in terms of what it may be said to be like, but in terms of precisely what it is seen to be. If knowledge of this sort could be had, it would be certain and irreformable. It would deliver man from the tension of inquiry and from the necessity of critical reflection and self-doubt. There will probably always be those whose desire for tension-free existence

leads them to make such claims, but Voegelin rejects this possibility on principle, since it conflicts radically with his basic conceptions of man, of human knowledge, and of the structure of existence.

3. Instead of certainty, one may have, at the very most, the confidence which comes from faith—the trust that reality as a whole is transcendentally ordered—and which also comes from the experienced harmony between one's thought and one's existence. The claimant to the certainty of *gnosis* lives in constant fear that reality may give the lie to his claims. He may bury the consciousness of this fear so deeply that it is virtually eclipsed for him, but there always remains a residue of anxiety that speaks to him of his finitude and of the impossibility of transcending it, even if that speech falls on deaf ears and survives only in the mute forms of frustration, anger, torment, or despair. Whatever his ideas of himself, man's experience is always human experience. This is the experience of existence within a whole of reality greater than man.

4. Voegelin's constant appeal is to experience, because it is another of his fundamental principles that the substance of reality is to be found on that level. Reality itself, that is, is experiential, and human experience is the point at which reality becomes conscious in man. Human experience, according to Voegelin, has certain universal features, even if these are not always clear and sometimes are not noticed at all. What is universal is finitude and the longing for what lies beyond the finite. This is the experience that Voegelin calls the tension of existence, a state of tending or longing toward what lies beyond all the imperfections of limited existence, beyond knowledge of particulars toward the true as such, beyond particular enjoyments toward the good as such.

5. Fully developed human consciousness, according to Voegelin, involves an experientially grounded theoretical distinction between transcendent and immanent, infinite and finite. The "differentiation of consciousness" that this distinction constitutes is the major advance in existential level possible to man. It is a qualitative leap that opens up the possibility of free, responsible commitment to the

essential order of being that discloses itself in the fundamental tension of existence. It makes clear man's transcendental obligations: he must be loyal to the true and the good as such, not particular truths and conceptions of the good, and his fundamental stance as an inquirer must be exploratory, both adventurous and humble, not defensive.

6. A person who has little tolerance for tension will not wish to allow himself to experience his finitude and the longing for what is beyond. Instead of the open existence which suffers the longing for transcendent perfection, he may choose the hoped-for security of the closed mode of existence, eclipsing the experience of existential tension and whatever would remind him of it, such as the awareness that texts do not have plain and simple meanings but must be interpreted, that human knowledge is symbolically mediated, that the symbols in which it is expressed do not provide precise pictures of facts but analogies, and that it is the abhorred tension itself that alone can serve as one's guide to the adequacy of the analogies, leading one to seek them out, to keep seeking for better ones, and ultimately to seek beyond them.

7. This tension expresses itself not only in rational inquiry but also in a manifold of ways including faith, hope, and love as basic modes of orientation toward transcendence. Reason is motivated and guided by these still more basic cognitive modes in that it is their sensitivity toward transcendental mystery that functions as the criterion for the adequacy of the analogical symbols through which reason reaches into the living mystery of existence. Existential truth, in Voegelin's thought, is not an idea, nor is it a fact; it is a life—a life that is both an action and a passion and that is known as such only from within, through the faith, hope, and love that are themselves its principal constituents.

8. It is this last point—that the entry into truth must be by means of faith and concern rather than by a method promising certainty or even a calculable probability—which will seem most disconcerting to those whose concept of knowledge has been shaped by scientistic ideals. Yet in this lies one of the greatest strengths of

Voegelin's thought. It is precisely his recognition that the thinker must ultimately take the risk of entrusting himself to reality as to something with coherence, order, and intelligibility, which reaches to man as he reaches toward it, that keeps Voegelin's thought open to whatever truth may disclose itself in experience. His thought is systematic in that it views experience in the light of a coherent, consistently applied set of theoretical principles, but it is not a closed system. Rather it is an avenue of entry into the study of the particulars of the finite world and its history in all of their variety. By its renunciation of the claim to certainty, moreover, Voegelin's way of thinking becomes the antidote to the dogmatic claims of those who demand exclusiveness and exhaustiveness for their pictures of reality. The wars of opinion that such claims generate have come close to destroying our civilization—intellectually, spiritually, and politically—and they threaten it still. Deliverance from this threat can come only from the acknowledgement that, in believing, one makes a choice of what to love and place one's trust in and that this choice must be grounded not in the infallibility of one's intuitions or that of a method but in one's recognition— partially adequate but partially always inadequate—of what is worthy to be loved. Despite what may sometimes seem its polemical flavor, Voegelin's message is one of reconciliation. His philosophy is not so much a picture of reality as it is a portal, both into reality and into the brotherhood of man. Its most fundamental feature is its principled openness, by which it acknowledges in advance the possibility of more comprehensive experience and alternative interpretive schemata. This opens up access to expressions of truth in many periods and cultures, and in fact much of Voegelin's work as an intellectual and cultural historian has involved the recovery of insights that were in danger of becoming lost through the widespread inability of modern societies to attend to the truth of other forms of expression than their own.

9. Voegelin is a fundamentally hopeful thinker, despite his criticisms of many historical developments that he sees falling away from openness of existence into cultivated illusions. His hopefulness

is based on his faith that the universal structure of human experience, to the extent that it realizes itself in openness of existence, is a condition of being ordered by the fundamental tension of existence toward transcendental perfection of being, toward the true as such and the good as such, and in fact toward a splendor and beauty far greater than such words as these can convey. His faith and hope are not at all facile, however. He is keenly aware of the massive forces, political and cultural, organized and spontaneous, that impede the recovery of openness he has tried to further. He recognizes also that openness of existence is openness to the suffering of love for a perfection that will always remain beyond man in his finitude. The price of existence in truth is the willingness to endure the "intolerable shirt of flame" of which T. S. Eliot spoke in "Little Gidding." To live in history—in the full and proper sense of that word as understood by Voegelin—is to live in fire. It is to burn with an unquenchable longing that reaches beyond history, beyond time and the world. And it is to do so with conscious intention. Openness of existence is not only a state of being drawn but also of perpetual voluntary seeking. The seeking and the being drawn are for Voegelin one and the same movement of the soul as it surrenders and gives itself to the love of God—which is the one universal ground of our hope.

Because it is not a closed system, Voegelin's thought is not an end but a beginning. As was said, it is an avenue of entry into the study of historical particulars. Much of Voegelin's own writing has been the beginning of such study, but vast as his historical coverage has been—for a single historian—it remains only a beginning. There are important areas of inquiry he has scarcely touched upon, but which can profit greatly from study in the light of his principles. His historical work has dealt primarily with Near Eastern and classical antiquity, the Western Middle Ages, and subsequent Western developments. He has discussed Asian thought only briefly and has not gone into it in any great depth, but eventually an approach in terms of Voegelin's principles should illumine many aspects of Asian thought. There is a need for similar study of the non-Christian religions in general. Voegelin discusses some of these in various places, but for the most part does not make them the focus of study. There is probably no area of thought, except perhaps in politics, where the war of dogmas has become so acute and fratricidal as in religion, and probably no other area is as much in need of and has so much potential to benefit from an analysis in terms of the type of philosophy for which Voegelin has become the most important modern spokesman. I might add that in my opinion there are areas of rich philosophical and religious experience that Voegelin has scarcely touched on in his writings—particularly patristic theology and the entire field of Eastern Orthodox thought and spirituality. At one time Voegelin had intended to devote two volumes of *Order and History* to the study of Christian civilization, but this plan was not realized. His treatment of Christianity has been sketchy and, except for a few references to later thinkers, has been confined almost entirely to parts of the New Testament. There is a great deal more of Christian thought, in all its periods, that needs to be examined from the point of view of Voegelin's philosophical principles.

Another notable omission is Jewish thought since the destruction of the Second Temple. Voegelin discusses the religion of Israel and early Judaism extensively in *Israel and Revelation*, but nowhere does he discuss the Rabbinic tradition, which has made its own distinctive contributions to the development of critically reflective religious thought in the West. Christianity and Judaism, closely linked as they are in their roots, remain largely strangers to one another, and Voegelin's thought contains much that could serve as a basis for their mutual recognition and reconciliation, but the working out of such possibilities remains to be done.

Voegelin has left comparatively undeveloped the area of practical political implications. Although he is primarily a political philosopher, his political thought has been almost entirely theoretical, and on the highly abstract level of first principles, at that. There is little in his writings to indicate even sketchily what practical political paths might best be followed in the confusion of our time.

Both the resolution of the major religious conflicts that divide Western civilization and the working out of practical solutions to the political challenges facing the various societies of the contemporary world remain urgent unfinished business. This is not, of course, a matter of reproach against Voegelin. No one person can be expected to do all the philosophical work that has been neglected for centuries, and Voegelin has already spread his efforts far more widely than almost any other living scholar. The major importance of Voegelin's contribution is foundational: he has articulated theoretical principles and provided a framework and starting point for the work of a generation of scholars. The magnitude of the work remaining to be done along the lines he has indicated is a measure of Voegelin's own stature as a thinker.

There is a lack of novelty, as he himself emphasizes, in his basic pattern of thought— or, to put it more positively, in the continuity of his thought with that of the formative thinkers of the Western cultural tradition. It might be better, really, to describe Voegelin as a spokesman for philosophy as such than to speak of "Voegelin's philosophical principles." They are not specifically his at all, except insofar as he has reappropriated them and given them new expression. Rather he has made himself a voice for experiences and ways of thinking that go back into ancient myths and for a heritage of theoretical reflection on these that is at least as old as the pre-Socratics.

The present study has attempted to make this clear. I hope it has also shown, at least in passing, that despite his emphasis on ancient sources, Voegelin is not at all isolated from major movements in contemporary thought, but is involved with questions that have come to occupy many of the more perceptive thinkers of our period. It is likely that historians in a later century will discern in the cultural turmoil of our own the emergence of a new intellectual horizon in which figures like Voegelin, Jaspers, Lonergan, Polanyi, Ricoeur, Gadamer, and others, building on age-old philosophical foundations that had become obscured by centuries of immanentizing and externalizing thought, gave a new, more explicit expression to the existential perspective of the whole human being and to his sense of the fullness of experience with its transcendental dimension. Among these thinkers, Voegelin is unique in the breadth of his historical coverage and in the way he combines a rare comprehensiveness and depth of philosophical vision with concreteness of historical focus. There are philosophers—though few who have penetrated so deeply into the heart of man and his existential situation—and there are even philosophical historians. Eric Voegelin stands out among these, however, for the way he integrates the most profound philosophical reflection with the most searching historical inquiry. His combination of learning, comprehensiveness, existential openness, and depth of insight has made him the great philosopher of history of our time.

Glossary

Agathon (ἀγαθόν). The Good. In Plato, the good as such. A term for the transcendental pole of the tension (q.v.) of existence.

Aitia (αἰτία). Cause.

Aletheia (ἀλήθεια). Truth, that which is "unhidden" or "uncovered." In Voegelin, especially "lived" truth, existential truth, the experienced manifestness of "existential consciousness" (q.v.). Equivalent to *episteme*.

Amathia (ἀμαθία). Usually translated as ignorance, folly, rudeness, boorishness. Term used by Plato in the *Laws* to refer to voluntary ignorance motivated by aversion to truth (consequently a stronger term than "folly" in English). Voegelin says its symptom is an unwillingness to discuss, but its underlying cause is an unwillingness to be drawn into consideration of the transcendental.

Amicitia. Literally, friendship. Aquinas's term for the mutual love between God and man.

Anamnesis (ἀνάμνησις). Remembrance or recollection. In Plato's *Meno*, the conception that whatever one learns in this life is recalled from the memory of what was known in a former life. In Voegelin's interpretation, a symbol for the recognition that the explication of experience is the bringing into consciousness of what had previously been implicitly present but unconscious.

Anima mundi. World soul. Latin term for Plato's animate cosmos in the *Timaeus*. One of the hypostases of Plotinus.

Apeiron (ἄπειρον). Unlimited, indefinite, unbounded. In Anaximander, the "unlimited" source of all particular things. Because it transcends all limits, it is in principle undefinable. Voegelin uses it (especially in *OH*, vol. 4) to refer to the pole of the *metaxy* (q.v.) standing opposite the One (the Beyond).

Aphtharsia (ἀφθαρσία). Imperishability. The characteristic of the gods as symbols of perfection of being. An aspect of the transcendental pole of the tension of existence or *metaxy* (q.v.).

APODICTIC. Certain or necessary. Used to refer to knowledge of what must be, as compared with what can be (and may even be).

APPERCEPTION. Leibniz's term for the introspective or reflective apprehension by the mind of its own inner states. Contrasts with "perception," which is awareness of something external. Used by Voegelin to refer to self-awareness, a combination of immediate and mediated, reflective self-awareness.

Arche (ἀρχή). Beginning, principle. Especially ultimate undemonstrable principle, or ultimate underlying substance.

Athanatizein (ἀθᾰνᾰτίζειν). To immortalize. See "immortalizing" and "exodus."

BALANCE OF CONSCIOUSNESS. Voegelin's term for the precarious awareness of the conditions of existence in the *metaxy* (q.v.), easily lost when the experience of being drawn toward the transcendental pole becomes sufficiently vivid to tempt one to expect escape from the *metaxy* and from the existential tension (q.v.) that characterizes it.

BETWEEN, THE. See *metaxy*.

BEYOND, THE. Translation of Greek *epekeina*. That which is ultimate and is itself indefinable because it surpasses all categories of understanding. The proportionate goal of the fundamental tension of existence.

Caritas. In Christianity, the love of God for man and of man for God or for fellow men when this is an expression of the love of God. Latin translation of the Greek *agape* (ἀγάπη). Cf. *amicitia*.

CLOSED EXISTENCE, CLOSURE. Voegelin's term for the mode of existence in which there are internal impediments to a free flow of truth into consciousness and to the pull of the transcendental. Contrasts with "open existence" (q.v.).

CLOSURE. See "closed existence."

Cognitio fidei (or *amoris*, or *spei*). Knowledge through or by faith (or love, or hope). A more fundamental (and compact, q.v.) cognitive mode, according to Voegelin, than reason. An important element in the preanalytic cognitive matrix from which reason develops.

COMMON SENSE. According to Voegelin's interpretation of representatives of the late eighteenth-century school of thought that goes by this name (particularly Thomas Reid), a compact (q.v.) form of rationality made up of good habits of judgment and conduct deriving historically from noetic experience, but without a differentiated knowledge of *noesis* (q.v.).

COMPACT. Voegelin's term for experience having distinguishable features yet to be noticed as distinct. Contrasts with "differentiated" (q.v.).

CONSUBSTANTIALITY. Term adopted by Voegelin from John A. Wilson (*The Intellectual Adventure of Ancient Man*) for the sensed underlying unity of reality, the common participation of all levels of being in the tension (q.v.) of existence toward transcendental (q.v.) perfection.

COSMOS. In Voegelin's usage, the whole of ordered reality including animate and inanimate nature and the gods. (Not to be confused with the modern conception of "cosmos" as the astrophysical universe.) Encompasses all of reality, including the full range of the tension of existence toward the transcendental (q.v.). Noetic and pneumatic differentiations (q.v.) of consciousness separate this cosmos into the immanent "world" and the transcendent "divine ground."

DECULTURATION. Voegelin's term for the loss of culture. He interprets culture as a process in which soul and character are formed through experiences of transcendence and the virtues (such as faith, love, hope, reason) inherent in "open existence" (q.v.). Equivalent to "deformation" (q.v.), but with greater emphasis on the social aspects of the process.

DEFORMATION. Voegelin's term for the destruction of the order of the soul, which should be "formed" by (i.e., should receive its vital principle from) the love of transcendental perfection inherent in the fundamental tension of existence.

DIALECTIC. Constructive exchange of thoughts. The characteristic mode of inquiry of genuine philosophy (q.v.) or *noesis* (q.v.). Characterized by critical reflectiveness and "openness" (q.v.).

DIFFERENTIATED. Voegelin's term for consciousness in which the distinguishable features of a previously "compact" field of experience are noticed as distinct.

DIFFERENTIATION OF CONSCIOUSNESS. Voegelin's general phrase for the process by which the discernible features of consciousness as such and its objects are noticed and given expression. May have either noetic (q.v.) or pneumatic (q.v.) emphases. Especially refers to the development of a sense of the distinction between transcendent (q.v.) and immanent (q.v.), e.g., between truth as such and particular truths, the good as such and particular goods, the transcendental divine ground and the world of immanence. The transcendental pole that is differentiated serves as a point of orientation that orders or structures consciousness.

Dikaiosune (δικαιοσύνη). Justice (considered as a quality of a person), righteousness.

Dike (δίκη). Justice, order, law, right.

DOGMATOMACHY. Voegelin's term for conflict over opinions; motivated by philodoxy (q.v.).

Doxa (δόξᾰ). Opinion, judgment. In Greek philosophy, an inferior grade of knowledge as compared with *episteme* (q.v.). In Parmenides, the realm of particular phenomena as compared with true being. In Plato, knowledge of the sensory world as compared with knowledge of ideas. Voegelin uses the term particularly to refer to externalizing conceptions.

DOXIC THINKING. In Voegelin's use, thinking that tends to focus on a *doxa* (q.v.) and to confuse the model with the reality it symbolically represents.

DOXOGRAPHY. A descriptive (not analytical) account of opinions.

ECLIPSE. Voegelin's term for the voluntary, perverse closure of consciousness against reality; a state that may become habitual and unconscious, but never entirely free from the pressure of reality and the anxiety produced by the attempt to evade it. Equivalent to "closed existence" (q.v.).

ECUMENICITY. Voegelin's term for the tendency of an imperial order (one that embraces a number of particular societies) to seek to attain genuine "universality" (q.v.) by extending its political domination throughout the *ecumene* (the full range of territory available for such domination).

EGOLOGICAL. Husserl's term for that which pertains to the ego or to egology, which is the study of the ego considered as pure consciousness (all other aspects of the thinking individual being "bracketed," i.e., placed outside consideration, in accord with phenomenological method).

Eikos mythos (εἰκός μῦθος). Likely or probable tale. In Plato, a myth that serves as an analogy for what ultimately lies beyond human comprehension.

Epekeina (ἐπέκεινα). The Beyond (q.v.).

Episteme (ἐπιστήμη). Theoretical knowledge. In Greek philosophy, true knowledge, as compared with *doxa*. In Voegelin, knowledge that is the explication of genuine philosophical experience; especially, experiential knowledge of existence as ordered by the love of transcendental perfection of being. Equivalent to *theoria* (q.v.).

EQUIVALENCE OF SYMBOLS. In Voegelin, the principle that two symbolisms are equivalent, despite differences of individual form, if they refer recognizably to the same structures in reality.

ERISTIC. From Greek *eris*: strife. In Plato, contentious reasoning, characteristic of philodoxy (q.v.). The opposite of "dialectic" (q.v.).

Eros (ἔρος). Desire, love, longing. Voegelin's use of the term, based on Plato's, does not refer (in the manner made popular by Freud) to specifically sexual desire, but to desire as such and especially to desire for the *summum bonum* (q.v.) implicit in all particular desires for limited goods. As such it is virtually equivalent in Voegelin's usage to the "tension of existence."

Eunomia (εὐνομία). Well-orderedness. In Voegelin's use, specifically existence ordered morally and cognitively by the tension of existence toward the pole of transcendental perfection of being.

EXISTENTIAL CONSCIOUSNESS. In Voegelin's use, the reflective self-awareness of human existence in the *metaxy* (q.v.), i.e., between poles of immanence and transcendence, finitude and infinity, imperfection and perfection, and so on. See also "truth of existence," "intentional consciousness."

EXODUS. In Voegelin, the process of transcendence. According to Voegelin "exodus from reality" (which would be escape from the tension of existence) is impossible; what is possible and is in fact the universal calling of humanity is "exodus within reality," i.e., open existence (q.v.) in the *metaxy* (q.v.) oriented toward its transcendental pole.

EXPERIENCE. In Voegelin, a "luminous perspective" within the process of reality. Voegelin generally follows Aristotle's conception of experience (*Met*. A, 1) as more than sense data, but less than art or "science" in the sense of *episteme* (q.v.).

Fides formata. Formed faith. Aquinas's term for the adequate orientation of the soul toward God, not only through correct teachings about Him but also through His love experienced within the soul. According to

Aquinas, it is love (*caritas*, q.v.) that is the soul or vital principle of faith. A higher level of faith than *fides informis* (q.v.), which, lacking love as its vital principle, is incomplete.

Fides informis. Unformed faith. Aquinas's term for a proper but rudimentary orientation toward God through the teachings of the Church. A lower level of faith than *fides formata* (q.v.).

Gnosis (γνῶσις). Knowledge. Originally a general term in Greek for knowledge of various sorts. Later, especially with the Gnostic movement of the early Christian era, a purported direct, immediate apprehension or vision of truth without the need for critical reflection; the special gift of a spiritual and cognitive elite. According to Voegelin, the claim to *gnosis* may take intellectual, emotional, and volitional forms.

GNOSTICISM. A type of thinking that claims absolute cognitive mastery of reality. Relying as it does on a claim to *gnosis* (q.v.), gnosticism considers its knowledge not subject to criticism. As a religious or quasi-religious movement, gnosticism may take transcendentalizing (as in the case of the Gnostic movement of late antiquity) or immanentizing forms (as in the case of Marxism).

GROUND. That upon which something is founded. In the sense of the "divine ground," Voegelin uses it to refer to the supreme, undefinable, transcendent reality which may be considered either as the source or origin (*arche*, q.v.) of both the world and the *metaxy* (q.v.) or as "the Beyond" (q.v.) that forms existence by drawing it into participation (q.v.).

Helkein (ἕλκειν). To draw, drag, pull. In Voegelin, the tension of existence when it is experienced as the power of attraction exercised by the transcendental. Correlative to *zetein* or *zetesis* (q.v.).

HISTORIOGENESIS. Term coined by Voegelin for the type of symbolism developed in speculation on the origin and cause of a society. Along with the other symbolisms of origin collectively (designated by the standard terms, anthropogony, cosmogony, and theogony), it is considered by Voegelin to be the mythic equivalent of a noetic quest for the ground of being.

HISTORIOMACHY. Voegelin's term for competing claims to prestigious status made by one society or cultural or religious group against another on the basis of its purported antiquity.

Homonoia (ὁμόνοια). Like-mindedness. In Aristotle, friendship based on likeness in participation in *nous* (q.v.); not the sharing of opinions or positions, but sharing in *nous* as the dynamic movement elicited by the attraction of transcendental perfection. In Christian thought, the participation of Christians in the *nous* of Christ. Alexander the Great used the term *homonoia* to refer to the ideal of peace among the subjects of his ecumenic empire.

HORIZON. In Voegelin's use, a general term for the experience of limitedness; symbol of the boundary between the known world and that which remains beyond it and consequently mysterious.

Hyperouranion (ὑπερούπάνιον). Beyond the heavens. Plato's term in the *Phaedrus* for the realm of ultimate reality beyond the home of the gods.

Hypostasis (ὑπόστᾱσις). A standing under, support, substance, hence a real being, an individual entity, a thing.

HYPOSTATIZING. Voegelin's term for the process by which features of the *metaxy* (q.v.), e.g., the transcendental or immanent poles of the tension of existence, are falsely conceived of as though they were individual entities.

IMMANENT. Literally "dwelling in." Present within limited, mundane reality. The opposite of "transcendent" (q.v.).

IMMORTALIZING (from Greek *athanatizein*). The process of transcendence considered as oriented toward the mode of existence (immortality) of the gods or of the divine "ground" (q.v.). See also exodus, *aphtharsia*.

IN-BETWEEN, THE. See *metaxy*.

INDEX. Term coined by Voegelin (used principally in "Eternal Being in Time" and "What Is Political Reality?") for the language symbols used in the exegesis of existence in the *metaxy* (q.v.). Such symbols speak in terms of objects but do not refer to independently existing things. They are neither names, concepts, nor definitions. Rather they indicate poles of the tension of existence. For example, to say that "man participates in being" is to use "man" and "being" not as the names of entities but as pointers with which to explicate the tension of existence. Intended to counter the tendency toward hypostatizing (q.v.) of such symbols.

INTENTIONAL CONSCIOUSNESS. Consciousness oriented toward cognitive objects. Contrasts in Voegelin's use with "existential consciousness" (q.v.).

INTENTIONALITY. The property of consciousness whereby it is oriented toward cognitive objects. The "intentional object" is not necessarily an actual entity; it is whatever consciousness is consciousness *of*.

INTUITION. Direct and immediate apprehension of anything, internal or external to the knowing subject. Gnosticism, as Voegelin uses the term, is characterized by intuitionist cognitive claims.

Ipsum Esse. Being Itself. In Aquinas, a term for God considered as unlimited, ontologically necessary Being, as compared with finite, contingent beings, which are dependent for their existence on the creative act of God.

Libido dominandi. Pleasure in dominating, especially intellectual domination.

Logos (λόγος). Reason, rational capacity, definition, intelligible structure, an analytical account (as compared with a myth). A central feature of *theoria* or *episteme* (q.v.).

Metalepsis (μετάληψις). Participation (q.v.).

Metastasis (μετάστασις). Change, transformation, revolution. Term introduced by Voegelin in *OH*, 1:452, to signify "the change in the constitution of being envisaged by the Israelite prophets." Subsequently used extensively to refer to all unrealistically expected transformations of man, society, the structure of existence, and so on. The fundamental form of such utopian expectation is that escape from the tension of existence will be possible through movement out of the *metaxy* (q.v.) toward identity or union with one of its poles.

Metaxy (μεταξύ). Between. Plato's symbol representing the experience of human existence as "between" lower and upper poles: man and the divine, imperfection and perfection, ignorance and knowledge, and so on. Equivalent to the symbol of "participation of being."

Methexis (μεθέξις). Participation (q.v.).

Mythos (μῦθος). Myth, story, tale, fable. Originally any speech or account, not necessarily fictitious. In Plato's philosophical use, an account in story form, as compared with *logos* (a conceptual, analytic account). *Eikos mythos*, a likely or probable story, i.e., an analogically illuminating account in the form of a story, as in the cosmogonic myth of the *Timaeus*, the story of Atlantis in the *Critias*, and the story of judgment after death in the *Gorgias* and the *Republic*.

MYTHO-SPECULATION. Voegelin's term for a speculation (especially regarding ultimate origins and ends) in the medium of myth. A combination of mythopoesis (myth-making) and *noesis* (q.v.) intermediate between the compactness of cosmological myth and noetic differentiation.

Noesis (νόησις). The activity of *nous* (q.v.), the process by which *episteme* (q.v.) is developed; reflective understanding involving critical self-awareness on the part of the inquirer based on understanding of the nature of inquiry as such. *Noesis* does not bring knowledge of a previously unknown reality, but differentiated insight into hitherto compactly experienced reality.

NOETIC DIFFERENTIATION. Voegelin's term for the process by which one moves from compact consciousness (which tends to express itself in mythic symbols) to a more differentiated, conceptually articulated awareness of the inquiring consciousness and its structure, including both its reflective character and its orientation toward the transcendental pole of the tension of inquiry, i.e., toward Truth as such. Historically, the birth of philosophy in classical Greece.

Nomos (νόμος). Law, measure.

Nous (νοῦς). In Voegelin's use, based primarily on Plato and Aristotle, the capacity of seeking *episteme* (q.v.) under the guidance of attraction toward the transcendental (q.v.).

OPEN EXISTENCE, OPENNESS. In Voegelin, the mode of existence in which consciousness is consistently and unreservedly oriented toward truth and toward the transcendental pole of the tension of existence. Contrasts with "closed existence" (q.v.).

Opsis (ὄψις). Vision. Platonic term interpreted by Voegelin as referring to the revelatory aspect of the mutual participation of divine and human in each other; what it reveals according to Voegelin is the fundamental order and direction of the process of reality.

Ousia (οὐσία). Essence. Aristotle's term for "being" or "entity." According to Voegelin, Aristotle's term expressed the "things" of the "cosmos" (q.v.), which included both immanent and transcendent dimensions, and should not be translated as "substance," a term in later, immanentistically conceived metaphysics.

PARTICIPATION (Greek *metalepsis, methexis, mimesis*). Refers to sharing the qualities of a supreme exemplar, in which they are present in their perfection. In "participation in being" being is an analogical term with varying degrees of applicability; it describes existence in the *metaxy* (q.v.) as a condition between higher and lower degrees of reality.

Pathos (πάθος). Experience, event, passion, what happens to one, what is undergone. Not to be confused with the popular use of "pitiableness."

Peitho (πείθω). Persuasion. In Voegelin (following Plato), the persuasive communication of (or invitation to) truth, especially the truth of existential order.

Periagoge (περιαγωγή). Turning around, conversion. Plato's term for the cognitive and moral reorientation toward the True and the Good as such.

Philia (φιλία). Love, especially in the sense of friendship.

PHILODOXY. Voegelin's term (based on Plato's *philodoxos*) for "love of opinion." Contrasts with "philosophy" (q.v.) or "love of wisdom" in that it conceives of truth in immanentistic rather than transcendental terms and tends to claim a perfect correspondence between ultimate reality and the ideas or interpretive models used to represent it. Another point of contrast is that whereas philosophy is inherently oriented toward further inquiry through openness to the Question (q.v.), philodoxy is the expression of a desire to put an end to questioning and thereby to escape from the "tension of existence" (q.v.). In this respect, philodoxy is a principal manifestation of "closed existence" (q.v.).

Philomythos (φιλόμῦθος). Lover of myth. Aristotle's term for one who thinks in the medium of myth and whom he describes as, in a sense, a philosopher (*Met.* 982b18 ss).

PHILOSOPHY. The love of wisdom in the sense of transcendental truth. As Voegelin (following Plato) conceives it, philosophy is characterized by the realization that one does not actually possess transcendental truth but is oriented toward it through love. Contrasts with philodoxy (q.v.).

Phronesis (φρόνησις). Intention, purpose; practical wisdom, prudence. In Aristotle, the understanding that guides ethical virtue. Plato had given the concept a more contemplative emphasis, sometimes treating it as virtually equivalent to *nous* (q.v.).

Pleonexia (πλεονεξία). A disposition to take more than one's share.

Pneuma (πνεῦμα). Wind, air, breath, spirit. In Voegelin's use, the presence of the transcendental pole of the tension of existence as a force ordering the soul from within. An equivalent symbol for *helkein* (q.v.).

PNEUMATIC DIFFERENTIATION. Voegelin's term for the awakening of the soul both by and to the experience of the pull (*helkein*, q.v.) in the tension of existence toward the pole of transcendental perfection; the emergent realization of the absolutely transcendent character of that pole. Historically, the realization among both ancient Israelites and early Christians of the absolute distinction between God and the created realm.

Pothos (πόθος). Desire, yearning, longing (for mundane fulfillments). Defined by Voegelin as "a powerful desire to reach out indefinitely toward the unknown and unheard of." Used especially to refer to Alexander the Great's unlimited ambitions.

Psyche (ψυχή). Breath, vital principle, soul. In Voegelin's use, a comprehensive term for the process in which the pull toward the transcendental pole of the tension of existence is sensed and responded to; includes varying degrees of consciousness.

QUESTION, THE. Voegelin's term for the tension of existence in its aspect as a questioning unrest seeking not simply particular truth, but still more the transcendental pole of truth as such: "not just any question but the quest concerning the mysterious ground of all being." Expresses itself in mythopoetic as well as noetic acts.

Realissimum. The "most real." Term for God or the divine ground considered as supreme reality.

REFLECTION. Consideration of experience by way of a mediating interpretive model. Contrasts with immediacy of experience.

REFLECTIVE DISTANCE. Voegelin's term for the realization of the difference between the experience of existence as an event of conscious "participation" (q.v.) in being and the expression of this event in language symbols. This is an essential ingredient, according to Voegelin, in the "balance of consciousness" (q.v.) and involves the conception of truth not as information but as a growth of luminosity in the process of reality. Contrasts with "doxic" thinking (q.v.) and claims to *gnosis* (q.v.).

SCIENTISM. The reductionist theory that all reality should be knowable by the methods of the natural sciences (especially mathematical, quantitative method). Tends to involve the expectation of control of man through scientific knowledge and technique.

Scotosis. Darkening, turning toward darkness. Voluntary ignorance. Term coined by Bernard Lonergan and used by Voegelin for the attitude seeking "eclipse of reality" (q.v.).

SECOND REALITY. Voegelin's term, drawn from Robert Musil, for a fictitious world imagined as true by a person using it to mask and thereby "eclipse" (q.v.) genuine reality.

SECULARIZATION. According to Voegelin (*OH*, 4:196), "a polite word for 'deculturation'" (q.v.).

Spoudaios (σπουδαῖος). Serious, earnest person. Aristotle's term for the "mature" rational and ethical person, the fully developed human being capable of intelligent thought and responsible decision and action.

SUBSTANCE. From Latin *substantia*: standing under. In Voegelin's use the underlying reality of anything. Not to be confused with the use of the term in traditional metaphysics, where it refers to an independently existing entity. See also *hypostasis*.

Summum bonum. The "greatest good." Equivalent Latin term for the *agathon* (q.v.) in Plato; the "divine measure," or "transcendental perfection."

SYMBOLISM (PRIMARY AND SECONDARY). In Voegelin's use of the term, "primary symbolism" expresses genuine philosophical or spiritual experience. Correct interpretation of it requires parallel experience on the part of the interpreter. "Secondary symbolism" replaces primary when the original symbol is separated from its engendering experience and used to refer to some experience (either actual or purported) differing from the original.

Telos (τέλος). End, purpose, goal, completion. The objective or completion of a process of development. In Aristotle, the purpose or "final cause" of a process.

TENSION. A condition of tending toward a goal. Voegelin uses the term especially to refer to what he calls the "tension of existence," the fundamental experience of longing for transcendental fulfillment, the Beyond (q.v.), the *summum bonum* (q.v.).

Thaumazein (θαυμάζειν). To wonder. The experience from which Aristotle said philosophy begins. An aspect of what Voegelin calls the "tension of existence"; equivalent to the Question (q.v.).

THEOPHANY. A manifestation of the divine.

Theoria (θεωρία). In Plato and Aristotle, contemplative wisdom; equivalent to *episteme* (q.v.).

THIRD GOD, THE. In Plato's *Laws*, *nous* (q.v.) considered as the divine source of order manifest after the ages of Kronos (the first god) and Zeus (the second god).

TRANSCENDENT. From Latin *transcendere*: to go beyond, surpass. General term for that which extends or lies beyond some set of limits; may be relative (beyond some particular limits) or absolute (beyond all possible limits). The opposite of "immanent" (q.v.). See also "the Beyond," "ground."

TRANSCENDENTAL. General term for that which is "transcendent" (q.v.), but tending to refer to absolute rather than relative transcendence. In medieval usage, the term for attributes that cannot be circumscribed by the boundaries of the Aristotelian categories; the medieval *transcendentia* or "transcendentals" are: *ens* (being), *unum* (one), *bonum* (good), *verum* (true), *res* (thing), and *aliquid* (something).

TRUTH OF EXISTENCE. Voegelin's term for transcendentally oriented conscious existence; involves the experience of: (1) finiteness and creatureliness; (2) dissatisfaction with imperfection and a sense of transcendental perfection; (3) the luminosity or manifestness of such experience in consciousness; (4) the self-transcending tendency of consciousness seeking fullness of truth.

UNIVERSALITY, UNIVERSAL. Voegelin's term for the experience of the pull (*helkein*, q.v.) of the transcendental in the tension of existence as the source of existential order for all human beings. Also refers to the order so constituted.

WORLD. In Voegelin's use, not a quantity of territory but a substantive order involving the experience of "universality" (q.v.). Contrasts in this respect with *ecumene*, which in Voegelin's interpretation is a territorial term. According to Voegelin, the symbol "world" developed historically when the "cosmos" (q.v.) separated in the differentiated consciousness of existence into its immanent (symbolized by "world") and transcendent (symbolized by "God") components. "World" in this sense involves an ordering orientation toward transcendental perfection of being.

Zetema (ζήτημα). Inquiry. In Voegelin's use (following Plato), an existential inquiry, the process of the conceptual self-illumination of the soul; a search for truth, both cognitive and existential.

Zetesis (ζήτησις). Search, seeking. In Voegelin's use, that aspect of the dynamics of the tension of existence in which it is experienced as a seeking or striving toward the transcendental pole of the tension. Correlative to *helkein* (q.v.).

Bibliography

This bibliography is in two parts. The first is a list in chronological order of all of the publications of Eric Voegelin. The second is a list in alphabetical order of secondary sources. The latter includes works referred to in the present study as well as works that proved especially important in the preparation of it. It does not include all of the many essays on Voegelin by other authors. For an extensive listing of such material from 1953 to 1977, see Stephen A. McKnight, ed., *Eric Voegelin's Search for Order in History* (Baton Rouge and London: Louisiana State University Press, 1978), pp. 202–7.

PUBLICATIONS BY ERIC VOEGELIN

1922   "Die gesellschaftliche Bestimmtheit soziologischer Erkenntnis." *Zeitschrift für Volkswirtschaft und Sozialpolitik*, n.s., 2:331–48.

1924   "Reine Rechtslehre und Staatslehre." *Zeitschrift für öffentliches Recht* 4:80–131.

"Die Zeit in der Wirtschaft." *Archiv für Sozialwissenschaft und Sozialpolitik* 53:186–211.

1925   "Über Max Weber." *Deutsche Vierteljahrsschrift für Literaturwissenschaft und Geistesgeschichte* 3:177–93.

1926   "Die Verfassungmäßigkeit des 18. Amendments zur United States Constitution." *Zeitschrift für öffentliches Recht* 5:445–64.

"Wirtschafts- und Klassengegensatz in America." *Unterrichtsbriefe des Instituts für angewandte Soziologie* 5:6–11.

1927   "Kelsen's Pure Theory of Law." *Political Science Quarterly* 42:268–76.

"La Follette und die Wisconsin-Idee." *Zeitschrift für Politik* 17:309–21.

"Zur Lehre von der Staatsform." *Zeitschrift für öffentliches Recht* 6:572–608.

1928 "Die ergänzende Bill zum Federal Reserve Act." *Nationalwirtschaft* 2:225–29.

"Die ergänzende Bill zum Federal Reserve Act und die Dollarstabilisation." *Mitteilungen des Verbandes österreichischer Banken und Bankiers* 10:321–28.

"Konjunkturforschung und Stabilisation des Kapitalismus." *Mitteilungen des Verbandes österreichischer Banken und Bankiers* 9:252–59.

"Der Sinn der Erklärung der Menschen- und Bürgerrechte von 1789." *Zeitschrift für öffentliches Recht* 8:82–120.

"Die Souveränitätstheorie Dickinsons und die reine Rechtslehre." *Zeitschrift für öffentliches Recht* 8:413–34.

Über die Form des amerikanischen Geistes. Tübingen: J. C. B. Mohr.

"Zwei Grundbegriffe der Humeschen Gesellschaftslehre. *Archiv für angewandte Soziologie* 1 (no. 2): 11–16.

1929 "Die Transaktion." *Archiv für angewandte Soziologie* 1 (no. 4–5): 14–21.

1930 "Die amerikanische Theorie vom Eigentum." *Archiv für angewandte Soziologie* 2:165–72.

"Die amerikanische Theorie vom ordentlichen Rechtsverfahren und von der Freiheit." *Archiv für angewandte Soziologie* 3:40–57.

"Die Einheit des Rechts und das soziale Sinngebilde Staat." *Internationale Zeitschrift für Theorie des Rechts* 1–2:58–89.

"Max Weber." *Kölner Vierteljahrshefte für Soziologie* 9:1–16.

"Die österreichische Verfassungsreform von 1929." *Zeitschrift für Politik* 19:585–615.

Translation of "Das Recht und der Staat," by Harold Laski. *Zeitschrift für öffentliches Recht* 10:1–27.

1931   "Das Sollen im System Kants." In *Gesellschaft, Staat und Recht*, edited by Alfred Verdrosz, pp. 136–73. Vienna: Springer.

        "Die Verfassungslehre von Carl Schmitt: Versuch einer konstruktiven Analyse ihrer staatstheoretischen Prinzipien." *Zeitschrift für öffentliches Recht* 11:80–109.

1932   "Nachwort." In Ernst Dimnet, *Die Kunst des Denkens*, pp. 279–96. Freiburg: Herder.

1933   *Rasse und Staat*. Tübingen: J. C. B. Mohr.

        Die Rassenidee in der Geistesgeschichte von Ray bis Carus. Berlin: Junker und Duennhaupt.

1934   "Le régime administratif: Avantages et inconvénients." *Mémoires de l'Académie Internationale de Droit Comparé* 2:126–49.

1935   "Rasse und Staat." In *Psychologie des Gemeinschaftslebens*, edited by Otto Klemm, p. 91–104. Jena: Fischer.

1936   *Der autoritäre Staat*. Vienna: Springer.

        "Josef Redlich." *Juridische Blätter* 65:485–86.

        "Volksbildung, Wissenschaft und Politik." *Monatsschrift für Kultur und Politik* 1:594–603.

1937   "Change in the Ideas on Government and Constitution in Austria since 1918." Austrian Memorandum No. 1–3. International Studies Conference on Peaceful Change, Paris.

        "Das Timurbild der Humanisten: Eine Studie zur politischen Mythenbildung." *Zeitschrift für öffentliches Recht* 17:545–82. Reprinted in Eric Voegelin, *Anamnesis* (1966); pp. 153–78.

1938   *Die politischen Religionen*. Vienna: Bermann-Fischer.

1939   Review of *The Ruling Class*, by Gaetano Mosca. *Journal of Politics* 1:434–36.

1940   "Extended Strategy: A New Technique of Dynamic Relations." *Journal of Politics* 2:189–200.

        "The Growth of the Race Idea." *Review of Politics* 2:283–317.

1941   "The Mongol Orders of Submission to European Powers, 1245–

1255." *Byzantion* 15:378–413. German translation in Voegelin, *Anamnesis* (1966), pp. 179–222.

"Right and Might." Review of *Law, the State, and the International Community*, by James Brown Scott. *Review of Politics* 3:122–23.

"Two Recent Contributions to the Science of Law." Review of *Introduction to the Sociology of Law*, by N. S. Timasheff, and *Jurisprudence*, by Edgar Bodenheimer. *Review of Politics* 3:399–404.

"Some Problems of German Hegemony," *Journal of Politics* 3:154–68.

1942   "The Theory of Legal Science: A Review." Review of *The Theory of Legal Science*, by Huntington Cairns. *Louisiana Law Review* 4:554–72.

Review of *The Structure of the Nazi Economy*, by Maxine Y. Sweezy, and *The Dual State*, by Ernst Fraenkel. *Journal of Politics* 4:269–72.

1944   "Nietzsche, the Crisis and the War." *Journal of Politics* 6:177–212.

"Political Theory and the Pattern of General History." *American Political Science Review* 38:746–54. Reprinted in *Research in Political Science*, edited by E. S. Griffith, pp. 190–201. Chapel Hill: University of North Carolina Press, 1948.

Review of *The Decline of Liberalism*, by John Hallowell. *Journal of Politics* 6:107–9.

"Siger de Brabant." *Philosophy and Phenomenological Research* 4:505–26.

1945   Review of *Contemporary Italy: Its Intellectual and Moral Origins*, by Count Carlo Sforza. *Journal of Politics* 7:94–97.

1946   "Bakunin's Confession." *Journal of Politics* 8:24–43. German translation in Voegelin, *Anamnesis* (1966), pp. 223–38.

Review of *Soviet Politics, At Home and Abroad*, by Fred L. Schuman. *Journal of Politics* 8:212–20.

Review of *The Lessons of Germany*, by G. Eisler et al. *American Political Science Review* 40:385–86.

1947   "Plato's Egyptian Myth." *Journal of Politics* 9:307–24.

Review of *The Myth of the State*, by Ernst Cassirer. *Journal of Politics* 9:445–47.

Review of *Post-War Governments of Europe*, edited by D. Fellman. *American Political Science Review* 41:595–96.

Review of *Soviet Legal Theory: Its Social Background and Development*, by Rudolph Schlesinger. *Journal of Politics* 9:129–31.

"Zu Sanders 'Allgemeiner Staatslehre.'" *Österreichische Zeitschrift für öffentliches Recht*, n.s., 1:103–35.

1948   "The Origins of Scientism." *Social Research* 15:462–94. Translation, "Wissenschaft als Aberglaube: Die Urspruenge des Scientifismus," *Wort und Wahrheit* 6 (1951) 341–60.

Review of *Homo Ludens*, by J. Huizinga. *Journal of Politics* 10:179–87.

1949   "The Philosophy of Existence: Plato's *Gorgias*." *Review of Politics* 11:477–98.

Review of *Western Political Thought*, by John Bowle. *Review of Politics* 11:262–63.

Review of *On Tyranny*, by Leo Strauss. *Review of Politics* 11:241–44.

1950   "The Formation of the Marxian Revolutionary Idea." *Review of Politics* 12:275–302. Reprinted in *The Image of Man*, edited by M. A. Fitzsimmons, T. McAvoy, and Frank O'Malley, pp. 265–81. Notre Dame: University of Notre Dame Press, 1959. Translation, "La Formacion de la idea revolucionaria marxista." *Hechos e Ideas* 12 (1951):227–50.

Review of *The New Science*, by Giovanni Battista Vico; translated by T. G. Bergin and M. A. Fisch. *Catholic Historical Review* 35:75–76.

1951   "Machiavelli's Prince: Background and Formation." *Review of Politics* 13:142–68.

       "More's Utopia," *Österrichische Zeitschrift für öffentliches Recht*, n.s., 3:451–68.

1952   *The New Science of Politics:* An Introduction. Chicago: University of Chicago Press. German translation with a foreword, *Die Neue Wissenschaft der Politik: Eine Einführung.* Munich: Puste, 1952. Italian translation, *La nuova Scienza politica*. Turin: Borla, 1968 with an introduction by A. Del Noce, "Eric Voegelin e la critica dell' idea di modernità."

       "Gnostische Politik." *Merkur* 4:301–17.

       "Goethe's Utopia." In *Goethe After Two Centuries*, edited by Carl Hammer, Jr., pp. 55–62. Baton Rouge: Louisiana State University Press.

1953   "The Origins of Totalitarianism." *Review of Politics* 15:68–85. With a reply by Hannah Arendt.

       "The Oxford Political Philosophers." *Philosophical Quarterly* 3:97–114. Translation, "Philosophia der Politik in Oxford." *Philosophische Rundschau* 1:23–48.

       Review of *Geschichtswissenschaft*, by F. Wagner. *American Political Science Review* 47:261–62.

       "The World of Homer." *Review of Politics* 15:491–523.

1954   Review of *Plato's Modern Enemies and the Theory of Natural Law*, by John Wild, and *In Defense of Plato*, by Ronald B. Levinson. *American Political Science Review* 48:859–62.

1955   Review of *Politique et philosophie chez Thomas Hobbes*, by Raymond Polin. *American Political Science Review* 49:597–98.

1956   *Order and History*. Vol. 1: *Israel and Revelation*. Baton Rouge: Louisiana State University Press.

1957   *Order and History*. Vol. 2: *The World of the Polis*. Baton Rouge: Louisiana State University Press.

Order and History. Vol. 3: *Plato and Aristotle.* Baton Rouge: Louisiana State University Press.

1958 "Der Prophet Elias." *Hochland* 50:325–39.

1959 *Wissenschaft, Politik und Gnosis.* Munich: Kösel. English translation by William J. Fitzpatrick in Voegelin, *Science, Politics, and Gnosticism* (1968), pp. 1–80.

"Demokratie im neuen Europa." *Gesellschaft-Staat-Erziehung* 4:293–300.

"Diskussionsbereitschaft." In *Erziehung zur Freiheit*, edited by Albert Hunold, pp. 355–72. Zurich: Erlenbach; and Stuttgart: Rentsch. Translation, "On Readiness to Rational Discussion." In *Freedom and Serfdom*, edited by Albert Hunold, pp. 269–84. Dordrecht, Holland: D. Reidel, 1961.

1960 "El concepto de la 'buena sociedad.'" *Cuadernos del Congresso por la Libertad de la Cultura*, supp. 40, pp. 25–28.

"Historiogenesis." *Philosophisches Jahrbuch* 68:419–46. Reprinted in *Philosophia Viva: Festschrift für Alois Dempf*, edited by Max Müller and Michael Schmaus, pp. 419–46. Freiburg and Munich: Albert, 1960. Reprinted in Voegelin, *Anamnesis* (1966), pp. 79–116. Translated and expanded in Voegelin, *The Ecumenic Age* (1974), pp. 59–114.

"Der Liberalismus und seine Geschichte." In *Christentum und Liberalismus: Studien und Bericht der Katholischen Akademie in Bayern*, edited by Karl Forster, 13:13–42. Munich: Zink. Translation, "Liberalism and Its History," translated by Mary and Keith Algozin. *Review of Politics* 37 (1974): 504–20.

"Religionsersatz: Die gnostischen Massenbewegungen unserer Zeit." *Wort und Wahrheit* 15:5–18. Translation, "Ersatz Religion." *Politeia* 1:2–13. Translation reprinted in Voegelin, *Science, Politics, and Gnosticism* (1968), pp. 81–114.

"La Société industrielle à la recherche de la raison." In *Colloques de Rheinfelden*, edited by Raymond Aron and George Kennan, pp. 44–64. Paris: Calmann-Levy. German translation, "Die industrielle Gesellschaft auf der Suche nach der Vernunft." In *Die Gesellschaft und die drei Welten*, pp. 46–64. Zurich: EVZ-Verlag, 1961. English translation, "Industrial Society in Search of Reason." In *World Technology and Human Destiny*, edited by R. Aron, pp. 31–46. Ann Arbor: University of Michigan Press, 1963.

"Verantwortung und Freiheit in Wirtschaft und Demokratie." *Die Aussprache* 10:207–13.

1961 "Les perspectives d'avenir de la civilisation occidentale." In *L'histoire et ses interprétations: Entretiens autour de Arnold Toynbee*, edited by Raymond Aron, pp. 133–51. The Hague: Mouton.

"Toynbee's History as a Search for Truth." In *The Intent of Toynbee's History: A Cooperative Appraisal*, edited by Edward T. Gargan, pp. 181–98. Chicago: Loyola University Press.

1962 "World Empire and the Unity of Mankind." *International Affairs* 38:170–88.

1963 "Das Rechte von Natur." *Österreichische Zeitschrift für öffentliches Recht*, n.s., 13:38–51. Reprinted in Voegelin, *Anamnesis* (1966), pp. 117–33. Translation, "What Is Right by Nature?" translated by Gerhart Niemeyer. Voegelin, *Anamnesis* (1978), pp. 55–70.

"Hacia una nueva Ciencia del Orden Social?" *Atlantida: Revista del Pensamiento Actual* 1:121–37.

1964 "Demokratie und Industriegesellschaft." *Die unternehmerische Verantwortung in unserer Gesellschaftsordnung*, pp. 96–114. Vol. 4 of the Walter-Raymond-Stiftung. Cologne and Opladen: Westdeutscher Verlag.

"Ewiges Sein in der Zeit." In *Zeit und Geschichte: Dankesgabe an Rudolph Bultmann zum 80. Geburtstag*, edited by Erich Dinker, pp. 591–614. Tübingen: J. C. B. Mohr. Also in *Die Philosophie und die Frage nach dem Fortschritt*. Munich: Pustet. Pp. 267–91. Reprinted in Voegelin, *Anamnesis* (1966), pp. 254–80. Translation, "Eternal Being in Time," translated by Gerhart Niemeyer. Voegelin, *Anamnesis* (1978), pp. 116–40.

"Der Mensch in Gesellschaft und Geschichte." *Österreichische Zeitschrift für öffentliches Recht*, n.s., 14:1–13.

1965 "Was ist Natur?" *Historica* 1:1–18. Reprinted in Voegelin, *Anamnesis* (1966), pp. 134–52. Translation, "What Is Nature?" Translated by Gerhart Niemeyer. Voegelin, *Anamnesis* (1978), pp. 71–88.

1966 *Anamnesis: Zur Theorie der Geschichte und Politik.* Munich: R. Piper. Pp. 395. Italian translation, *Anamnesis: Teoria della Storia e della Politica.* Milan: Giuffré. Translated in part in Voegelin, *Anamnesis* (1978).

"Die deutsche Universität und die Ordnung der deutschen Gesellschaft." In *Die deutsche Universität im Dritten Reich*, edited by Helmut Kuhn, et al., pp. 241–82. Munich: Piper. Proceedings of a series of lectures at the University of Munich in 1960.

"Universität und Oeffentlichkeit: Zur Pneumopathologie der deutschen Gesellschaft." *Wort und Wahrheit* 21:497–518.

"Was ist politische Realität?" *Politische Vierteljahresschrift* 7:2–54. Reprinted in Voegelin, *Anamnesis* (1966), pp. 283–354. Translation, "What Is Political Reality?" translated by Gerhart Niemeyer. Voegelin, *Anamnesis* (1978), pp. 141–213.

1967 "On Debate and Existence." *Intercollegiate Review* 3:143–52.

"Immortality: Experience and Symbol." *Harvard Theological Review* 60:235–79.

1968 *Science, Politics, and Gnosticism.* Chicago: Henry Regnery. Translation of *Wissenschaft, Politik und Gnosis* (1959) and *Religionsersatz* (1960). With a foreword to the American edition.

"Configurations of History." In *The Concept of Order*, edited by Paul G. Kuntz, pp. 23–42. Seattle and London: University of Washington Press.

Zwischen Revolution und Restauration: Politisches Denkens in England in 17 Jahrhundert, edited by Eric Voegelin. Munich: List.

1969 "History and Gnosis." In *The Old Testament and Christian Faith*, edited by Bernhard W. Anderson, pp. 64–89. New York: Herder and Herder.

1970   "The Eclipse of Reality." In *Phenomenology and Social Reality*, edited by Maurice Natanson, pp. 185–94. The Hague: Martinus Nijhoff.

      "Equivalences of Experience and Symbolization in History." In *Eternità e Storia: I valori permanenti nel divenire storico*, pp. 215–34. Florence: Valecchi. *Il Mito del Mondo Nuovo*, translated by A. Munari. Milan: Rusconi.

1971   "The Gospel and Culture." In *Jesus and Man's Hope*, 2 vols., edited by Donald G. Miller and Dikran Y. Hadidian, 2:59–101. Pittsburgh: Pittsburgh Theological Seminary.

      "Henry James' 'The Turn of the Screw.'" *Southern Review*, n.s., 7:3–48. Contains: (1) Prefatory note by Robert B. Heilman. (2) Letter to Robert B. Heilman. (3) Postscript: "On Paradise and Revolution."

      "On Hegel: A Study in Sorcery." *Studium Generale* 24:335–68.

1973   "On Classical Studies." *Modern Age* 17:2–8.

      "Philosophies of History." *New Orleans Review* 2:135–39.

1974   "Reason: The Classic Experience." *Southern Review*, n.s., 10:237–64. Reprinted in Voegelin, *Anamnesis* (1978).

      Order and History. Vol. 4: *The Ecumenic Age*. Baton Rouge: Louisiana State University Press.

1975   *From Enlightenment to Revolution*. Edited by John H. Hallowell. Durham, N.C.: Duke University Press.

      "Response to Professor Alitzer's 'A New History and a New but Ancient God.'" *Journal of the American Academy of Religion* 43: 765–72.

1978   *Anamnesis*. Translated and edited by Gerhart Niemeyer. Notre Dame: University of Notre Dame Press. Contains parts of Voegelin, *Anamnesis* (1966), plus "Reason: The Classic Experience" and a new essay, "Remembrance of Things Past."

SECONDARY SOURCES

Adler, Mortimer J. "Little Errors in the Beginning." *The Thomist* 38 (1974): 27–48.

Albright, William F. Review of *Israel and Revelation*, by Eric Voegelin. *Theological Studies* 22 (1961): 270–79. Reprinted in *History, Archeology, and Christian Humanism*. London: Black, 1965.

Algozin, Keith. "Faith and Silence in Plato's *Gorgias*." *The Thomist* 41 (1977): 237–46.

Altizer, Thomas J. J. "A New History and a New but Ancient God?" *Journal of the American Academy of Religion* 43 (1975): 757–64. With a response from Eric Voegelin, pp. 765–72.

Anderson, Bernhard W. "Politics and the Transcendent: Voegelin's Philosophical and Theological Exposition of the Old Testament in the Context of the Ancient Near East." In *Eric Voegelin's Search for Order in History*, edited by Stephen A. McKnight, pp. 62–100. Baton Rouge: Louisiana State University Press, 1978. Originally published in a shorter form in *Political Science Reviewer* 1 (1971): 1–29.

Annice, M. "Historical Sketch of the Theory of Participation." *The New Scholasticism* 26 (1952): 47–79.

Anonymous. *The Cloud of Unknowing*. Translated with an introduction by Clifton Wolters. Baltimore: Penguin Books, 1961.

Aquinas, St. Thomas. *An Introduction to the Metaphysics of St. Thomas Aquinas*. Texts selected and translated by James F. Anderson. Chicago: Henry Regnery, 1969.

————. *On Being and Essence*. Translated with an introduction and notes by Armand Maurer. Toronto: Pontifical Institute of Medieval Studies, 1949.

————. *Summa Theologiae*. Vol. 31: *Faith (2a 2ae, 1–7)*. Latin text, English translation, introduction, notes, appendixes, and glossary. Translated and edited by Thomas C. O'Brien. London: Eyre and Spottiswood; New York: McGraw-Hill, 1974.

————. *The Summa Theologica of St. Thomas Aquinas*. Translated by Fathers of the English Dominican Province. Revised by Daniel J. Sullivan. *Great Books of the Western World*, vols. 19 and 20. Chicago: William Benton, 1952.

Aristotle. *The Basic Works of Aristotle*. Edited by Richard McKeon. New York: Random House, 1941.

Atkins, Anselm. "Eric Voegelin and the Decline of Tragedy." *Drama Survey* 5 (1966): 280–85.

Aufricht, Hans. "A Restatement of Political Theory: A Note on Voegelin's *The New Science of Politics*." In *Eric Voegelin's Search for Order in History*, edited by Stephen A. McKnight, pp. 46–61. Baton Rouge: Louisiana State University Press, 1978. Originally published in *Western Political Quarterly* 6 (1953): 458–68.

Augustine, St. *Confessions*. 2 vols. With an English translation by William Watts. Cambridge, Mass.: Harvard University Press, 1912.

————. *Enarrationes in Psalmos*. Edited by D. E. Dekkers and J. Fraipont. *Corpus Christianorum*, series Latina, vols. 38–40. Turnholti: Brepols, 1956.

Barrett, William. *Irrational Man: A Study in Existential Philosophy*. Garden City, N.Y.: Doubleday, 1962.

Bettenson, Henry Scowcroft, ed. *Documents of the Christian Church*. 2d ed. London: Oxford University Press, 1963.

Brown, Peter. *Augustine of Hippo: A Biography*. Berkeley and Los Angeles: University of California Press, 1967.

Burke, Kenneth. *The Philosophy of Literary Form: Studies in Symbolic Action*. Baton Rouge: Louisiana State University Press, 1941.

Burrell, David. *Analogy and Philosophical Language*. New Haven: Yale University Press, 1973.

Chenu, Marie-Dominique, O.P. *Nature, Man, and Society in the Twelfth Century: Essays on New Theological Perspectives in the Latin West*. Edited and translated by Jerome Taylor and Lester K. Little. Chicago: University of Chicago Press, 1968.

Cooper, Barry. "A Fragment from Eric Voegelin's *History of Western Political Thought*." Review of *From Enlightenment to Revolution*, by Eric Voegelin. *Political Science Reviewer* 7 (1977): 23–52.

Copleston, Frederick. *A History of Philosophy*. Vol. 3: *Late Medieval and Renaissance Philosophy*. Part 1: *Ockham to the Speculative Mystics*. Garden City, N.Y.: Doubleday, 1963.

Corrington, John William. "Order and Consciousness/Consciousness and History: The New Program of Voegelin." In *Eric Voegelin's Search for Order in History*, edited by Stephen A. McKnight, pp. 155–95. Baton Rouge: Louisiana State University Press, 1978.

————, ed. "A Symposium on Eric Voegelin." *Denver Quarterly* 10, no. 3 (1975): 93–138.

———. "Order and History: The Breaking of the Program." *Denver Quarterly* 10, no. 3 (1975): 115–22.

Daniélou, Jean. *From Glory to Glory: Texts from Gregory of Nyssa's Mystical Writings*. Edited and translated by Herbert Musurillo. New York: Charles Scribner's Sons, 1961.

Demiéville, Paul. *Le Concile de Lhasa: Une controverse sur le quiétisme entre bouddhistes de l'Inde et de la Chine au VIII. siècle de l'ère chrétienne.* Paris: Imprimerie nationale de France, 1952.

Dempf, Alois, Hannah Arendt, and Friedrich Engel-Janosi, eds. *Politische Ordnung und menschliche Existenz: Festgabe für Eric Voegelin.* Munich: C. H. Beck, 1962.

Dodds, E. R. *The Greeks and the Irrational.* Berkeley and Los Angeles: University of California Press, 1951.

Doresse, Jean. "La Gnose." In *Histoire des religions*, edited by H.-C. Puech, vol. 2, pp. 364–429. Paris: Gallimard, 1972.

———. "L'Hermétisme égyptianisant." In *Histoire des religions*, edited by H.-C. Puech, vol. 2, pp. 430–97. Paris: Gallimard, 1972.

Douglass, Bruce. "A Diminished Gospel: A Critique of Voegelin's Interpretation of Christianity." In *Eric Voegelin's Search for Order in History*, edited by Stephen A. McKnight, pp. 139–54. Baton Rouge: Louisiana State University Press, 1978.

———. "The Gospel and Political Order: Eric Voegelin on the Political Role of Christianity." *Journal of Politics* 38 (1976): 25–45.

———. "The Break in Voegelin's Program." Review of *The Ecumenic Age*, by Eric Voegelin. *Political Science Reviewer* 7 (1977): 1–21.

Ebeling, Gerhard. *Word and Faith.* Translated by James W. Leitch. Philadelphia: Fortress Press, 1963.

Ehrlich, Leonard H. *Karl Jaspers: Philosophy as Faith.* Amherst: University of Massachusetts Press, 1975.

Eliade, Mircea. *The Forge and the Crucible: The Origins and Structures of Alchemy.* Translated by Stephen Corrin. New York: Harper and Row, 1962.

———. *The Sacred and the Profane: The Nature of Religion.* Translated by Willard R. Trask. New York: Harcourt, Brace and World, 1959.

Engel-Janosi, Friedrich. *. . . . aber ein stolzer Bettler: Erinnerungen aus einer verlorenen Generation.* Graz: Styria, 1974.

———. Review of *Order and History* (I–III), by Eric Voegelin. *Wort und Wahrheit* 13 (1958): 538–44.

Engelmann, Paul. *Letters from Ludwig Wittgenstein, With a Memoir*. Translated by L. Furtmüller. Edited by B. F. McGuinness. New York: Horizon Press, 1967.

Fabro, Cornelio. "The Intensive Hermeneutics of Thomistic Philosophy: The Notion of Participation." *Review of Metaphysics* 27 (1974): 449–91.

———. "Platonism, Neo-Platonism and Thomism: Convergencies and Divergencies." *The New Scholasticism* 48 (1974): 69–100.

Fay, Thomas A. "Bonaventure and Aquinas on God's Existence: Points of Convergence." *The Thomist* 41 (1977): 585–95.

Florovsky, Georges. *Bible, Church, Tradition: An Eastern Orthodox View*. Belmont, Mass.: Nordland Pub. Co., 1972.

Frame, Douglas. *The Myth of Return in Early Greek Epic*. New Haven: Yale University Press, 1978.

Frankfort, Henri and H. A., John A. Wilson, Thorkild Jacobsen, and William A. Irwin. *The Intellectual Adventure of Ancient Man*. Chicago: University of Chicago Press, 1948.

Frankl, Victor. *The Unconscious God: Psychotherapy and Theology*. New York: Simon and Schuster, 1975.

Gadamer, Hans-Georg. *Philosophical Hermeneutics*. Translated and edited by David E. Linge. Berkeley and Los Angeles: University of California Press, 1976.

———. *Truth and Method*. New York: Seabury Press, 1975.

Gelven, Michael. *Winter, Friendship, and Guilt: The Sources of Self-Inquiry*. New York: Harper and Row, 1972.

Germino, Dante. *Beyond Ideology: The Revival of Political Theory*. New York: Harper and Row, 1967.

———. "Eric Voegelin's *Anamnesis*." *Southern Review*, n.s., 7 (1971): 68–88.

———. "Eric Voegelin: The In-Between of Human Life." In *Contemporary Political Philosophers*, edited by Anthony de Crespigny and Kenneth R. Minogue, pp. 100–119. New York: Dodd, Mead and Co., 1975.

———. Review of *The Ecumenic Age*, by Eric Voegelin. *Journal of Politics* 37 (1975): 847–48.

———. "Two Conceptions of Political Philosophy." In *The Post-Behavioral Era: Perspectives on Political Science*, edited by George J. Graham, Jr., and George W. Carey, pp. 243–57. New York: David McKay, 1972.

Gilkey, Langdon. *Reaping the Whirlwind: A Christian Interpretation of History.* New York: Seabury Press, 1976.

Graham, George J., Jr., and George W. Carey, eds. *The Post-Behavioral Era: Perspectives on Political Science.* New York: David McKay, 1972.

Gueguen, John A. "Voegelin's *From Enlightenment to Revolution*: A Review Article." *The Thomist* 42 (1978): 123–34.

Hadas, Moses. Review of *Order and History* (I–III), by Eric Voegelin. *Journal of the History of Ideas* 19 (1958): 442–44.

Hallowell, John H. "Existence in Tension: Man in Search of His Humanity." In *Eric Voegelin's Search for Order in History*, edited by Stephen A. McKnight, pp. 101–26. Baton Rouge: Louisiana State University Press, 1978. Originally published in *Political Science Reviewer* 2 (1972): 162–84.

Havard, William C. "Voegelin's Changing Conception of History and Consciousness." In *Eric Voegelin's Search for Order in History*, edited by Stephen A. McKnight, pp. 1–25. Baton Rouge: Louisiana State University Press, 1978. Originally published in a shorter form in *Southern Review*, n.s., 7 (1971): 49–67.

———. "The Disenchantment of the Intellectuals." In *Politische Ordnung und menschliche Existenz: Festgabe für Eric Voegelin*, edited by Alois Dempf and Friedrich Engel-Janosi, pp. 271–86. Munich: C. H. Beck, 1962.

———. "The Method and Results of Philosophical Anthropology in America. *Archiv für Rechts- und Sozialphilosophie* 57 (1961): 395–415.

———. "Notes on Voegelin's Contributions to Political Theory." *Polity* 10 (1977): 33–64.

———. "Voegelin's Diagnosis of the Western Crisis." *Denver Quarterly* 10, no. 3 (1975): 127–34.

Heidegger, Martin. *Being and Time.* Translated by John Macquarrie and Edward Robinson. New York: Harper and Row, 1962.

Hollweck, Thomas. *Thomas Mann.* Munich: List Verlag, 1975.

Husserl, Edmund. *The Crisis of European Sciences and Transcendental Phenomenology: An Introduction to Phenomenological Philosophy.* Translated with an introduction by David Carr. Evanston: Northwestern University Press, 1970.

Ilien, Albert. *Wesen und Funktion der Liebe im Denken des Thomas von Aquin.* Freiburg: Herder, 1975.

Jacobsen, Thorkild. *The Treasures of Darkness: A History of Mesopotamian Religion.* New Haven: Yale University Press, 1976.

Jaeger, Werner. *Aristotle: Fundamentals of the History of His Development*. 2d ed. Translated by Richard Robinson. London: Oxford University Press, 1962.

—————. *Gregor von Nyssa's Lehre vom Heiligen Geist*. Edited by H. Dörries. Leiden: E. J. Brill, 1966.

—————. *Paideia: The Ideals of Greek Culture*. Translated by Gilbert Highet. 3 vols. New York: Oxford University Press, 1939–44.

—————. *The Theology of the Early Greek Philosophers*. Translated by Edward S. Robinson. Oxford: The Clarendon Press, 1947.

Janik, Allan and Stephen Toulmin. *Wittgenstein's Vienna*. New York: Simon and Schuster, 1973.

Jaspers, Karl. *The Origin and Goal of History*. Translated by Michael Bullock. London: Routledge and Kegan Paul, 1953.

—————. "Philosophical Autobiography." Translated by Paul A. Schilpp and Ludwig B. Lefebre. In *The Philosophy of Karl Jaspers*, edited by Paul Arthur Schilpp. New York: Tudor Publishing Co., 1957.

—————. *Philosophy*. Translated by E. B. Ashton. 3 vols. Chicago: University of Chicago Press, 1969–71.

—————. *Psychologie der Weltanschauungen*. 6th ed. Berlin and New York: Springer-Verlag, 1971.

—————. *Reason and Existenz: Five Lectures*. Translated with an introduction by William Earle. New York: Noonday Press, 1955.

Johnston, William. *The Mysticism of "The Cloud of Unknowing."* Foreword by Thomas Merton. St. Meinrad, Ind.: Abbey Press, 1975.

Kierkegaard, Søren. *Concluding Unscientific Postscript*. Translated by David F. Swenson and Walter Lowrie. Princeton: Princeton University Press, 1941.

—————. *The Journals of Søren Kierkegaard: A Selection*. Translated by Alexander Dru. London: Oxford University Press, 1961.

—————. *The Sickness Unto Death, combined with Fear and Trembling*. Translated by Walter Lowrie. Garden City, N.Y.: Doubleday, 1954.

Kirby, John. "Symbolism and Dogmatism: Voegelin's Distinction." *The Ecumenist* 13 (1975): 26–30.

Kirk, Russell. "Behind the Veil of History." *Yale Review* 46 (1957): 466–76.

Kremer, Klaus. *Die Neuplatonische Seinsphilosophie und ihre Wirkung auf Thomas von Aquin*. Leiden: E. J. Brill, 1971.

Lewis, Clive Staple. *Surprised by Joy: The Shape of My Early Life*. New York: Harcourt, Brace and World, 1955.

Lonergan, Bernard J. F., S.J. *Insight: A Study of Human Understanding*. 3d ed. New York: Philosophical Library, 1970.

———. *Method in Theology*. New York: Herder and Herder, 1972.

———. *A Second Collection*. Edited by William F. J. Ryan and Bernard J. Tyrell. Philadelphia: Westminster Press, 1974.

———. "Theology and Praxis." In Catholic Theological Society of America, *Proceedings of the Thirty-Second Annual Convention*, Toronto, 1977, pp. 1–16.

———. *Verbum: Word and Idea in Aquinas*. Edited by David B. Burrell. Notre Dame: University of Notre Dame Press, 1967.

McDonald, Neil A., and James N. Rosenau. "Political Theory as Academic Field and Intellectual Activity." *Journal of Politics* 30 (1968): 311–44.

McKnight, Stephen A., ed. *Eric Voegelin's Search for Order in History*. Baton Rouge: Louisiana State University Press, 1978.

———. "The Evolution of Voegelin's Theory of Politics and History, 1944–1975." In *Eric Voegelin's Search for Order in History*, edited by Stephen A. McKnight, pp. 26–45. Baton Rouge: Louisiana State University Press, 1978.

———. "The Renaissance Magus and the Modern Messiah." *Religious Studies Review* 5 (1979):81–89.

Macquarrie, John. *An Existentialist Theology: A Comparison of Heidegger and Bultmann*. London: SCM Press, 1955.

Marcel, Gabriel. *Être et avoir*. Paris: Aubier, 1935.

Maritain, Jacques. *Distinguish to Unite, or The Degrees of Knowledge*. Translated by Gerald B. Phelan. New York: Charles Scribner's Sons, 1959.

Mead, Walter B. "Christian Ambiguity and Social Disorder." *Interpretation* 3 (1973): 221–42.

Merlan, Philip. *From Platonism to Neoplatonism*. 3d ed., rev. The Hague: Martinus Nijhoff, 1968.

Merleau-Ponty, Maurice. *Consciousness and the Acquisition of Language*. Translated by Hugh J. Silverman. Evanston: Northwestern University Press, 1973.

Murray, Michael. *Modern Philosophy of History: Its Origins and Destination*. The Hague: Martinus Nijhoff, 1970.

Natanson, Maurice. *Edmund Husserl: Philosopher of Infinite Tasks.* Evanston: Northwestern University Press, 1973.

Nicolson, Marjorie Hope. *The Breaking of the Circle: Studies in the Effect of the "New Science" upon Seventeenth-Century Poetry.* Rev. ed. New York: Columbia University Press, 1960.

Niebuhr, H. Richard. *The Meaning of Revelation.* New York: Macmillan, 1941.

Niebuhr, Reinhold. *The Nature and Destiny of Man: A Christian Interpretation.* 2 vols. London: Nisbet, 1941–43.

Niemeyer, Gerhart. "The Depth and Height of Political Order." *Review of Politics* 21 (1959): 588–96.

———. "Eric Voegelin's Achievement." *Modern Age* 9 (1965): 132–40.

———. "Eric Voegelin's Philosophy and the Drama of Mankind." *Modern Age* 20 (1976): 28–39.

———. "The Order of Consciousness." *Review of Politics* 30 (1968): 251–56.

———. "The Order of History and the History of Order." *Review of Politics* 19 (1957): 403–9.

O'Brien, Thomas C. "'Sacra Doctrina' Revisited: The Context of Medieval Education." *The Thomist* 41 (1977): 475–509.

Ockham, William of. *Philosophical Writings: A Selection.* Edited and translated by Philotheus Boehner. Edinburgh: Thomas Nelson, 1957.

Otto, Rudolf. *The Idea of the Holy: An Inquiry into the Non-rational Factor in the Idea of the Divine and Its Relation to the Rational.* Translated by John W. Harvey. London: Oxford University Press, 1923.

Peters, F. E. *Greek Philosophical Terms: A Historical Lexicon.* New York: New York University Press, 1967.

Plato. *The Collected Dialogues of Plato.* Edited by Edith Hamilton and Huntington Cairns. New York: Pantheon Books, 1961.

Polanyi, Michael. *Personal Knowledge: Towards a Post-Critical Philosophy.* Corrected ed. Chicago: University of Chicago Press, 1962.

Porter, J. M. "A Philosophy of History as a Philosophy of Consciousness." *Denver Quarterly* 10, no. 3 (1975): 96–104.

Pritchard, J. B. Review of *Israel and Revelation,* by Eric Voegelin. *American Historical Review* 63 (1958): 640–44.

Rank, Otto. *Will Therapy and Truth and Reality.* Translated by Jessie Taft. New York: Alfred A. Knopf, 1945.

Richardson, Alan. *History: Sacred and Profane.* Philadelphia: Westminster Press, 1964.

Ricoeur, Paul. *The Conflict of Interpretations: Essays in Hermeneutics.* Edited by Don Ihde. Evanston: Northwestern University Press, 1974.

————. *Fallible Man.* Translated by Charles Kelbley. Chicago: Henry Regnery, 1965.

————. *Freud and Philosophy: An Essay on Interpretation.* Translated by Denis Savage. New Haven: Yale University Press, 1970.

————. *The Symbolism of Evil.* Translated by Emerson Buchanan. Boston: Beacon Press, 1969.

Robinson, James M., ed. *The Nag Hammadi Library in English.* Translated by the members of the coptic Gnostic Library Project of the Institute for Antiquity and Christianity. San Francisco: Harper and Row, 1977.

Rosen, Stanley. "Order and History." *Review of Metaphysics* 12 (1958): 257–76.

Rowley, H. H. Review of *Israel and Revelation*, by Eric Voegelin. *Journal of Biblical Literature* 76 (1957): 157–58.

Ryle, Gilbert. *The Concept of Mind.* New York: Barnes and Noble, 1949.

Sandoz, Ellis. "Eric Voegelin and the Nature of Philosophy." *Modern Age* 13 (1969): 152–68.

————. "The Foundations of Voegelin's Political Theory." *Political Science Reviewer* 1 (1971): 30–73.

————. "The Philosophical Science of Politics Beyond Behavioralism" In *The Post-Behavioral Era*, edited by George J. Graham, Jr., and George W. Carey, pp. 285–305. New York: David McKay, 1972.

————. Review of *Order and History* (I-III), by Eric Voegelin. *Social Research* 28 (1961): 229–34.

————. "Voegelin's Idea of Historical Form." *Cross Currents* 12 (1962): 41–63.

————. "Voegelin Read Anew: Political Philosophy in the Age of Ideology." *Modern Age* 17 (1973): 257–63.

Schilpp, Paul Arthur, ed. *The Philosophy of Karl Jaspers.* New York: Tudor Publishing Co., 1957.

Sebba, Gregor. "Eric Voegelin: From Enlightenment to Universal Humanity." *Southern Review*, n.s., 11 (1975): 918–25.

————. "Order and Disorders of the Soul: Eric Voegelin's Philosophy of History." *Southern Review*, n.s., 3 (1967), 282–310.

———. "Prelude and Variations on the Theme of Eric Voegelin." *Southern Review*, n.s., 13 (1977), 646–76.

———. "The Present State of Political Theory." *Polity* 1 (1968): 259–70.

Shinn, Roger L. "Another 'Leap of Being.'" *Christian Century* 55 (1958): 1053–54.

———. "Societies and Symbols." *Christian Century* 54 (1957): 894.

Snell, Bruno. *The Discovery of the Mind: The Greek Origins of European Thought.* Translated by T. G. Rosenmeyer. Cambridge, Mass.: Harvard University Press, 1953.

Starr, David E. *Entity and Existence: An Ontological Investigation of Aristotle and Heidegger.* New York: Burt Franklin and Co., 1975.

Stewart, J. A. *Plato's Doctrine of Ideas.* Oxford: The Clarendon Press, 1909.

Trilling, Lionel. *Sincerity and Authenticity.* Cambridge, Mass.: Harvard University Press, 1972.

Vico, Giambattista. *The New Science.* Translated by T. G. Bergin and M. H. Fisch. Ithaca: Cornell University Press, 1948.

Vondung, Klaus. *Magie und Manipulation: Ideologischer Kult und politische Religion des Nationalsozialismus.* Göttingen: Vandenhoeck und Ruprecht, 1971.

Von Mises, Ludwig. *Notes and Recollections.* South Holland, Ill.: Libertarian Press, 1977.

Waismann, Friedrich. *Wittgenstein und der Wiener Kreis: Aus dem Nachlass.* Edited by B. F. McGuinness. Oxford: Basil Blackwell, 1967.

Wallraff, Charles F. *Karl Jaspers: An Introduction to His Philosophy.* Princeton: Princeton University Press, 1970.

Walsh, David J. "Philosophy in Voegelin's Work." Presented at the Annual Meeting of the American Politicial Science Association, September 3, 1976.

Webb, Eugene. *The Dark Dove: The Sacred and Secular in Modern Literature.* Seattle and London: University of Washington Press, 1975.

———. "Eric Voegelin's Theory of Revelation." *The Thomist* 42 (1978): 95–122.

White, Hayden V. *Metahistory: The Historical Imagination in Nineteenth-century Europe.* Baltimore: Johns Hopkins University Press, 1973.

Wilhelmsen, Frederick D. "The New Voegelin." Review of *The Ecumenic Age*, by Eric Voegelin. *Triumph*, January 1975, pp. 32–35.

Wiser, James L. "Eric Voegelin and the Eclipse of Philosophy." *Denver Quarterly* 10, no. 3 (1975): 108–14.

————. "Philosophy and Human Order." *Political Science Reviewer* 2 (1972): 137–61.

————. "Philosophy as Inquiry and Persuasion." In *Eric Voegelin's Search for Order in History*, edited by Stephen A. McKnight, pp. 127–38. Baton Rouge: Louisiana State University Press, 1978.

Wittgenstein, Ludwig. *Philosophical Investigations*. Translated by G. E. M. Anscombe. New York: Macmillan, 1967.

————. *Tractatus Logico-Philosophicus*. Translated by D. F. Pears and B. F. McGuinness. Introduction by Bertrand Russell. London: Routledge and Kegan Paul, 1961.

Zernov, Nicolas. "Christianity: The Eastern Schism and the Eastern Orthodox Church." In *The Concise Encyclopedia of Living Faiths*, edited by R. C. Zaehner, pp. 77–93. London: Hutchinson, 1977.

Index

Abraham, 166–67
Aeschylus, 146, 175
Agathon, 112n24, 114, 174, 178, 180, 277. *See also* Good
Alchemy, 199–201
Aletheia, 103, 107, 116, 158–59, 182, 187–88, 277
Amicitia (friendship), between man and God, 189–90, 262–63, 265, 277
Analogia entis (analogy of being), 72–73
Analogy, 103, 107, 123, 141, 158, 220, 269. *See also* Language, analogical; Myth
Anamnesis (memory), 17, 104n, 277
Anamnesis (book by Voegelin), 33n
"Anamnetic Experiments," 35–37
Anaxagoras, 183
Anaximander, 263
Anima mundi, 124, 277
Anthes, Rudolf, 65n
Anxiety, 240–41, 270
Apeiron, 263, 277
Apocalypticism, 200, 253
Apollinaris, 233
Aquinas, Saint Thomas, 216, 235–36; on beauty, 28n; on faith, 189, 212, 219, 262–63; on God, 70–72, 193; on the good, 83n; on *gratia unionis*, 232n; on knowledge of God, 114; participationism in, 70–73; philosophical myth in, 127n; and Plato, 72n29; *verbum mentis*, 76. *See also Amicitia*

Arete, 173–74
Aristotle, 178, 181–83, 185, 235n; concept of experience in, 53–55, 75; on *episteme*, 196–97; his ethical thought, 179; on relation between man and God, 262; on relation between myth and philosophy, 98–99, 133; on religion, 212–13; *spoudaios*, 113, 179; Voegelin's criticism of, 138n, 142
Augustine, Saint, 39, 41n, 42, 44, 50, 53n, 55n3, 68n20, 82, 120, 177n, 253
Austria, 21
Atomic bomb, 6n6
Ayer, A. J., 82n39

Babylon, 162
Bakunin, Mikhail, 206
Balance of consciousness, as theme in Voegelin, 121, 189, 264n, 278
Barfield, Owen, 194n
Barth, Karl, 230
Baudelaire, Charles, 47
Beckett, Samuel, 48, 242
"Before" and "After": as symbols, 257, 259–60. *See also* Epochal
Being: continuum of, 70; essential vs. participated, 72; God of (*Seinsgott*), 137–38; universal vs. particular, transcendent vs. immanent (Being vs. beings), 73n30, 73n31, 163. *See also* Existence
Bergson, Henri, 20, 147, 192

311